MACHINE
LEARNING

A
Theoretical
Approach

Sponsoring Editor   *Bruce Spatz*
Production Editor   *Sharon Montooth*
Cover Designer   *Our House Design Studio*
Copyeditor   *Bob Klinginsmith*

Library of Congress Cataloging-in-Publication Data

Natarajan, Balas Kausik.
   Machine learning : a theoretical approach / Balas Kausik
Natarajan.
      p.   cm.
   Includes bibliographical references and index.
   ISBN 1-55860-148-1
   1. Machine learning.   I. Title.
Q325.5.N38   1991
006.3'1--dc20   91-14432
                                                              CIP

Morgan Kaufmann Publishers, Inc.
Editorial Office:
        2929 Campus Drive, Suite 260
        San Mateo, CA 94403
        (415) 578-9911

MACHINE LEARNING

A Theoretical Approach

BALAS K. NATARAJAN

Morgan Kaufmann Publishers, Inc.
San Mateo, California

Contents

Chapter 1   Introduction   1
  1.1 Bibliographic Notes   5

Chapter 2   Learning Concepts on Countable Domains   7
  2.1 Preliminaries   8
  2.2 Sample Complexity   14
  2.3 Dimension and Learnability   17
  2.4 Learning Concepts with One-Sided Error   31
  2.5 Summary   34
  2.6 Appendix   34
  2.7 Exercises   36
  2.8 Bibliographic Notes   40

Chapter 3   Time Complexity of Concept Learning   41
  3.1 Preliminaries   41
  3.2 Polynomial-Time Learnability   46
  3.3 Occam's Razor   51
  3.4 One-Sided Error   63
  3.5 Hardness Results   64
  3.6 Summary   66
  3.7 Appendix   67
      3.7.1 Randomized Algorithms   67
      3.7.2 Chebyshev's Inequality   67
  3.8 Exercises   68
  3.9 Bibliographic Notes   71

Chapter 4   Learning Concepts on Uncountable Domains   73
  4.1   Preliminaries   73

  4.2   Uniform Convergence and Learnability   76

  4.3   Summary   94

  4.4   Appendix   94
    4.4.1   Measurability and Probability Distributions   94
    4.4.2   Bounds for the Binomial Distribution   95

  4.5   Exercises   95

  4.6   Bibliographic Notes   97

Chapter 5   Learning Functions   99
  5.1   Learning Functions on Countable Domains   99
    5.1.1   Dimension and Learnability   101
    5.1.2   Time Complexity of Function Learning   109

  5.2   Learning Functions on Uncountable Domains   113
    5.2.1   Learning with Respect to Metrics   118

  5.3   Summary   122

  5.4   Exercises   122

  5.5   Bibliographic Notes   123

Chapter 6   Finite Automata   125
  6.1   Preliminaries   125

  6.2   A Modified Framework   130

  6.3   Summary   144

  6.4   Exercises   145

  6.5   Bibliographic Notes   145

Chapter 7   Neural Networks   147
  7.1   Preliminaries   147

  7.2   Bounded-Precision Networks   149

  7.3   Efficiency Issues   155

  7.4   Summary   164

  7.5   Appendix   164
    7.5.1   Hyperplanes and Half-Spaces   164

7.6   Exercises.   165

7.7   Bibliographic Notes   166

Chapter 8   Generalizing the Learning Model   167
8.1   Preliminaries.   167

8.2   Sample Complexity.   169

8.3   Time Complexity.   171

8.4   Prediction   175
       8.4.1   Hardness Results   178

8.5   Boosting.   179
       8.5.1   Confidence Boosting   180
       8.5.2   Precision Boosting   182

8.6   Summary.   193

8.7   Exercises.   193

8.8   Bibliographic Notes   195

Chapter 9   Conclusion   197
9.1   The Paradigm.   197

9.2   Recent and Future Directions.   199

9.3   An AI Perspective   201

Index   215

Preface

The field of machine learning concerns computer programs that can imitate the learning behavior of humans. This book presents a mathematically rigorous, yet accessible, treatment of the theoretical foundations of machine learning. The discussion is based on the recently developed model of *probably approximately correct* learning, which is gaining acceptance as a fundamental paradigm.

The book is intended for use in an introductory graduate course and is derived from such a course presented by the author while at Carnegie Mellon University. Some familiarity with the board notions of computational complexity and probability theory is assumed, while more technical tools are introduced in appendices. These appendices are likely to be superfluous to the reader with a theoretical background. Running examples are included in the text to enhance readability, and several exercises are listed at the end of each chapter. Notation is introduced within the text, in flagged paragraphs following the first occurrence or useage. Frequently used notation is also collectively presented at the end of the book.

Since the field is developing rather fast, it is difficult to decide which of the results in the literature will have a lasting impact and, therefore, must be included in the textbook. The material included here reflects the author's bias in this regard, and it is certainly true that many interesting results have been omitted. In the main, this book is meant to be an introductory text that might at best compose the core part of a course. It is expected that the instructor will expand on the material along directions most appealing to him or her.

Complexity hardness results are treated in a peculiar manner that requires some explanation. Specifically, some hardness theorems are stated without proof, depending on their importance and difficulty. This is because hardness proofs are often disproportionately difficult in comparison to their contribution to the intuitive understanding of the broader audience. It is hoped that readers interested in the omitted proofs will pursue them in the references listed in the Bibliography. Others may proceed without digression.

Many thanks to all those who helped with this effort: Don Loveland for getting me started; David Bourne and Susan Manning for encouraging me to continue; Dana Angluin, Alan Demers, David Haussler, Michael Kearns, Lenny Pitt, Prasad Tadepalli, Ron Rivest, Robert Schapire, and Les Valiant for helpful discussions, comments, and papers; and Alex Drukarev, Fred Kitson, Konstantinous Konstantinides and the rest of the group at Hewlett Packard for the facilities, encouragement and patience. Many special thanks to the reviewers Eric

Bach, John Paxton, Jude Shavlik, and Carl Smith, who helped immeasurably with their comments and suggestions.

I would like to dedicate this book to my parents.

BKN
Palo Alto, CA

1

Introduction

The process of learning has long fascinated psychologists, philosophers, scientists of all sorts, and, more generally, the parents of young children. Yet, it is difficult for us to agree upon a precise definition of the process. In the main, our understanding of the process depends on our viewpoint. As psychologists, we would be interested in studying the learning behavior of humans or animals and would define the process in the context appropriate for such purposes: *the modification of behavior through practice, training, or experience* (from the Random House Dictionary). As teachers, we would be interested in learning in the classroom sense and might define it in that setting: *to acquire knowledge or skill in by study, instruction, or experience.* (This is the second meaning listed in the Random House Dictionary.) As computer scientists, we find these definitions to be short of precise. Specifically, they fail to rigidly stipulate the conditions under which the learning occurs, so that reproducing the conditions would lead to identical results. Such repeatability is possible and desirable in computers, although it is rarely achievable with humans or animals. Hence, we must identify the factors that are of interest to us and then construct a rigorous and abstract model of the learning phenomenon.

Our interest in the subject is motivated by a desire to make computers think like human beings. Actually, the notion of thought is rather hard to define, so we will settle for computers that imitate the cognitive behavior of humans. Whether or not they think like humans is not of great concern to us, as long as they appear to do so when observed from the outside.

Suppose that we agree that the human brain is nothing more than a very large computer. (This is a controversial supposition. We do not debate the issue here, but merely perform a thought experiment.) Then, it must be possible to simulate the brain on a sufficiently large computer. We could subject this model to the same experiences as a human, thereby causing it to learn from experience. Afterward, the computer would indeed behave like a human with exactly the same set of experiences. In order to carry out such a simulation, we must construct a rather detailed model of the brain and run this model on a computer. At the present time, we have a rather incomplete model of the brain in terms of neurons and interconnections. Even with this incomplete model, given that the brain has about 10^{10} neurons, simulating a single cycle of a neural model of the brain would take about 10^4 seconds on a computer capable of 10^6 operations per second. This is rather long compared to the time taken by the human brain to perform a typical function. On the other hand, such a simulation might be feasible if carried out on a "neural network"—a computer with millions of processors interlinked in a brainlike structure. While such massive networks are the subject of ongoing research, their practical realization appears to be out of reach at the moment. Thus, a general simulation of the brain faces two obstacles: (a) We do not know the detailed structure of the brain. (b) We do not have computers fast enough to simulate the brain, even if we did know the details of its structure.

Having eliminated the general model of the brain as impractical at the moment, we must settle for models that mimic specific and limited human behaviors. For instance, we might seek to construct a program that spoke and understood a natural language, such as English: We would like the program to respond to input sentences just like the average human would. To this end, we could hand-code all the syntactic and semantic rules of English into one very large program—a daunting task indeed. Or, we could construct a skeletal program that starts with a limited ability to understand the language and then learns the rules of the language from experience during the course of its life. This alternative corresponds to the learning of natural languages by humans, and we are interested in understanding this alternative better. Notice that we have placed no restriction on the architecture of the machine on which the program is to be implemented—it could vary from a single-processor sequential computer to a massively parallel neural network.

Thus, we have narrowed the focus of our interest considerably. We are interested in constructing programs that learn to imitate a class of input/output behaviors. The rest of this book involves the analysis of such programs under various assumptions and conditions. Until recently, such analysis has been undertaken under two broad categories that are indicative of the methodology involved. The first and more popular category falls under the label of artificial intelligence. Much of the work in this category tends to be less formal in direction and experimental in nature. The second category is termed inductive inference. This work is formal in direction and is largely based on E. M. Gold's paradigm of "identification in the limit." Within the paradigm, a learning algorithm is presented with an infinite stream of examples for an unknown set. An example for a set is an element from the domain of interest, with a label indicating its membership in the set. At each example, the algorithm conjectures a hypothesis for the unknown set. The algorithm is said to converge in the limit if its hypotheses converge to the unknown set after finitely many examples. Such convergence is required over *all* admissible streams, i.e., those streams that list only and all examples for the unknown set.

Gold's model and the subsequent work on it provide many insights into learning as a process of computational inference. What interests us is the particular task of placing a complexity measure on Gold's paradigm. Such a measure would evaluate the progress of the learning algorithm as a function of the number of examples seen, with respect to the consumption of computational resources such as time and space. To measure the progress of a learning algorithm, we must be able to measure the error of the hypotheses conjectured by the learning algorithm. If this measure of error were independent of the stream of examples seen by the algorithm, the measure would be too stringent to be considered natural. To illustrate this, we consider the student-teacher setting of the classroom. In such a setting, a measure that is "independent of the stream" would test a student with absolutely no regard to the teacher who taught him. A good student, when taught and tested by professors with similar inclinations, will perform well in the test. However, even a good student is likely to perform poorly if he is taught by one professor and tested by another with completely different inclinations. The poor performance would reflect more on the stringency of the test than on the abilities of the student. In short, the worst-case demand of the student's success in the face of completely disparate teachers and examiners is unreasonable in the human setting, and hence, undesirable in a theoretical model of the learning process.

In light of the above, it seems appropriate to define a complexity measure that takes into account the properties of the stream of examples presented to the learning algorithm. Unfortunately, this task proved more elusive than one might expect, and while several complexity measures were suggested in the inductive inference literature, none enjoyed practical import.

More recently, L. G. Valiant proposed the paradigm of "probably approximately correct" (PAC) learning. To a large extent, this paradigm can be viewed as the addition of a probabilistic flavor to Gold's paradigm. Valiant characterized streams of examples by their statistical properties, and measured the error in the hypothesis of the learning algorithm with respect to the same statistical properties. This characterization permits the desired dependence of the error measure on the properties of the stream. At the same time, as is typical of statistical characterizations, Valiant's characterization is compact and facilitates technical analysis.

Thus, the PAC paradigm appears to be a good model of the natural learning process while lending itself to analysis. Since its introduction, the paradigm has continued to gain acceptance as a fundamental model of learning. Our discussions are based on this paradigm and its generalizations.

We now examine briefly the two classes of input/output behaviors that interest us. The first class we consider is that of *concept recognition*, as it is called in the artificial intelligence literature. We use the term *concept* in a technical sense to mean a subset of a universe of objects. For instance, the concept of a cup is the set of all objects that are cups. This is distinct from the procedures or rules that one may actually use to recognize cups. For example, consider the following logical rule for recognizing cups:

(*has handle*) ∧ (*is open*) ∧ (*is container*).

The concept associated with this rule is not the rule itself, but the set of objects satisfying the rule. The problem of recognizing the concept of a cup is: Given an object as input, output a "yes" or a "no" to indicate whether the object is a cup. In other words, concept recognition is evaluating set membership. Note that humans learn to identify cups by trial and error, i.e., from examples and counterexamples. Our interest here is to consider algorithms that can learn from similar experiences.

The second form of input/output behavior we consider is the obvious extension of evaluating set membership to evaluating the value of a function. Once again, we are interested in algorithms that learn to compute functions, given the value of the function on some sample points. The familiar problem of numerical interpolation is an example of such learning.

Chapter 2 presents a formal framework for algorithms that learn classes of concepts defined on countable universes, such as the strings of a finite alphabet. The framework is analyzed with respect to the number of examples required for learning. Chapter 3 concerns the computational efficiency of learning in the framework of Chapter 2. Chapter 4 concerns learning concepts on uncountable domains, such as the set of real numbers. Chapter 5 considers learning general functions as opposed to concept learning, with respect to both countable and uncountable domains. Chapter 6 examines the learnability of concepts represented as deterministic finite automata, while Chapter 7 examines the learnability of concepts representable as neural networks. Chapter 8 concerns a relaxation of the learning model, expanding the class of classes that can be learned in a computationally efficient manner. Chapter 9 discusses the significance of the results presented in the earlier chapters. It also points to some of the results otherwise omitted by the book and examines the directions of current research in the field.

A note on the notation used in this book. When each notational convention is used for the first time, the paragraph following the first use is flagged "Notation:" and contains a detailed description of the usage. It is hoped that this will provide for smoother reading, as compared to *in situ* descriptions. Frequently used notation is also collectively presented at the end of the book.

1.1 Bibliographic Notes

Gold's paradigm of identification in the limit appeared in Gold (1967). An overview of the area of inductive inference and a discussion of Gold's paradigm may be found in Angluin and Smith (1983) and in Osherson, Stob, and Weinstein (1986). Amongst others, Pitt (1989) and Daley and Smith (1986) examine the question of placing complexity measures on Gold's paradigm of identification in the limit. There are a number of books on the artificial intelligence approach to machine learning, including Pearl (1988), Michalski, Mitchell, and Carbonell (1986), Shavlik and Diettrich (1990), and Weiss and Kulikowski (1991). The paradigm of probably approximately correct learning was introduced by Valiant (1984).

2

Learning Concepts on Countable Domains

To us, a concept is a subset of the objects in a predefined domain. An example for a concept is an object from the domain together with a label indicating whether the object belongs to the concept. If the object belongs to the concept, it is a positive example, otherwise it is a negative example. Concept learning is the process in which a learner constructs a good approximation to an unknown concept, given a small number of examples and some prior information on the concept to be learned. This prior information is also called the learner's *prior knowledge* or *bias*. If the learner has no prior information on the concept to be learned, then he can say little about objects that he has not seen as examples. That is, unless the concept is exhaustively enumerated, the learner has little hope of learning the concept. On the other hand, if the learner knows that the unknown concept is, say, one of two predetermined concepts, then a single well-chosen example would suffice. Thus, the number of examples the learner requires is intimately linked with his prior information. We are interested in the following question: What is the quantitative relationship between the number of examples required and the learner's prior information? In order to answer this question, we construct a formal model of the learning process and then analyze it.

In this chapter, we limit the discussion to concepts defined on countable domains. In later chapters, we examine concepts defined on uncountable domains, such as the real numbers.

2.1 Preliminaries

A concept is a subset of the objects in a predefined domain. For example, the concept of a chair is the set of all objects in the world that we would call chairs. Formally, we define concepts on the binary strings, with the understanding that these are symbolic representations for the objects in the domain of interest. Let $\Sigma = \{0, 1\}$ be the Boolean alphabet and let Σ^* be the set of all strings of finite length on Σ. In this chapter, Σ^* is the domain of interest in our formal discussions. A *concept f* is any subset of Σ^*.

To illustrate our notions in a concrete setting, consider the set of all words on the English alphabet as the domain of interest. In particular, let W be the English alphabet and W^* be the set of all strings on it. W^* is the domain of interest. Let $\aleph \subseteq W^*$ be the set of all nouns in English, i.e., the concept of a noun. For the purpose of this discussion, we assume that this set is well-defined in that there is a clearly identifiable set of words that we would call nouns. This is an oversimplification with respect to English; it is more appropriate for structured languages, such as Sanskrit.

An example for a concept is an object in the domain together with a label indicating its classification with respect to the concept. If the object is a member of the concept, we call it a positive example, and if the object is not a member of the concept, we call it a negative example. Formally, an *example* for a concept f is a pair (x, y) where $x \in \Sigma^*$, $y \in \{0, 1\}$ and $y = f(x)$. Thus, an example is an element of $\Sigma^* \times \{0, 1\}$. If $y = f(x) = 1$, (x, y) is a *positive* example; otherwise, it is a *negative* example.

> Notation: For any set S, I_S denotes the *indicator function* of S, i.e., $I_S(x) = 1$ if $x \in S$ and $I_S(x) = 0$ otherwise. In the interest of simplicity, we use S to denote the set S and its indicator function I_S, relying on the context for clarity. Thus, $I_S(x) = S(x) = 1$ if $x \in S$ and $I_S(x) = S(x) = 0$ if $x \notin S$.

Revisiting $\aleph$, the concept of a noun on W^*: The strings *ball* and *car* are elements of $\aleph$, while the strings *crooked* and *honest* are not elements of $\aleph$. Thus, we may write $\aleph(car) = 1$ and $\aleph(crooked) = 0$. It follows that (*ball*, 1) and (*car*, 1) are positive examples for $\aleph$ while (*honest*, 0) is a negative example.

Having defined what we mean by a concept and an example for it, we consider the notion of "learning a concept from examples." Informally speaking, the problem of learning a concept from examples is the following: Given some examples for an unknown concept and some prior information on it, compute a good approximation to the concept. The concept for which examples are provided is known as the *target concept*. Returning to the concept $\aleph$, suppose that: (a) we are provided with the prior information "all words beginning with capital letters are nouns"; (b) we are given a number of positive and negative examples for $\mathfrak{N}$; and (c) we are required to construct an approximation to $\mathfrak{N}$. This approximation is to be "good" in that it agrees with $\mathfrak{N}$ on "most" of the strings in W^*, including strings that were not seen as examples. Defined this way, concept learning is the extrapolation (over the domain of interest) of an unknown set from a given collection of data points. The number of data points needed for a good approximation will depend on our prior information about the target concept. Since we are interested in a precise characterization of this dependence, we need to construct a formal model of concept learning.

Let us focus on the notion of prior information. First, notice the similarity between the informal definition of concept learning given above and the problem of numerical extrapolation (or interpolation). In numerical extrapolation, we are given the value of a function at a few sample points and required to extrapolate the function over some interval. Note that we are to construct a good approximation to the function over the entire interval, including points that were not seen as sample points. If we are told that the unknown function is a polynomial of degree 10, we could rule out all functions that are not polynomials of degree 10 since these cannot be candidates for the unknown function. We are then free to pick a polynomial of degree 10 that best fits the observed data. Thus, our prior information serves to rule out all functions that are not consistent with the information. Similarly, for the concept $\mathfrak{N}$ of nouns on W^*: Given that "all words beginning with capital letters are nouns," any concept on W^* that does not contain all such words cannot be a candidate for the target concept and can be eliminated *a priori*. In concept learning, concepts on the domain that are not consistent with the prior information cannot be candidates for the target concept and can be ruled out. What remains is a set of concepts on the domain, one of which is indeed the target concept. Let us define a *class* of concepts F to be any set of concepts. Then, we can say that the prior information allows us to carve out a class of concepts around the target concept—the class consisting of all the concepts on the domain that are consistent with the prior information. We call this class of concepts the *target class* of the prior information. Notice that the target class is independent of the exact manner in which the prior information is expressed. This independence is desirable since it permits us to use the target class as an abstract model of the prior information. Thus, our learning paradigm will be in terms of target classes rather than in terms of prior information. On occasion, we will interpret the paradigm in terms of the prior information.

There are other possible forms that the prior information may take. For instance, the prior information might tell us something about the probability of seeing each object in the domain, thereby indicating the importance of correctly classifying each object with respect to the unknown concept. For now, we will not consider such forms.

We now introduce our learning paradigm. The paradigm is probabilistic in nature and is perhaps best introduced by returning to $\mathfrak{N}$, the concept of a noun. Suppose a certain Mr. A is unsure of his grammar and wishes to learn $\mathfrak{N}$. He enlists the help of Mr. B, who is known to be knowledgeable on the subject. First, Mr. B gives Mr. A a few rules of thumb on recognizing nouns. This is Mr. A's prior information. Then, Mr. B picks up a copy of the *New York Times* and reads it aloud word-by-word, correctly classifying each word as a noun or otherwise. After a few hours of such activity, Mr. A would have a reasonable idea of the concept of a noun. By this we mean that for any word picked out of the newspaper, Mr. A and Mr. B are likely to agree on whether it is a noun. In essence, the words in the newspaper represent a random sample of the words in the language. Mr. B, the teacher, classified this sample, thereby providing random examples of the concept of a noun for Mr. A, the learner. These are the "training examples" for Mr. A. After seeing a sufficiently large number of these examples, Mr. A constructs a good approximation of the concept of a noun. Mr. A's approximation is good in the sense that he is likely to correctly classify a word chosen at random from the newspaper, including those words that were not read aloud by Mr. B.

There are several interesting issues that arise here. What if none of the words read aloud by Mr. B is a noun? If such is the case, Mr. A would have a rather poor idea of a noun. While this is extremely unlikely, it is certainly possible. Hence, we can say only that it is likely, but not certain, that Mr. A will learn a good approximation of the concept of a noun.

Is it possible that the approximation constructed by Mr. A is a bad one with respect to, say, the *Journal of Fluid Mechanics*? The set of words used in the *New York Times* differs considerably from that used in the *Journal of Fluid Mechanics*. Hence, it is possible that Mr. A will be unable to correctly classify words chosen at random from the *Journal of Fluid Mechanics*. But this does not reflect on Mr. A's ability to learn. If Mr. A were a good learner, he would learn an approximation that is good for the *Journal of Fluid Mechanics*, so long as his examples were picked from there as well. The same situation is encountered in the classroom: A good student is likely to perform well if he is taught and tested by the same person. If the test is set by someone with leanings far divergent from those of the teacher, we can hardly demand guarantees from the student regarding his performance.

In the above, probability considerations entered at two important points. Firstly, a concept is a good approximation to the target concept if it is likely to agree with it on a randomly chosen element of the domain. Secondly, it is likely, but not certain, that the learner will learn a good approximation to the target concept.

Let us construct an abstract model of our learning experiment as follows: Place a probability distribution P on W^*. The learner is given a description of the target class F to which the target concept is known to belong. Thus, the target concept could be any one of the concepts in F. In addition, the learner is provided with examples of the target concept, the examples being randomly chosen according to the distribution P. After a small number of such examples, the learner is to construct his approximation to the target concept. With high probability, this is to be a good approximation. A concept is a good approximation to the target concept if it is likely to agree with the target concept on a word chosen at random according to the distribution P. Thus, the learner is taught using examples chosen at random according to the distribution P and is tested with examples chosen at random according to P. If the learner is a good one, he is likely to succeed.

There is one other interesting feature in the above learning experiment that we should examine. It is reasonable to expect that learning to classify the nouns used in the *New York Times* is somewhat harder than learning to classify the nouns used in *Grimm's Fairy Tales*. This is because there is a wider range of words used in the *Times*, and these words tend to be longer than those in *Grimm's Fairy Tales*. Thus, we can characterize the difficulty of the learning task in terms of the size of the domain that is relevant to the learner. Specifically, let us say that the longest word appearing in *Grimm's Fairy Tales* has 7 characters, while the longest word appearing in the *New York Times* has 23 characters. In our abstract model, this will be characterized in terms of the probability distribution P: When learning from *Grimm's Fairy Tales*, the probability of seeing a word of length greater than 7 is zero, i.e., P is zero on words of length greater than 7. When learning from the *New York Times*, the probability of seeing a word of length greater than 23 is zero. That is, P is zero on words of length greater than 23. The question arises as to whether the learner should be given this bound on the relevant length *a priori* or be required to infer it from observation. In the practical learning situation, the learner will certainly have to do the latter. Yet, in what follows, we assume that the learner is given the bound at the start of the learning process as a "length parameter." This permits technical simplicity in our discussions. In the Appendix to this chapter, we show that the learner could equally well infer the bound from observation without affecting any of our results. The material in the Appendix is not directly required in support of the rest of this chapter and may be skipped at the first reading.

We can now formalize our learning paradigm. Let F be a class of concepts on the domain Σ^*. The target concept f may be any concept in F. A *learning algorithm* for F is an algorithm that attempts to construct an approximation to the target concept from examples for it. The learning algorithm takes as input three parameters: the *error parameter* $\varepsilon \in (0, 1]$, the *confidence parameter* $\delta \in (0, 1]$, and the *length parameter* $n \in \mathbf{N}$. As will be described shortly, the error parameter ε specifies the error allowed in a good approximation, while the confidence parameter δ controls the likelihood of constructing a good approximation. The length parameter n bounds the portion of the domain that is relevant to the learner. The learning algorithm has at its disposal a subroutine EXAMPLE, which at each call produces a single example for the target concept *f*. The probability that a particular example $(x, f(x))$ will be produced at a call of EXAMPLE is $P(x)$, where P is an arbitrary and unknown probability distribution on $\Sigma^{[n]}$. The choice of the distribution P is independent of the target concept f. The output of the learning algorithm is a concept $g \in F$ such that with probability at least $(1-\delta)$, g is a good approximation to f. By "probability at least $(1-\delta)$," we mean that if the algorithm is run infinitely many times with the same inputs and the same target concept f, a fraction of at least $(1-\delta)$ of the runs will result in a good approximation for f. By "good approximation," we mean that the probability that f and g differ on a randomly chosen string is at most ε, i.e., $P(f\Delta g) \leq \varepsilon$. A bird's-eye view of the paradigm is given in Figure 2.1.

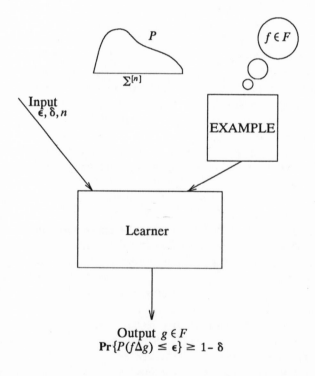

Figure 2.1 _____

The schematic of the learning paradigm.

Notation: $\mathbf{N}$ is the set of natural numbers. $\mathbf{R}$ is the set of real numbers, and $(0, 1]$ is the half-open interval on $\mathbf{R}$ from 0 to 1, i.e., including 1 but excluding 0. Σ^n is the set of all strings of length n in Σ^*, and $\Sigma^{[n]}$ is the set of all strings of length at most n. That is,

$$\Sigma^{[n]} = \bigcup_{i \leq n} \Sigma^i.$$

For any two sets f and g, $f \Delta g$ denotes the symmetric difference $(f - g) \cup (g - f)$. For random variable q and distribution P, $P(q)$ denotes the expectation of q. For a set S we use S and I_S interchangeably and, hence, write $P(S)$ to denote $P(I_S)$. Note that

$$P(I_S) = \sum_{x \in \Sigma^*} I_S(x) P(x) = \sum_{x \in S} P(x).$$

Thus, $P(S)$ is simply the "weight" of P on S.

In essence, the learning algorithm takes as input ε, δ, and n and produces as output a concept $g \in F$. With probability at least $(1 - \delta)$, $P(f \Delta g) \leq \varepsilon$, where f is the target concept and P is zero on all strings of length greater than n. That is, the algorithm is $(1 - \delta)$ confident that the error in its output is at most ε. For instance, if $\delta = 0.01$ and $\varepsilon = 0.05$, the algorithm is 99% sure that its output is 95% correct. Thus, the output of the learning algorithm is *probably* a good *approximation* to the target concept.

We must address one additional issue before we can bring together all of the above in a formal definition. Recall that the output of the learning algorithm is a concept from F. What is the form of this output? The answer to this question depends on the focus of our inquiry, and we consider two foci. The first inquires into the number of examples required for learning, independent of the time needed to process the examples. This is the sample complexity of learning. The second focus inquires into the time required for learning, i.e., the time required by the learning algorithm to process the examples. This is the time complexity of learning. In the familiar student-teacher setting of human learning, the sample complexity is a measure of the amount of student-teacher interaction required for learning, whereas the time complexity is a measure of the amount of work the student must do, both in class and at home. In this chapter, we will be concerned only with the sample complexity of learning. The form of the learning algorithm's output does not affect the sample complexity of learning, and we will leave it unspecified. In the next chapter, we will consider the time complexity of learning, and the form of the output of the learning algorithm will factor into the discussion.

Bringing together all of the above:

DEFINITION _____

An algorithm A is a *probably approximately correct* (PAC) learning algorithm for a class of concepts F if

(a) A takes as input $\varepsilon \in (0, 1]$, $\delta \in (0, 1]$, and $n \in \mathbf{N}$ where ε and δ are the error and confidence parameters, respectively, and n is the length parameter.

(b) A may call EXAMPLE, which returns examples for some $f \in F$. The examples are chosen randomly according to an arbitrary and unknown probability distribution P on $\Sigma^{[n]}$.

(c)   For all concepts $f \in F$ and all probability distributions P on $\Sigma^{[n]}$, A outputs a concept $g \in F$, such that with probability at least $(1 - \delta)$, $P(f \Delta g) \leq \varepsilon$.

_____

Note that the above definition requires the learning algorithm to learn over all probability distributions P, even though the distribution is unknown. This is in keeping with our earlier observation that a good learner should learn with respect to any distribution, as long as the teaching and testing distributions are the same. As we shall see later in this chapter, this is not as demanding as may appear at first glance.

2.2 Sample Complexity

The central aim of our study is to establish a quantitative relationship between the number of examples required for learning and the properties of the class of concepts in question. Toward this aim, we set up a complexity measure for learning algorithms to measure the number of examples required by the algorithm as a function of the various parameters.

DEFINITION _____

Let A be a learning algorithm for a concept class F. The *sample complexity* of A is the function $s : \mathbf{R} \times \mathbf{R} \times \mathbf{N} \rightarrow \mathbf{N}$ such that $s(\varepsilon, \delta, n)$ is the maximum number of calls of EXAMPLE by A, the maximum being taken over all runs of A on inputs ε, δ, and n, with the target concept f ranging over all $f \in F$ and the probability distribution P ranging over all distributions on $\Sigma^{[n]}$. If no finite maximum exists, $s(\varepsilon, \delta, n) = \infty$.

_____

To illustrate the above definition, we give a recipe to compute the sample complexity of A for a particular choice of ε, δ, and n. The recipe serves for clarity and is a thought experiment, not a computational procedure. Run A on inputs ε, δ and n, for all target concepts $f \in F$ and all probability distributions P on $\Sigma^{[n]}$. For each choice of P and f, repeat the runs over all possible outcomes of the sequence of calls to EXAMPLE. The maximum number of calls to EXAMPLE over all these runs is $s(\varepsilon, \delta, n)$. If no finite maximum exists, $s(\varepsilon, \delta, n)$ is infinite.

Let us revisit $\aleph$, the concept of a noun on W^*. Let F be the target class corresponding to the prior information that all words beginning with capital letters are nouns. That is, F is the class of concepts that contain all words beginning with capital letters. Suppose A is a learning algorithm for F with sample complexity $n/(\varepsilon\delta)$. As before, let us say that the length of the longest word in the *New York Times* is 23 characters and that the length of the longest word in *Grimm's Fairy Tales* is 7 characters. Then, the distribution P of words in the *New York Times* will be nonzero only on words of length 23 or less. And the distribution P of words in *Grimm's Fairy Tales* will be nonzero only on words of length 7 or less. Fix $\varepsilon = 0.05$ and $\delta = 0.1$. When learning to classify nouns from the *New York Times*, algorithm A will require 4,600 examples. When learning to classify nouns from *Grimm's Fairy Tales*, algorithm A will require only 1,400 examples. In other words, to learn the nouns in the *New York Times* to an accuracy of 95% and a confidence of 90%, the algorithm would require 4,600 examples. To learn the nouns in *Grimm's Fairy Tales* to the same accuracy and confidence, the algorithm would require 1,400 examples.

Thus, the sample complexity of algorithm A is the number of examples required by it as a function of the input parameters. If this function is bounded by a polynomial in $1/\varepsilon$, $1/\delta$ and n, we consider the learning task to be feasible. (The reciprocal of ε and δ are used because we wish to study the sample complexity as these parameters approach zero.) If the function is superpolynomial, i.e., grows faster than any polynomial, the number of examples required will be hopelessly large for all but small values of n and large values of ε and δ. With this in mind, we give the following definition:

DEFINITION

A class F is said to be *polynomial-sample learnable* if there exists a learning algorithm A for F with sample complexity $p(1/\varepsilon, 1/\delta, n)$, where p is a polynomial function of its arguments.

Example 2.1   Consider j Boolean variables $a_1, a_2, \ldots, a_j$. Each string $x \in \Sigma^*$ of length j corresponds to an assignment of the j variables, where the ith bit of x is the value of a_i. A string not of length j is not a valid assignment to the variables. Using this correspondence between strings and assignments, we can view a Boolean formula as a concept on Σ^*. Specifically, the concept defined by a formula f on j variables is simply the set all strings that satisfy f. Notice that strings not of length j are not valid assignments and, hence, cannot satisfy f. We follow the convention that the null formula has no satisfying assignments. Also, abusing notation, we use f to denote a formula f as well as the concept defined by it, depending on the context for clarity.

Note that a Boolean formula may not explicitly carry information as to the variables it is defined on. For instance, the formula $a_1 \wedge a_3$ does not tell us whether the formula is defined on just two variables a_1 and a_3, or whether there are four variables involved, a_1, a_2, a_3, and a_4. Since the set of variables is important to us, we assume that each formula is defined on a sequence of variables of the form $a_1, a_2, \ldots, a_j$ and that each formula carries with it a header of the form

$$(a_1 \vee \neg a_1) \wedge (a_2 \vee \neg a_2) \wedge \cdots \wedge (a_j \vee \neg a_j).$$

The header precedes the rest of the formula as a conjunct, and being a tautology, it does not affect the truth value of the formula. The header is a technicality, and unless we explicitly refer to it, the reader should pretend that it does not exist.

A monotone monomial is a Boolean formula of the form

$$\bigwedge_{i \in S} a_{i,} \text{ where } S \subseteq 1, 2, \ldots, j.$$

In words, a monotone monomial is a formula consisting solely of the conjunction of some subset of the variables $a_1, a_2, \ldots, a_j$. The concept defined by a monotone monomial formula is called a monotone monomial concept. Let F be the class of monotone monomial concepts defined by all the monotone monomials, for all values of j.

In Example 2.5 we will show that there exists a learning algorithm for F, with sample complexity

$$\frac{1}{\varepsilon} \left[(n+1)^2 \ln(2) + \ln \left[\frac{1}{\delta} \right] \right].$$

Verify that the above expression is bounded from above by a polynomial in $1/\varepsilon$, $1/\delta$, and n. Since we can always introduce some dummy calls of EXAMPLE in the algorithm, we can ensure that the number of calls of EXAMPLE is exactly polynomial in the parameters of interest. Hence, we can conclude that the monotone monomials are polynomial-sample learnable.   ■

We have now made precise our notion of concept learning. In the following section, we establish the relationship between the properties of a target class and the sample complexity of a learning algorithm for it.

2.3 Dimension and Learnability

We now turn our attention to a measure of complexity for a class of concepts.

DEFINITION _____

Let F be a class of concepts on a domain X. We say that F *shatters* a set $S \subseteq X$ if the set $\{f \cap S \mid f \in F\}$ is the power set of S.

_____

> Notation: The power set of S is the set of all subsets of S and is denoted by 2^S.

Example 2.2   Let $X = \mathbf{R}^2$ be the real plane. Let G be the class of all axis-parallel rectangles on X, i.e., rectangles with sides parallel to the coordinate axes. G shatters the set of four points shown as dots in Figure 2.2. Specifically, for any subset of the four points, there exists an axis-parallel rectangle that includes those points and excludes the rest of the four.

As another example, let X be the integers, let S be the set $\{0, 1, 2\}$, and let F be the class of sets $\{0, 2, 4\}, \{0, 4\}, \{2\}, \{4\}, \{0, 2\}, \{0, 1, 2\}, \{1, 2\}, \{1, 4\}, \{0, 1, 4\}$. F shatters S. To see this, take any subset of S, say $S_1 = \{0, 1\}$. Then, $\{0, 1, 4\} \in F$ and $\{0, 1, 4\} \cap S = \{0, 1\}$. The same holds for any other subset S_1 of S.

Finally, let F be the monotone monomials of Example 2.1. The set $S = \{0111, 1011, 1101, 1110\}$ is shattered by F. To see this, pick any subset S_1 of S, say $S_1 = \{0111, 1101\}$. Let f be the monotone monomial formula $f = a_2 \wedge a_4$. Then $f \in F$, and $f \cap S = S_1$.   ∎

The significance of the above definition is that if F shatters a set S, then each string x in S is "independent" of the others. That is, for any concept $f \in F$, knowing whether $x \in f$ tells us nothing about the membership in f of any other string in S. Thus, the size of the largest set shattered by a class is a measure of the number of "degrees of freedom" possessed by it. With this in mind, we define the following:

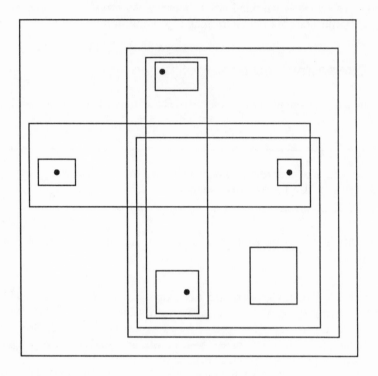

Figure 2.2 _____

Four points shattered by the axis-parallel rectangles. In the interest of
clarity, not all the rectangles involved are shown.

DEFINITION _____

Let F be a class of concepts on a domain X. The *Vapnik-Chervonenkis
dimension* of F, denoted by $D_{VC}(F)$, is the greatest integer d such that there
exists a set of cardinality d that is shattered by F.

Notice that the Vapnik-Chervonenkis dimension is a purely combinatorial
concept and has no direct connection with the geometric notion of dimension as
used in "three-dimensional space," etc.

The following lemma establishes a relationship between the cardinality $|F|$ of a class F and its Vapnik-Chervonenkis dimension $\mathbf{D}_{VC}(F)$.

Notation: For a set S, $|S|$ is the cardinality of X. For a string x, $|x|$ is the length of x.

LEMMA 2.1 _____

Let X be any finite set and let F be a class of concepts on X. If $d = \mathbf{D}_{VC}(F)$, then

$$2^d \le |F| \le (|X|+1)^d.$$

Proof: The first inequality is immediate from the definition of $\mathbf{D}_{VC}(F)$ and the definition of shattering. The second inequality is proved by induction on $|X|$.

Basis: Clearly true for $|X| = 1$.

Induction: Assume the claim holds for $|X| = k$ and prove true for $k+1$. Let $|X| = k+1$. Pick any $x \in X$ and partition X into the two sets $\{x\}$ and $X_1 = X - \{x\}$. Let F_1 be the set of all sets in F that are reflected about x. That is, for each f_1 in F_1, there exists $f \in F$ such that f differs from f_1 only in that f does not contain x. Formally,

$$F_1 = \{f_1 | f_1 \in F, \text{ there exists } f \in F, f \ne f_1 \text{ and } f_1 = f \cup \{x\}\}.$$

Let $F_2 = F - F_1$. Surely, the concepts in F_2 can be distinguished on the elements of X_1. That is, no two concepts in F_2 can differ only on x by virtue of our definition of F_1. Hence, we can consider F_2 as a class of concepts on X_1. Since $F_2 \subseteq F$, F_2 cannot shatter a set larger than the largest set shattered by F. Hence, $\mathbf{D}_{VC}(F_2) \le d$. Since $|X_1| \le k$, by the inductive hypothesis we have $|F_2| \le (|X_1|+1)^d$.

Now consider F_1. Again, the sets of F_1 are all distinct on X_1. Suppose F_1 shattered a set $S \subseteq X_1, |S| \ge d$. Then, F would shatter $S \cup \{x\}$. But, $|S \cup \{x\}| \ge d+1$, which is impossible by assumption. Hence, F_1 shatters a set of at most $(d-1)$ elements in X_1. By the inductive hypothesis, we have

$$|F_1| \le (|X_1|+1)^{d-1}$$

Combining the two bounds, we have

$$
\begin{aligned}
|F| &= |F - F_1| + |F_1| \\
&= |F_2| + |F_1| \le (|X_1|+1)^d + (|X_1|+1)^{d-1} \\
&= (k+1)^d + (k+1)^d - 1 = (k+2)(k+1)^{d-1} \le (k+2)^d \\
&= (|X|+1)^d.
\end{aligned}
$$

Thus, the claim is proved.

□

We also define an asymptotic form of the Vapnik-Chervonenkis dimension as follows:

DEFINITION _____

Let F be a class of concepts on Σ^* and let $f \in F$. The *projection* $f^{[n]}$ of f on $\Sigma^{[n]}$ is simply the set of strings of length at most n in f, i.e., $f^{[n]} = f \cap \Sigma^{[n]}$. Similarly, the projection $F^{[n]}$ of F on $\Sigma^{[n]}$ is given by $F^{[n]} = \{f^{[n]} | f \in F\}$.

DEFINITION _____

The *asymptotic dimension* of a class of concepts F is the function $d : \mathbf{N} \to \mathbf{N}$ such that for all n, $\mathbf{D}_{VC}(F^{[n]}) = d(n)$. We denote the asymptotic dimension of F by $\mathbf{D}(F)$.

For simplicity, we drop the prefix asymptotic, relying on the context for clarity. If $\mathbf{D}(F)$ is $O(p(n))$ for some polynomial p, we say that F is of polynomial dimension.

Notation: Let $a : \mathbf{N} \to \mathbf{N}$ and $b : \mathbf{N} \to \mathbf{N}$. We say a is $O(b(n))$ if there exists positive real c_1 and $n_0 \in \mathbf{N}$ such that for all $n \ge n_0$, $a(n) \le c_1 b(n)$. We say that a is $\Omega(b(n))$ if there exists positive real c_2 such that for infinitely many n, $a(n) \ge c_2 b(n)$. Some authors in the literature use "a is $\Omega(b(n))$" to mean "b is $O(a(n))$." The reader should note this difference.

Example 2.3 Let F be the monotone monomials of Example 2.1. In Example 2.2 we showed that F shatters the set $S = \{0111, 1011, 1101, 1110\}$. Since every string in S is of length 4, for any $f \in F$, $f \cap S = f_4 \cap S$. Thus, F shatters S if and only if $F^{[4]}$ shatters S. It follows that $F^{[4]}$ shatters S. Similarly, we can show that $F^{[5]}$ shatters $S = \{01111, 10111, 11011, 11101, 11110\}$ and in general that $F^{[n]}$ shatters a set of n strings. Hence, $\mathbf{D}_{VC}(F^{[n]}) \geq n$ and $\mathbf{D}(F)$ is $\Omega(n)$. ∎

The following lemma is the asymptotic corollary of Lemma 2.1. The lemma is central to the proof of Theorem 2.1, which establishes a relationship between the sample complexity and the properties of a target class.

LEMMA 2.2 _____

Let $d = \mathbf{D}_{VC}(F^{[n]})$. Then,

$$2^d \leq |F^{[n]}| \leq 2^{(n+1)d}$$

Proof: We need only substitute $F^{[n]}$ for F and $\Sigma^{[n]}$ for X in Lemma 2.1. Now, $|X| \leq 2^{n+1} - 1$. Hence,

$$2^d \leq |F^{[n]}| \leq (2^{n+1} - 1 + 1)^d \leq 2^{(n+1)d}.$$

□

Example 2.4 Consider the monotone monomials of Example 2.1. There are 2^j monotone monomials definable on j variables, and $F^{[n]}$ is simply the set of all monotone monomial concepts definable on $n, n-1, n-2, \ldots, 1, 0$ variables. Thus,

$$|F^{[n]}| = 2^n + 2^{n-1} + \cdots + 2^0 = 2^{n+1} - 1.$$

Invoking Lemma 2.2, we have $\mathbf{D}_{VC}(F^{[n]}) \leq \log |F^{[n]}| \leq n + 1$. By Example 2.1, we have $\mathbf{D}_{VC}(F^{[n]}) \geq n$. Thus $\mathbf{D}(F)$ is both $O(n)$ and $\Omega(n)$. ∎

We need the following supporting definition before we can give the main results of this chapter.

DEFINITION _____

Let $f: X \to Y$ be any function. An example for f is a pair $(x, f(x))$, and the set of all examples for f is denoted by graph(f). That is, graph$(f) = \{(x, y) \mid x \in X, y = f(x)\}$. We say f is *consistent* with a set $S \subseteq X \times Y$ if $S \subseteq$ graph(f).

_____

For a concept f, we use graph(f) to denote graph(I_f), the graph of the indicator function of f. We say f is consistent with a set of examples S if $S \subseteq$ graph(f). Thus, a concept is consistent with a set of examples if it "agrees" with them in the intuitive sense.

THEOREM 2.1 _____

Let F be a class of concepts on Σ^*. Then, there exists a learning algorithm for F with sample complexity

$$s(\varepsilon, \delta, n) = \frac{1}{\varepsilon} \left[(n+1)\mathbf{D}_{\mathrm{VC}}(F^{[n]})\ln(2) + \ln\left(\frac{1}{\delta}\right) \right].$$

_____

Proof: Algorithm $A_{2.1}$ below is a learning algorithm for F.

Learning Algorithm $A_{2.1}$
input: ε, δ, n;
begin:
    let $m = \dfrac{1}{\varepsilon} \left[(n+1)\mathbf{D}_{\mathrm{VC}}(F^{[n]})\ln(2) + \ln\left(\dfrac{1}{\delta}\right) \right]$;
    make m calls of EXAMPLE;
    let S be the set of examples seen;
    pick a concept $g \in F$ consistent with S;
    output g;
end

Actually, we require that $A_{2.1}$ call EXAMPLE as many times as the smallest integer greater than m. For $m > 0$, $\lceil m \rceil$, read "ceiling m," denotes the smallest integer greater than m. Similarly, we have "floor m," $\lfloor m \rfloor$, the largest integer less than m. In the interest of clarity, throughout this book we omit ceilings and floors, with the understanding that the reader will supply them as necessary.

We now show that $A_{2.1}$ does indeed satisfy our requirements. Let f be the target concept. We require that with probability exceeding $(1-\delta)$, $A_{2.1}$ should output a concept $g \in F$, such that $P(f \Delta g) \le \varepsilon$.

Let $g^{[n]} \in F^{[n]}$ be such that $P(f^{[n]} \Delta g^{[n]}) \ge \varepsilon$. For a particular such $g^{[n]}$, the probability that any call of EXAMPLE will produce an example consistent with $g^{[n]}$ is at most $(1-\varepsilon)$. Hence, the probability that m calls of EXAMPLE will produce examples all consistent with $g^{[n]}$ is at most $(1-\varepsilon)^m$. It follows that the probability that m calls of EXAMPLE will produce examples all consistent with any such choice of $g^{[n]}$ is at most $(1-\varepsilon)^m$ summed over all the choices for $g^{[n]}$. Now, there are at most $|F^{[n]}|$ choices for $g^{[n]}$. Hence, this probability is at most $|F^{[n]}|(1-\varepsilon)^m$. We will make m sufficiently large to bound this probability by δ. That is,

$$|F_n|(1-\varepsilon)^m \le \delta.$$

By Lemma 2.2,

$$|F^{[n]}| \le 2^{(n+1)\mathbf{D}_{VC}(F^{[n]})}.$$

Hence, we want

$$2^{(n+1)\mathbf{D}_{VC}(F^{[n]})}(1-\varepsilon)^m \le \delta.$$

Taking natural logarithms on both sides of the inequality, we get

$$(n+1)\mathbf{D}_{VC}(F^{[n]})\ln(2) + m\ln(1-\varepsilon) \le \ln(\delta).$$

Using the approximation $\ln(1+\alpha) \le \alpha$, it suffices if

$$(n+1)\mathbf{D}_{VC}(F^{[n]})\ln(2) - \frac{m}{\varepsilon} \le \ln(\delta).$$

Simplifying, we get

$$m \ge \frac{1}{\varepsilon}\left[(n+1)\mathbf{D}_{VC}(F^{[n]})\ln(2) + \ln\left(\frac{1}{\delta}\right)\right].$$

Hence, if m examples are drawn, with probability at least $(1-\delta)$, any concept $g^{[n]} \in F^{[n]}$ consistent with the examples will be such that $P(f^{[n]} \Delta g^{[n]}) \le \varepsilon$. Notice that $f^{[n]} \Delta g^{[n]} = (f \Delta g) \cap \Sigma^{[n]}$. Since P is a distribution on $\Sigma^{[n]}$, it follows that $P(f \Delta g) = P(f^{[n]} \Delta g^{[n]})$. Also, all the examples drawn involve strings from $\Sigma^{[n]}$, and $g^{[n]}$ will be consistent with these examples if and only if g is consistent with them. It follows that, with probability at least $(1-\delta)$, any $g \in F$ that is consistent with all the examples drawn will be such that $P(f \Delta g) \le \varepsilon$.

This completes the proof.

□

Note the simplicity of learning algorithm $A_{2.1}$. It simply calls for a certain number of examples and then picks a concept that agrees with the examples seen. Such algorithms are often called "consistent" algorithms. In fact, many of the algorithms that we will examine in this book will be of this form. Also, notice that the sample complexity of $A_{2.1}$ varies as $D_{VC}(F^{[n]})$, $1/\varepsilon$, and $\ln(1/\delta)$. In Theorem 2.2 we will see that the first dependency is necessary, and in Chapter 4, we will see that latter dependencies are necessary as well.

To see the import of Theorem 2.1, suppose the learner's prior information on the target concept corresponds to a target class F. Then the number of examples sufficient to learn the target concept is proportional to the dimension of F. We illustrate this with an example.

Example 2.5   Let F be the monotone monomials. In Example 2.2 we showed that $D_{VC}(F^{[n]}) \le n+1$. Algorithm *learn_monomial* below is a learning algorithm for F and is based on $A_{2.1}$.

Learning Algorithm *learn_monomial*;
input: ε, δ, n;
begin

$$\text{let } m = \frac{1}{\varepsilon}\left[(n+1)^2\ln(2) + \ln\left[\frac{1}{\delta}\right]\right];$$

make m calls of EXAMPLE;
let S be the set of examples seen;
delete all the negative examples from S;
if $S = \emptyset$ **then**
    output the null formula and halt;
else let $j = |x|$, $(x, y) \in S$;
let $g = a_1 \wedge a_2 \wedge \cdots \wedge a_j$;
for each example $(x, 1) \in S$ **do**
    for each a_i **do**
        if $a_i = 0$ in x **then**
            delete a_i from f;
end
output g;
end

The main difference between *learn_monomial* and $A_{2.1}$ is that *learn_monomial* specifies the manner in which it picks a concept consistent with the examples seen. If all the examples in S are negative, then *learn_monomial* outputs the null formula, which corresponds to the empty concept. If S contains positive examples, then the target monotone monomial must be defined on j variables, where $j = |x|$, $(x, y) \in S$. In this case, *learn_monomial* constructs a monotone monomial formula g on j variables consistent with the examples in S. Specifically, g is initialized to be $a_1 \wedge a_2 \wedge \cdots \wedge a_j$, the most restrictive nonempty monotone monomial on the variables $a_1, a_2, \ldots, a_j$, Then, conjuncts are removed from g to allow the positive examples in S to satisfy g. Therefore, g will be the most restrictive monotone monomial to be satisfied by the positive examples in S, and none of the negative examples in S will satisfy g. Hence, g is consistent with S. For a more rigorous proof that g is consistent with S, see Example 2.7.   ∎

COROLLARY 2.1 _____

A class of concepts F is polynomial-sample learnable if it is of polynomial dimension.

_____

Proof: By Theorem 2.1, there exists a learning algorithm for F with sample complexity

$$\frac{1}{\varepsilon}\left[(n+1)\mathbf{D}_{\mathrm{VC}}(F^{[n]})\ln(2) + \ln\left[\frac{1}{\delta}\right]\right].$$

If F is of polynomial dimension, there exists a polynomial $p(n)$ such that for all n,

$$\mathbf{D}_{\mathrm{VC}}(F^{[n]}) \leq p(n).$$

Combining the two equations and simplifying, we get

$$\frac{1}{\varepsilon}\left[(n+1)p(n)\ln(2) + \ln\left[\frac{1}{\delta}\right]\right].$$

It follows that there exists a learning algorithm for F with sample complexity polynomial in $1/\varepsilon$, $1/\delta$, and $1/n$. Hence F is polynomial-sample learnable.

□

We now establish a lower bound on the sample complexity of a learning algorithm for a class of concepts. The thrust of Theorem 2.2 is that the sample complexity of any learning algorithm for a class F must be asymptotically comparable to $\mathbf{D}(F)$. First, we need a technical detour.

Thus far, we have placed no restriction on the kind of computational procedures we will permit as learning algorithms. We now require the restriction of statistical measurability, as given below. In placing this restriction, it is convenient to define the notion of the learning operator Ψ, associated with a learning algorithm A, by replacing the calls to EXAMPLE with a sequence of examples provided as input. In words, Ψ takes as input ε, δ, n, and σ, where σ is a sequence of examples. Then, Ψ runs A on inputs ε, δ, and n. When A calls EXAMPLE, Ψ gives A successive examples from σ, rather than allow A to obtain random examples from EXAMPLE. If the number of examples demanded by A exceeds the number of examples in σ, $\Psi(\varepsilon, \delta, n, \sigma)$ is undefined. Else, Ψ outputs the concept output by A.

DEFINITION

The *learning operator* associated with a learning algorithm A is given by:

Learning Operator Ψ
input: $\varepsilon, \delta, n, \sigma$;
begin
    let $\sigma = (x_1, y_1), (x_2, y_2), \ldots$
    run A on inputs ε, δ, and n;
    simulate EXAMPLE as follows;
        at the ith call of EXAMPLE by A
            if σ has fewer than i examples then
                Ψ is undefined;
            else give A the example (x_i, y_i);
    output A's output;
end

We will require that the learning algorithm A be such that certain statistical properties of Ψ are well defined—we require that Ψ computes a random function. By this we mean that for each set of inputs ε, δ, n, and σ, and each output x, the probability that $\Psi(\varepsilon, \delta, n, \sigma)$ will output x should be defined. We say A is *admissible* if Ψ satisfies the above property. Note that if A is deterministic, Ψ computes a function and, hence, A is definitely admissible. It is easy to see that even if A tosses coins and uses the results in its computations, A would still be admissible. But if A were non-deterministic, A might or might not be admissible.

THEOREM 2.2 _____

Let F be a class of concepts on Σ^*, and let A be an admissible learning algorithm for F, with sample complexity $s(\varepsilon, \delta, n)$. Then, for $\varepsilon < 1/4$ and $\delta < 1/2$, and all values of n, $s(\varepsilon, \delta, n) \geq \frac{1}{2} D_{VC}(F^{[n]})$.

_____

Proof: Suppose not. For $\varepsilon < 1/4$ and $\delta < 1/2$, pick n such that $D_{VC}(F^{[n]}) > 2s(\varepsilon, \delta, n)$. Let $d = D_{VC}(F^{[n]})$ and let $m = s(\varepsilon, \delta, n)$. By definition, $F^{[n]}$ shatters a set S such that $|S| = d$. Let x^m be an element of S^m.   ∎

Notation: For set S, S^m is the $m$fold Cartesian product of S. Each x^m in S^m is an ordered list of m items. For instance, N^3 is the set of ordered triples of natural numbers. Recall the notation that Σ^n is the set of all strings of length n on Σ. While this appears to clash with the notation being introduced currently, there is essentially no difference between an m-tuple and a string.

Let P be the probability distribution that is uniform on S and zero elsewhere and let Ψ be the learning operator corresponding to A. For $f \in F$, let $f(x^m)$ denote the sequence of examples obtained from x^m. That is, if $x^m = (x_1, x_2, \ldots, x_m)$, $f(x^m)$ is the sequence of examples $(x_1, f(x_1))$, $(x_2, f(x_2)), \ldots, (x_m, f(x_m))$. Let $G \subseteq F$ be such that G shatters S and $|G| = 2^{|S|}$.

In what follows, we remind the reader that the output of A is not completely determined by its inputs and the examples provided to it. We only know that A is an admissible algorithm, and, hence, we can only measure the statistical properties of its output. Let $A(\varepsilon, \delta, n)$ denote the output of A when run on input ε, δ and n, with f as the target concept. Since A is a PAC learning algorithm for F, for each $f \in G$, the probability that $P(f \Delta A(\varepsilon, \delta, n)) \geq \varepsilon$ is at most δ. That is,

$$\mathbf{Pr} \left\{ P(f \Delta A(\varepsilon, \delta, n)) > \varepsilon \right\} \leq \delta. \tag{2.1}$$

Notation: For any event E, $\mathbf{Pr}\{E\}$ denotes the probability of the event occurring.

Using the learning operator Ψ of A, we can write

$$\mathbf{Pr}\left\{P(f\Delta A(\varepsilon, \delta)) > \varepsilon\right\} =$$

$$\sum_{x^m \in S^m} \mathbf{Pr}\left\{P(f\Delta\Psi(\varepsilon, \delta, n, f(x^m))) > \varepsilon\right\}\mathbf{Pr}\left\{f(x^m)\right\}. \qquad (2.2)$$

In the above, $\mathbf{Pr}\left\{f(x^m)\right\}$ is the probability that $f(x^m)$ is the sequence of examples obtained by m calls of EXAMPLE.

Substituting (2.2) in (2.1) gives us

$$\sum_{x^m \in S^m} \mathbf{Pr}\left\{P(f\Delta\Psi(\varepsilon, \delta, n, f(x^m))) > \varepsilon\right\}\mathbf{Pr}\left\{f(x^m)\right\} \le \delta.$$

Summing both sides of the above over all f in G, we get

$$\sum_{f \in G}\sum_{x^m \in S^m} \mathbf{Pr}\left\{P(f\Delta\Psi(\varepsilon, \delta, n, f(x^m))) > \varepsilon\right\}\mathbf{Pr}\left\{f(x^m)\right\} \le \sum_{f \in G}\delta.$$

Flipping the order of the sums in the above, we get

$$\sum_{x^m \in S^m}\sum_{f \in G} \mathbf{Pr}\left\{P(f\Delta\Psi(\varepsilon, \delta, n, f(x^m))) > \varepsilon\right\}\mathbf{Pr}\left\{f(x^m)\right\} \le \sum_{f \in G}\delta. \qquad (2.3)$$

We will estimate the inner sum in (2.3):

$$\sum_{f \in G} \mathbf{Pr}\left\{P(f\Delta\Psi(\varepsilon, \delta, n, f(x^m))) > \varepsilon\right\}. \qquad (2.4)$$

It is convenient to define a switch function $\theta: \{\text{true, false}\} \to N$ as follows. For any predicate E

$$\theta(E) = \begin{cases} 1, \text{ if } E \text{ is true} \\ 0 \text{ otherwise} \end{cases}.$$

Using the switch function, we can expand (2.4) as follows:

$$\sum_{f \in G}\sum_{h \in G} \theta\left[P(f\Delta h) > \varepsilon\right]\mathbf{Pr}\left\{S\cap h = S\cap\Psi(\varepsilon, \delta, n, f(x^m))\right\}. \qquad (2.5)$$

Fix x^m. We claim that for each $f \in G$, there exists $g \in G$ such that $g(x^m) = f(x^m)$ and, for all $h \in G$, at least one of the following inequalities must hold:

$$P(f \Delta h) > \varepsilon, \ \ P(g \Delta h) > \varepsilon.$$

To see this, consider the set $[x^m]$.

Notation: We use $[x^m]$ to denote the set of distinct items occurring in a sequence $x^m \in S^m$, i.e., $[x^m] = \{x \in S \mid x \text{ occurs in } x^m\}$.

Pick $g \in G$ such that g agrees with f on all of $[x^m]$ and disagrees with f on all of $S - [x^m]$. We denote such a choice of g by pair(f). Clearly, $g(x^m) = f(x^m)$. Now, h must disagree on at least half the elements in $S - [x^m]$ with either f or g. Since P is uniform on S, one of the following must hold:

$$P(f \Delta h) \geq \frac{|S - [x^m]|}{2|S|}, \ \ P(g \Delta h) \geq \frac{|S - [x^m]|}{2|S|}.$$

But $|[x^m]| \leq m \leq |S|/2$, and, hence, $|S - [x^m]| \geq |S|/2$. Substituting this in the above and noting that $\varepsilon < 1/4$ by assumption, the claim follows.

Now split G into disjoint sets G_1 and G_2 such that for each $f \in G_1$, pair$(f) \in G_2$ and vice versa. The split is not unique, but any such split will suffice. Let $\zeta(f)$ denote the event $S \cap h = S \cap \Psi(\varepsilon, \delta, n, f(x^m))$. We can now write (2.5) as

$$\sum_{f \in G_1} \sum_{h \in G} \theta \left[P(f \Delta h) > \varepsilon \right] \Pr \{\zeta(f)\} +$$

$$\sum_{g \in G_2} \sum_{h \in G} \theta \left[P(g \Delta h) > \varepsilon \right] \Pr \{\zeta(g)\}. \tag{2.6}$$

If $g = \text{pair}(f)$, then $f(x^m) = g(x^m)$. Hence, $\zeta(f) = \zeta(g)$, and we can write (2.6) as

$$\sum_{f \in G_1} \sum_{h \in G} \left[\theta \left[P(f \Delta h) > \varepsilon \right] + \theta \left[P(\text{pair}(f) \Delta h) > \varepsilon \right] \right] \Pr \{\zeta(f)\}. \tag{2.7}$$

Since at least one of $P(f \Delta h) > \varepsilon$, $P(\text{pair}(f) \Delta h) > \varepsilon$ must hold, we have

$$\theta \left[P(f \Delta h) > \varepsilon \right] + \theta \left[P(\text{pair}(f) \Delta h) > \varepsilon \right] \geq 1.$$

Substituting the above in (2.7) and noting that (2.7) was derived from (2.4), we get

$$\sum_{f \in G} \mathbf{Pr} \left\{ P(f \Delta \Psi(\varepsilon, \delta, n, f(x^m))) > \varepsilon \right\}$$

$$\geq \sum_{f \in G_1} \sum_{h \in G} \mathbf{Pr} \left\{ \zeta(f) \right\}$$

$$= \sum_{f \in G_1} \sum_{h \in G} \mathbf{Pr} \left\{ S \cap h = S \cap \Psi(\varepsilon, \delta, n, f(x^m)) \right\}$$

$$= \sum_{f \in G_1} 1 = 1/2 \sum_{f \in G} 1. \tag{2.8}$$

The last equality follows from the fact that $|G_1| = |G_2| = |G|/2$. Substituting (2.8) in the left-hand side of (2.3), we get

$$1/2 \sum_{x^m \in S^m} \sum_{f \in G} \mathbf{Pr} \left\{ f(x^m) \right\} = 1/2 \sum_{f \in G} \sum_{x^m \in S^m} \mathbf{Pr} \left\{ f(x^m) \right\}$$

$$= 1/2 \sum_{f \in G} 1. \tag{2.9}$$

Substituting (2.9) in (2.3), we get

$$1/2 \sum_{f \in G} 1 \leq \sum_{f \in G} \delta.$$

The above implies that $1/2 \leq \delta$, which is a contradiction since $\delta < 1/2$.

□

COROLLARY 2.2 _____

A class of concepts F is polynomial-sample learnable by an admissible learning algorithm only if F is of polynomial dimension.

_____

Proof: Let f be of superpolynomial dimension $d(n)$. By Theorem 2.2, for $\varepsilon < 1/4$ and $\delta < 1/2$, the sample complexity of any admissible learning algorithm A for F is $\Omega(d(n))$. Thus, the sample complexity of A is superpolynomial in n, and, hence, F is not polynomial-sample learnable.

□

Example 2.6   Let F be the class of the regular sets. We claim that F is not polynomial-sample learnable. To show this, we will prove that F is of superpolynomial dimension and then invoke Corollary 2.2. Consider $F^{[n]}$ for any n. Since every finite set is regular, $F^{[n]}$ is the power set of $\Sigma^{[n]}$. It follows that $F^{[n]}$ shatters $\Sigma^{[n]}$ and $D_{VC}(F^{[n]}) \geq 2^n$. By Corollary 2.2, F is not polynomial-sample learnable.   ∎

As an immediate consequence of Corollaries 2.1 and 2.2. we have:

THEOREM 2.3 _____

A class of concepts F is polynomial-sample learnable by an admissible algorithm if and only if F is of polynomial dimension.

_____

2.4 Learning Concepts with One-Sided Error

We now consider a learning framework in which the learning algorithm is required to be conservative in its approximation—the output concept must be a subset of the target concept. We call this learning with one-sided error since the error in the approximation produced by the learner can only be to the "safe side" of the target concept, i.e., the errors can only be errors of omission. In situations such as medical diagnosis or military decisions, such conservative behavior might be desirable. Our notion of one-sided error is somewhat related to the notion of Type I errors in the area of statistical hypothesis testing. However, since the relationship is not direct, we leave it to the reader to pursue it in the references listed in the Bibliographic Notes.

DEFINITION _____

Algorithm A learns F with *one-sided error* if (a) A is a PAC learning algorithm for F; and (b) the concept output by A is always a subset of the target concept.

_____

Essentially, A learns with one-sided error if, on any run of A, the concept g output by A is a subset of the target concept f. Thus, the errors in g are all errors of omission, in that some elements of f are missing from g. We will now obtain the analogs of Theorems 2.1, 2.2, and 2.3 in this setting. The following supporting definitions are required:

DEFINITION _____

Let $S \subseteq \text{graph}(f)$ for some $f \in F$. The *least* $g \in F$ consistent with S is such that (a) g is consistent with S; and (b) for all $h \in F$ consistent with S, $g \subseteq h$.

_____

Notice that g must be unique in the above, by definition.

DEFINITION

We say F is *minimally consistent* if, for each $f \in F$ and each nonempty and finite subset S of graph(f), there exists a least $g \in F$ consistent with S.

Example 2.7   The class F of monotone monomial concepts is minimally consistent. Let f be a monotone monomial and let S be a finite subset of graph(f). We need to show that there exists a least concept in F consistent with S. Let S^+ be the set of positive examples in S. If S^+ is empty, then the null monotone monomial concept is the least concept consistent with S. Otherwise, let $j = |x|$, $(x, y) \in S^+$. Consider the following monotone monomial on the j variables $a_1, a_2, \ldots, a_j$:

$$h = a_1 \wedge a_2 \cdots \wedge a_j.$$

Let V be the set of variables that are zero in at least one of the examples of S^+. That is,

$$V = \{a_i \mid \text{there exists } (x, 1) \in S^+, a_i = 0 \in x\}.$$

Delete all the variables in V from h to obtain the monotone monomial g. We claim that g is the least concept in F consistent with S. To see this, note that any $\hat{g} \in F$ consistent with S must be defined on j variables. Furthermore, since $\hat{g}$ cannot contain the variables in V, $\hat{g}$ can be obtained by deleting some variables from g. But, if $\hat{g}$ is obtained by deleting variables from g, then $g \subseteq \hat{g}$. Hence, g is the least monotone monomial consistent with S.

It follows that the monotone monomials are minimally consistent. See also Exercise 2.4. ∎

THEOREM 2.4

Let F be any class of concepts on Σ^*. If F is minimally consistent, there exists a learning algorithm for F with one-sided error and sample complexity

$$\frac{1}{\varepsilon} \left[(n+1) \mathbf{D}_{\mathrm{VC}}(F^{[n]}) \ln(2) + \ln \left[\frac{1}{\delta} \right] \right].$$

Proof: Algorithm $A_{2.2}$ below is a learning algorithm for F.

Learning Algorithm $A_{2.2}$
input: ε, δ, n;
begin:

$$\text{let } m = \frac{1}{\varepsilon}\left[(n+1)\mathbf{D}_{VC}(F^{[n]})\ln(2) + \ln\left[\frac{1}{\delta}\right]\right];$$

make m calls of EXAMPLE;
let S be the set of examples seen;
let g be the least concept in F
        consistent with S;
    output g;
end

Let f be the target concept. Since g is the least concept consistent with S, surely $g \subseteq f$. Using arguments identical to those used in our proof of Theorem 2.1, we can show that with probability greater than $(1-\delta)$, $P(f-g)$ $= P(f\Delta g) \leq \varepsilon$ will hold.

□

Example 2.8   In light of Example 2.7, we know that the algorithm of Example 2.5 for the monotone monomials actually learns with one-sided error. See also Exercises 2.4 and 2.5.   ■

THEOREM 2.5 _____

Let F be a class of concepts on Σ^* and let A be any admissible learning algorithm for F with one-sided error and sample complexity $s(\varepsilon, \delta, n)$. Then (a) F is minimally consistent; and (b) for fixed $\varepsilon < 1/4$ and $\delta < 1/2$, $s(\varepsilon, \delta, n) \geq \frac{1}{2}\mathbf{D}_{VC}(F^{[n]})$.

_____

Proof: We first show that F is minimally consistent. Let S be a nonempty and finite subset of graph(f) for some $f \in F$. Let P be the uniform distribution on S. Run the learning algorithm A for inputs $\varepsilon < 1/|S|$ and $\delta = 1/2$. Since $\varepsilon < 1/|S|$, with probability $1/2$ A must output a concept g such that g is consistent with S. Suppose that g is not the least concept consistent with S, i.e., there exists a concept $h \in F$ consistent with S such that g is not a subset of h.

Then, A does not learn with one-sided error, since h could well have been the target concept. This is a contradiction, and, hence, g must be the least concept consistent with S. Since S is arbitrary, F is minimally consistent.

By arguments identical to those of our proof of Theorem 2.1, we can show part (b) of the theorem. This completes the proof.

□

Finally, as a direct consequence of Theorems 2.4 and 2.5, we have:

THEOREM 2.6 _____

A class F is polynomial-sample learnable with one-sided error by an admissible algorithm if and only if it is of polynomial dimension and is minimally consistent.

2.5 Summary

We introduced the notion of PAC learning for classes of concepts defined on the countable domain of the strings of the binary alphabet. The number of examples required by a learning algorithm was formally measured by its sample complexity. The prior information available to the algorithm was quantified by the Vapnik-Chervonenkis dimension of the class of the concepts to be learned. We then obtained theorems linking the sample complexity and the dimension of a class of concepts. We also examined learning with one-sided error, wherein the output approximation of the learning algorithm was restricted to errors of omission only. Using the notion of minimal consistency of a class, we obtained analogs of the above results in this context.

Additional readings on the topics of this chapter are suggested in the Bibliographic Notes.

2.6 Appendix

We show that eliminating the length parameter n as input to the learning algorithm leaves the results of this chapter invariant in spirit.

Let us call the learning paradigm presented in the body of the chapter Framework 1. We define Framework 2 as follows:

DEFINITION _____

An algorithm A is a PAC learning algorithm for F if A is such that

(a) A takes as input ε, δ.

(b) A may call EXAMPLE, which returns examples for some $f \in F$. The examples are chosen randomly and independently according to an arbitrary and unknown probability distribution P on Σ^*.

(c)   For all concepts $f \in F$ and all probability distributions P on Σ^*, A outputs a concept $g \in F$, such that with probability at least $(1 - \delta)$, $P(f \Delta g) \leq \varepsilon$.

_____

The length of an example (x, y) is $|X|$, the length of x.

DEFINITION _____

Let A be a learning algorithm for a class F. The *sample complexity* of A is the function $s : \mathbf{R} \times \mathbf{R} \times \mathbf{N} \to \mathbf{N}$ such that $s(\varepsilon, \delta, n)$ is the maximum number of calls of EXAMPLE by A, the maximum being taken over all runs of A on inputs ε, δ, during which n is the length of the longest example seen by A, with the target concept ranging over all concepts in F and the probability distribution P ranging over all distributions on Σ^*. If no finite maximum exists, $s(\varepsilon, \delta, n) = \infty$.

_____

Suppose that A is a learning algorithm for a class of concepts F in Framework 2 with sample complexity $s(\varepsilon, \delta, n)$. We show how to construct a learning algorithm $\hat{A}$ for F in Framework 1 with the same sample complexity. On inputs ε, δ, and n, $\hat{A}$ runs A on inputs ε, δ and outputs A's output. Since the distribution P is on $\Sigma^{[n]}$, the length of the longest example seen by A will be n, and, hence, the number of calls of example will not exceed $s(\varepsilon, \delta, n)$. Also, the run time of $\hat{A}$ is but an additive constant over the run time of A.

Conversely, let A be a learning algorithm for F in Framework 1 with sample complexity $s(\varepsilon, \delta, n)$. The following is a learning algorithm $\hat{A}$ for F in Framework 2. In words, $\hat{A}$ first estimates a length n such that with probability at least $(1 - \delta/3)$, $\sum_{|x| \leq n} P(x) \geq 1 - \varepsilon/2$. Then, $\hat{A}$ runs A with inputs $\varepsilon/2, \delta/3$, and n. $\hat{A}$ has to make sure that A never receives an example of length greater than n. To achieve this, $\hat{A}$ draws a suitable number of examples so that with probability at least $(1 - \delta/3)$, a sufficient number of the examples obtained will be of length at most n. $\hat{A}$ then discards the examples longer than n and uses the remainder in its simulation of A. A formal proof that $\hat{A}$ is indeed a learning algorithm for F in Framework 2 follows the proof of Theorem 2.1 and is left to the reader as an exercise.

Learning Algorithm $\hat{A}$
input: ε, δ;
begin

      make $\left\lceil \dfrac{2}{\varepsilon} \right\rceil \ln \left\lceil \dfrac{3}{\delta} \right\rceil$ calls of EXAMPLE;

      let n be the length of the longest example seen;
      let $m = s(\varepsilon/2, \delta/3, n)$;

      make $\dfrac{m}{\ln(2/\varepsilon)} \ln \left\lceil \dfrac{3m}{\delta} \right\rceil$ calls of EXAMPLE;

      let σ be the sequence of examples so obtained;
      delete from σ examples whose lengths exceed n;
      if σ has fewer than m examples **then** halt;
      else
            run A on input $(\varepsilon/2, \delta/3, n)$;
            on the ith call of EXAMPLE by A
                give A the ith example from S;
            output A's output;
      end
end

Thus, F is polynomial-sample learnable in Framework 2 if and only if it is polynomial-sample learnable in Framework 1.

2.7 Exercises

2.1.   Prove that every finite class of concepts is polynomial-sample learnable.

2.2.   A literal is a Boolean variable c or its complement $\neg c$. A monomial on j variables is a formula consisting of the conjunction of literals. For instance, $a \wedge \neg b \wedge c$ is a monomial. Give a learning algorithm for the monomials, such as the one for monotone monomials given in Example 2.5.

2.3.   A Boolean formula is in disjunctive normal form (DNF) if it consists of the disjunctions of a number of terms, where each term is the conjunction of literals. For instance, on the variables a, b, c, and d,

$(a \wedge b \vee \neg d) \vee (a \wedge c \wedge b)$ is in DNF, consisting of two terms with two conjuncts per term. For fixed integer k, a k-DNF formula is a Boolean formula in disjunctive normal form, with no more than k conjuncts per term. Following the conventions of Example 2.1, consider the class of k-DNF concepts. Prove that for fixed k, this class is polynomial-sample learnable with one-sided error.

2.4.   Let F be a class of concepts on Σ^*. F is said to be closed under countable intersection if for every countable $G \subseteq F$,

$$\left[\bigcap_{g \in G} g \right] \in F.$$

Show that if F is closed under countable intersection, then F is minimally consistent. Also, show that it is not sufficient if F is closed under finite intersection. The converse is not true, i.e., F may be minimally consistent but not closed under countable intersection. Hint: Consider the case when $f \cap g$ is infinite.

2.5.   Using the above, prove that the monotone monomials are minimally consistent. Hence, show that the algorithm of Example 2.5 learns with one-sided error.

2.6.   As with a k-DNF formula, a k-CNF formula consists of the conjunction of some number of clauses, where each clause is the disjunction of literals. (CNF stands for conjunctive normal form.) For instance, $(a \vee b) \wedge (b \vee c)$ is in 2-CNF. Following the conventions of Example 2.1, consider the class of k-CNF concepts. Prove that for fixed k, this class is polynomial-sample learnable with one-sided error.

2.7.   Is the class of k-DNF concepts polynomial-sample learnable with one-sided error?

2.8.   Let F be a minimally consistent class, let $f \in F$, and let S be a nonempty and finite subset of $f \times \{1\}$. Suppose that S is of minimum cardinality among all sets $\hat{S}$ such that f is the least concept in F consistent with $\hat{S}$. Show that F shatters S.

2.9.   Tighten Lemma 2.1 by showing that

$$|H| \leq \Phi(|X|, d) \leq \left\lceil \frac{e |X|}{d} \right\rceil^{d+1}$$

where $\Phi(k, d) = \sum_{i=0}^{d} \binom{k}{i}$ and e is the base of the natural logarithm.

Hint: Show that

$$\Phi(k,d) = \Phi(k-1, d) + \Phi(k-1, d-1).$$

2.10.   Consider the following "generate and test" paradigm for concept learning. Suppose you are given a black box G that can enumerate the concepts in a class F without repetition. Consider the following learning algorithm for F. If f is the target concept, does the algorithm guarantee that with probability at least $1-\delta$, $P(f\Delta g) \le \varepsilon$ at termination? If not, modify the algorithm so that it does.

Learning Algorithm A
input: ε, δ, n;
begin
    $i = 1$;
    repeat forever
        make $\dfrac{1}{\varepsilon}\ln\left(\dfrac{1}{\delta}\right)$ calls of EXAMPLE;
        let S be the set of examples so obtained;
        let g be the ith concept output by G;
        if g is consistent with S **then**
            output g and halt;
        else $i = i +1$;
    end
end

2.11.   Suppose we modify the routine EXAMPLE() so that it takes a Boolean-valued argument, to be used by the learning algorithm to choose between positive and negative examples for the target concept. Let f be the target concept. If f is empty, EXAMPLE(1) returns nothing; otherwise, EXAMPLE(1) returns a positive example for the target concept, drawn according to the conditional distribution P_1 over all the strings in the target concept f. P_1 is given by

$$P_1(x) = \begin{cases} \eta_1 P(x), \text{ if } x \in f \\ 0 \text{ otherwise} \end{cases}$$

where

$$\eta_1 = \frac{1}{\sum_{x \in f} P(x)}.$$

Similarly, EXAMPLE(0) returns negative examples drawn according to the conditional distribution P_0 on all strings not in the target concept. If $f = \Sigma^*$, EXAMPLE(0) returns nothing.

Show that all the results of this chapter hold under this modified definition of EXAMPLE().

2.12. Let F be a class of concepts on a finite domain X. For each $f \in F$, a discriminant of f is a set of examples such that f is the only concept in f that is consistent with the set. A discriminant of minimum cardinality is denoted by $D(f)$. Assume F is finite. Prove or disprove each of the following assertions:

(a) For all $f \in F$, $|D(f)| \leq \mathbf{D}_{VC}(F)$.

(b) For all $f \in F$, $|D(f)| \leq \log |F|$.

(c) $\sum_{f \in F} |D(f)| \leq |F| \, \mathbf{D}_{VC}(F)$.

(d) $\sum_{f \in F} |D(f)| \leq |F| \log |F|$.

2.13. Let Γ be a context-free grammar generating some subset of Σ^*. A sentential form α of Γ is any string composed of terminals and nonterminals derivable from the start symbol of Γ. The set $L(\alpha, \Gamma)$ is the set of all strings in Σ^* derivable from the sentential form α, using the production rules of Γ. Consider the class of concepts

$$F = \{L(\alpha, \Gamma) \mid \alpha \text{ is a sentential form of } \Gamma\}.$$

Show that if Γ is an unambiguous context-free grammar, then F is minimally consistent.

2.14. Let F and G be two minimally consistent classes. Let H be the class given by

$$H = \{f \cap g \mid f \in F, g \in G\}.$$

Show that H is minimally consistent.

2.8 Bibliographic Notes

The paradigm of PAC learning was introduced by Valiant (1984). The notion of shattering and the Vapnik-Chervonenkis dimension is from Vapnik and Chervonenkis (1971), as adapted by Blumer, Ehrenfeucht, Haussler, and Warmuth (1990). Also see Pollard (1986), Chapter 2. More general forms of Theorems 2.1 and 2.2 are given in Blumer, Ehrenfeucht, Haussler, and Warmuth (1990) and Ehrenfeucht, Haussler, Kearns, and Valiant (1989), and are discussed in Chapter 4. Lemma 2.1 and its tighter form of Exercise 2.9 are proved in Assouad (1983) and in Vapnik and Chervonenkis (1971). It also appears in a somewhat different form in Nilsson (1990), pages 32–35. The material in Section 2.4 is from Natarajan (1991). A useful necessary condition for learning with one-sided error is given in Shvaytser (1990). For a discussion of statistical hypothesis testing and errors of Types I and II, see Brownlee (1960), pages 98–99. Exercise 2.6 is from Valiant (1984). Exercise 2.10 is from Kearns, Li, Pitt, and Valiant (1987a) and Angluin (1986a). A discussion of the pathologies involved in Framework 2 of the Appendix may be found in Pitt and Warmuth (1989). Haussler, Kearns, Littlestone, and Warmuth (1988) discuss the equivalence of several models of learnability, such as those with distinct sources of positive and negative examples as in Exercise 2.11. Exercise 2.12 is from Statman (1987), and Exercise 2.13 is from Natarajan (1989c).

3

Time Complexity of
Concept Learning

Thus far, we have concerned ourselves with the sample complexity of learning, i.e., the number of examples required to learn. In this chapter, we consider the time complexity of learning, i.e., the time required to process the examples.

3.1 Preliminaries

In the previous chapter, we used the term *algorithm* in a very broad sense. This was because we were interested in only the sample complexity of learning and desired our results to hold over the broadest possible definition. Indeed, we will continue to use the broader meaning of the term when sample complexity is our sole interest. When we are interested in time complexity, as we are in this chapter, we must use the term *algorithm* in the traditional sense to mean a finitely representable program with respect to some fixed computing system. For concreteness, we embrace the Turing machine as our system.

A technical issue arises when we limit the learning algorithm to be a Turing machine. The parameters ε and δ cannot be arbitrary precision real numbers if they are to be meaningfully presented as input. To overcome this difficulty, we restrict ε and δ to be the reciprocals of integers and provide these integers in binary form as input to the learning algorithm. This does not alter the spirit of the PAC learning model.

In order to permit interesting measures of time complexity, we must specify the manner in which the learning algorithm identifies its approximation to the target concept. In particular, we will require the learning algorithm to identify its output concept using some predetermined naming scheme. To this end, we define the notion of a representation for a class of concepts. In essence, a representation for a class F is an assignment of names for each concept f in F. The names are simply strings in Σ^*, and each concept in F may have more than one name, as long as two distinct concepts do not share a name. The choice that each name be a string in Σ^* is only in the interest of simplicity. We could equally well define names to be strings in some other alphabet if that were more convenient.

DEFINITION

For a class of concepts F, a *representation* is a function $R : F \to 2^{\Sigma^*}$. For each $f \in F, R(f)$ is the set of *names* for f. R must be such that

(a)   Each $f \in F$ has at least one name, i.e., for all $f \in F$, $R(f) \neq \varnothing$.

(b)   No two concepts share a name, i.e., for any two distinct f and g in F, $R(f) \cap R(g) = \varnothing$.

The length or size of a name $r \in R(f)$ is simply the string length $|r|$ of r. Thus, the shortest name for f is the shortest string in $R(f)$. We denote the length of the shortest name for f by $l_{\min}(f, R)$. When R is clear from the context, we simply use $l_{\min}(f)$.

As an aside, we note that if each concept in F were to have a name of finite length, F would have to be of countable cardinality.

Example 3.1   When a Boolean formula is written in terms of variables and logical symbols, we say it is in standard form. The standard form also includes the tautological header mentioned in Example 2.1.

The length of a formula in standard form is simply the number of variables and logical symbols occurring in the formula. For instance, the formula $(a_1 \vee \neg a_1) \wedge (a_2 \vee \neg a_2) \wedge (a_1 \wedge a_2)$ is of length 19.

We encode Boolean formulae in binary as follows. First, we encode Boolean formulae using integers and the comma. Then we will show how to transform this encoding into binary.

The logical symbols are written as integers, as follows:

(	1
)	2
$\vee$	3
$\wedge$	4
$\neg$	5

A variable a_i is written as the integer $i+5$. For instance, a_4 would be written as 9. Variables and symbols are separated by commas. Thus, $a_1 \wedge a_2$ would be written as 6,4,7.

Now, we introduce a special binary encoding for the integers and the comma. The string 10 stands for 0, and 11 stands for 1. For instance, the binary encoding for 3 would be 1111, and the binary encoding for 4 would be 111010. The string 00 stands for the comma. Hence, $a_1 \wedge a_2$ would be encoded as 1111100011101000111111.

It is clear that a Boolean formula of length l in standard form can be defined on at most l variables. It follows that a Boolean formula of length l in standard form can be encoded in binary in length $O(l \log(l))$.

We will make use of the above encoding throughout this book and will refer to it simply as the "binary encoding of a Boolean formula."

Recall the class F of monotone monomial concepts of Example 2.1. Let M be the set of all monotone monomial formulae, encoded in binary. By definition, the mapping $R : F \rightarrow 2^M$, from concepts in F to the corresponding monotone monomial formulae, is a representation for this class. Specifically, for each $f \in F, R(f)$ is the set of all monotone monomial formulae for which f is the set of satisfying assignments. That is,

$$R(f) = \{r \mid r \in M, \text{ and } f \text{ is its satisfying assignments}\}.$$

Notice that each monotone monomial concept has at least one name in R, and perhaps many. Also, note that no two distinct concepts share a name. We call R the representation of monotone monomial formulae for F.

As another example, suppose that F were the set of regular sets. One possible representation for F would be the mapping R from the regular sets to sets of equivalent regular expressions (more precisely, the binary encodings of the regular expressions). For instance, consider the set f of all strings that end in 1. It is well known that f is regular. In fact, the regular expression $r_1 = (0+1)^* 1$ generates f and, hence, is a name for it in R, i.e., $r_1 \in R(f)$. Similarly, $r_2 = (0+1)^* 1^* 0^* 1$ also generates f and $r_2 \in R(f)$.

Another possible representation for the regular sets is the mapping from the regular sets to sets of the corresponding finite automata.   ∎

We say that a learning algorithm A learns a concept class F in representation R if it identifies its output concept using names in R. Formally, we have the following:

DEFINITION _____

An algorithm A is a PAC learning algorithm for F in R if

(a) A takes as input ε, δ, and $n \in \mathbf{N}$.

(b) A may call EXAMPLE, which returns examples for some $f \in F$. The examples are chosen randomly according to an arbitrary and unknown probability distribution P on $\Sigma^{[n]}$.

(c) For all concepts $f \in F$ and all probability distributions P on $\Sigma^{[n]}$, A outputs $r \in R(g)$ for some $g \in F$, such that with probability at least $(1 - \delta)$, $P(f \Delta g) \le \varepsilon$.

_____

Example 3.2   Recall the class of monotone monomial concepts with the representation of the (binary encodings of) monotone monomial formulae, as in Example 3.1. The learning algorithm *learn_monomial* of Example 2.5 identifies its output concepts as monotone monomial formulae. If we changed *learn_monomial* so that it would output the binary encoding of its output formula, the resulting algorithm would learn the monotone monomial concepts in the representation of the monotone monomial formulae.

It is clear that converting a Boolean formula in standard form to its binary encoding can be carried out simply and efficiently by lexical substitution. With this in mind, we will view the standard form and the binary encodings as interchangeable and simply say that *learn_monomial* learns F in R as it stands. In fact, we will employ this interchangeability throughout this book.   ■

Although formality demands that we specify both F and R in the above definition, it can be cumbersome to write "algorithm A learns F in R." Often, F and R are naturally associated, and it is superfluous to give both. For instance, if R is the representation of the monotone monomial formulae, it is natural for F to be the class of monotone monomial concepts. Taking advantage of this association, we simply write "A learns the monotone monomial formulae" to mean that "A learns the monotone monomial concepts in the representation of the monotone monomial formulae." Similarly, if R is the representation of the finite automata, it is natural for F to be the class of regular sets. Thus, we write "A learns the finite automata" to mean that "A learns the class of regular sets in the representation of the finite automata."

Since the aim of this chapter is to examine the time complexity of learning, we must construct a measure of the computational time expended by a learning algorithm. In what follows, we will assume that each call of EXAMPLE costs unit time. Note that this is the cost of obtaining each example. The cost of reading and processing an example will depend on the length of the example and is not included in the cost of obtaining the example. Surely, the time expended by the learning algorithm will depend on the length of its output. To account for this dependence, we will include the length of the shortest name of the target concept as a parameter in the time complexity measure.

DEFINITION _____

Let A be a learning algorithm for a concept class F in representation R. The *time complexity* of A is the function $t : R \times R \times N \times N \to N$ such that $t(\varepsilon, \delta, n, l)$ is the maximum number of computational steps consumed by A, the maximum being taken over all runs of A in which the inputs are ε, δ, and n, with the target concept f ranging over all $f \in F$ such that $l_{min}(f) \leq l$, and the probability distribution P ranging over all distributions on $\Sigma^{[n]}$. If no finite maximum exists, $t(\varepsilon, \delta, n, l) = \infty$.

_____

To illustrate the above definition, we give a recipe to compute the time complexity of A for a particular choice of ε, δ, n, and l. The recipe serves for clarity and is a thought experiment, not a computational procedure. Run A on inputs ε, δ, and n for all target concepts $f \in F$ such that $l_{min}(f) \leq l$ and all probability distributions P on $\Sigma^{[n]}$. For each choice of P and f, repeat the runs over all possible outcomes of the sequence of calls to EXAMPLE. The maximum number of time steps consumed by A over all these runs is $t(\varepsilon, \delta, n, l)$. If no finite maximum exists, $t(\varepsilon, \delta, n, l)$ is infinite.

Thus, the time complexity of A is the time required by A as a function of ε, δ, $l_{min}(f)$, and n. If this function is bounded by a polynomial in these parameters, we consider the algorithm to be efficient. With this in mind, we give the following definition:

DEFINITION _____

F is *polynomial-time learnable* in R if there exists a deterministic learning algorithm for F in R, with time complexity $p(1/\varepsilon, 1/\delta, n, l)$, where p is a polynomial function of its arguments.

_____

It is important to note that polynomial-sample learnability and polynomial-time learnability are not comparable notions. This is because the polynomial-sample learnability of a class F does not involve a specific representation R. On the other hand, polynomial-time learnability involves a specific representation R, and the number of calls of EXAMPLE may depend on $l_{min}(f)$, the length of the shortest name in R for the target concept f. Thus, F may be polynomial-time learnable in R, without F being polynomial-sample learnable—Exercise 3.7 illustrates this point. Of course, the converse is true as well.

For concept classes and representations that are naturally associated with each other, we use the shortened notation that we mentioned before. For instance, we will say that the "monotone monomial formulae are polynomial-time learnable," or that "finite automata are not polynomial-time learnable," and so on.

Example 3.3   As pointed out in Example 3.2, algorithm *learn_monomial* of Example 2.5 learns the monotone monomial concepts in the representation of the monotone monomial formulae. In our shorthand notation, we can simply say that *learn_monomial* learns the monotone monomial formulae. We now estimate the run time of the algorithm. Each call of EXAMPLE costs unit time. Also, it takes $O(j)$ time to process each example in S. Since $j \le n$, the time required to process all the examples is $O(mn)$. Thus, the overall time expended is $O(mn)+m$, which is $O(mn)$.

Now,

$$m = \frac{1}{\varepsilon} \left[(n+1)^2 \ln(2) + \ln\left[\frac{1}{\delta}\right] \right].$$

Hence, the overall time expended by the algorithm is polynomial in $1/\varepsilon$, $1/\delta$, and n, and, hence, the monotone monomial formulae are polynomial-time learnable.   ∎

3.2 Polynomial-Time Learnability

We are interested in identifying the family of pairs F and R, such that F is polynomial-time learnable in R. Let us examine learning algorithm $A_{2.1}$ again. If each call of EXAMPLE costs unit time, then the only step that could be computationally expensive is that of picking a concept consistent with the examples seen. In light of this, we give the following definitions:

DEFINITION _____

Algorithm Q is said to be a *fitting* for a class F in representation R if

(a) Q takes as input a set of examples $S \subseteq \Sigma^* \times \{0, 1\}$.

(b) If there exists a concept in F that is consistent with S, Q outputs the name of such a concept. That is, if there exists $f \in F$ such that $S \subseteq \text{graph}(f)$, Q outputs $r \in R(g)$, such that $g \in F$ and $S \subseteq \text{graph}(g)$.

_____

In the above, we say that g is the concept identified by Q in its output. Abusing notation, we extend $l_{min}()$ to sets of examples as follows. For a set of examples S, $l_{min}(S)$ is the length of the shortest name of any concept in F consistent with S, i.e., $l_{min}(S) = \min \{l_{min}(f) | f \in F, S \subseteq \text{graph}(f)\}$. If no concept in F is consistent with S, $l_{min}(S) = \infty$.

DEFINITION _____

Let Q be a deterministic program that is a fitting for F in R. If on input S, Q runs in time polynomial in the length of its input and $l_{min}(S)$, we say Q is a *polynomial-time fitting*.

_____

With these definitions in hand, we can state the following theorem:

THEOREM 3.1 _____

Let F be a class of concepts of polynomial dimension and let R be a representation for F. F is polynomial-time learnable in R if there exists a polynomial-time fitting for F in R.

_____

Proof: Let Q be a polynomial-time fitting for F in R. Algorithm $A_{3.1}$ below is a polynomial-time learning algorithm for F in R:

Learning Algorithm $A_{3.1}$
input: ε, δ, n;
begin:

$$\text{let } m = \frac{1}{\varepsilon} \left[(n+1)\mathbf{D}_{\text{VC}}(F^{[n]})\ln(2) + \ln\left[\frac{1}{\delta}\right] \right];$$

make m calls of EXAMPLE;
let S be the set of examples seen;
output $Q(S)$;
end

We can prove that $A_{3.1}$ is a PAC learning algorithm for F using the methods of the proof of Theorem 2.1. It remains to bound the run time of the algorithm. Since each call of EXAMPLE costs unit time, A runs in time polynomial in $1/\varepsilon$, $1/\delta$, and n, except for the time taken to run Q. Now, Q runs in time polynomial in the size of its input and in $l_{\min}(S)$, and we will estimate both these quantities. By definition, $l_{\min}(S) \leq l_{\min}(f)$. The length of the description of S is the size of Q's input. Since each example in S is of the form (x, y), where $|x| \leq n$ and $|y| = 1$, the length of the description of S is at most $m(n+1)$ and, hence, is polynomial in n, $1/\varepsilon$ and $1/\delta$. It follows that A runs in time polynomial in $1/\varepsilon$, $1/\delta$, n, and $l_{\min}(f)$.

□

Example 3.4   Consider the class F of all finite axis-parallel rectangles on $N \times N$, i.e., finite rectangles with sides parallel to the axes. For technical convenience, we include the empty set in F.

A point (u,v) in $N \times N$ is encoded as a string x (of even length) in Σ^* as follows: The first half of x is the binary encoding of u, and the second half of x is the binary encoding of v. Thus, F can be viewed as a class of concepts on Σ^*. Now, each rectangle is uniquely identified by either of its diagonals. Thus, the number of distinct concepts on $\Sigma^{[n]}$ is at most the number of distinct pairs of strings we can choose from $\Sigma^{[n]}$. The latter is at most $|\Sigma^{[n]}| \times |\Sigma^{[n]}| \leq 2^{2n+2}$. Hence, by Lemma 2.2, $\mathbf{D}(F) \leq 2n+2$.

Consider the representation R, where for each rectangle $f \in F$, the names in $R(f)$ are the string encodings of the lower-left and upper-right vertices of f. We now show that F has a polynomial-time fitting Q in R. Specifically, we exhibit an algorithm that takes as input a set of examples S and identifies an axis-parallel rectangle that is consistent with S.

Fitting Q
input: S: set of examples.
begin
    compute x_{max} and x_{min}, the maximum and minimum
        values of the x-coordinates of the positive examples of S.
    compute y_{max} and y_{min}, the maximum and minimum
        values of the y-coordinates of the positive examples of S.
    output $(x_{min}, y_{min}), (x_{max}, y_{max})$
end

From Theorem 3.1, it follows that the class of axis-parallel rectangles is polynomial-time learnable in the representation of diagonal points. ∎

We now prove a weak form of the converse of Theorem 3.1. To do so, we need the following definitions. (Readers unfamiliar with the notion of a randomized algorithm, please see Appendix at the end of this chapter.)

DEFINITION _____

Let Q be a randomized fitting for F in R. If Q runs in time polynomial in the length of its input and in $l_{min}(S)$, we say it is a *random polynomial-time fitting*.

The following definition concerns the complexity of testing for membership in a concept $f \in F$, given a name $r \in R(f)$.

DEFINITION _____

R is *polynomial-time computable* if there exists a deterministic algorithm B and a fixed polynomial q such that:

(a) B takes as input a pair of strings $r, x \in \Sigma^*$.

(b)   If $r \in R(f)$ for some $f \in F$, B halts in time $q(|x| + |r|)$ and outputs $f(x)$.

THEOREM 3.2 _____

Let F be a class of concepts and let R be a polynomial-time computable representation for F. F is polynomial-time learnable in R only if F has a random polynomial-time fitting in R.

_____

Proof: Assume that F is polynomial-time learnable in R by an algorithm A and that R is polynomial-time computable by a program B. We show that there exists a random polynomial-time fitting Q for F.

Fitting Q
input: S:set of examples;
begin
    Let $\varepsilon = \dfrac{1}{|S|+1}$ and $\delta = \dfrac{1}{4}$;
    Let $n = \max \{|x| \,|(x, y)\in S\}$;
    Run A on inputs ε, δ, n;
    for each call of EXAMPLE by A **do**
        give A a randomly chosen element of S;
    Let r be the name output by A;
    if for each $(x, y)\in S, B\,(r, x) = y$, **then** output r ;
    else output nothing;
end

In essence, the fitting Q runs A with S as examples. If $\varepsilon < 1/|S|$ and $\delta = 1/4$, the name output by A must be that of a concept consistent with S with probability at least $(1-\delta) = 3/4$. By invoking the program B, Q checks to see whether A's output is consistent with S. If so, Q halts successfully. If not, Q outputs nothing. Thus, with probability 3/4, Q outputs the name of a concept in F that is consistent with S.

It remains to show that Q runs in polynomial time. Since A is a polynomial-time learning algorithm, A runs in time polynomial in $1/\varepsilon$, $1/\delta$, n and in $l_{min}(f)$, where f is the target concept. But, f could be any concept in F consistent with S, and so A must run in time polynomial in $l_{min}(S)$. Thus, Q runs in time polynomial in the size of its input and in $l_{min}(S)$ and, hence, is a random polynomial-time fitting.

□

3.3 Occam's Razor

This section is somewhat technical in nature and may be skipped at the first reading.

Theorem 3.1 is limited to the case where F is of polynomial dimension. In the following, we consider a weaker model of polynomial-time learning, one that is almost identical to the earlier definition except that we only require the run time of the learning algorithm to be "usually" polynomial in the various parameters. Note that the learning algorithm is still deterministic, with the probabilistic nature being introduced by the random examples.

DEFINITION _____

F is *learnable in usually polynomial time*[1] in R if there exists a deterministic learning algorithm for F in R such that on every set of inputs ε, δ, and n, for every target concept $f \in F$ and probability distribution P on $\Sigma^{[n]}$, with probability at least $1/2$, the algorithm halts in time $p(1/\varepsilon, 1/\delta, n, l_{min}(f))$, where p is a polynomial function of its arguments.

_____

In the following, we define a stronger notion of a fitting. We say that a fitting is Occam[2] if the names it outputs are of minimum length, give or take a polynomial factor. The polynomial factor is a function of the length and number of the examples given as input to the fitting.

DEFINITION _____

Let Q be a fitting for F in R. Q is *Occam* if there exists a fixed polynomial q and fixed real $0 \le \alpha < 1$ such that for all inputs S, the output of Q is of length at most $q(n, l_{min}(S))m^{\alpha}$, where $m = |S|$ and $n = \max\{|x| \mid (x, y) \in S\}$.

_____

We call q and α the bounding polynomial and bounding exponent, respectively, of Q. If Q is deterministic and runs in time polynomial in the length of its input and in $l_{min}(S)$, we say Q is a polynomial-time Occam fitting.

---

1. This is almost equivalent to saying "polynomial Blum time" in the terminology of Gill (1977).

2. W. Ockham (1285–1349), more often spelled Occam. Philosopher, credited with the principle of Occam's Razor: "*non sunt multiplicanda entia praeter necessitatem.*" This literally means "entities should not be multiplied unnecessarily," but is commonly interpreted to mean "the simplest explanation of the observed phenomena is most likely to be a correct one."

Using the above definitions, we have the following:

THEOREM 3.3

Let F be a class of concepts with representation R. F is usually polynomial-time learnable in R if there exists a polynomial-time Occam fitting for F in R and R is polynomial-time computable.

Proof: Let Q be a polynomial-time Occam fitting for F with bounding polynomial q and exponent α. Also let R be polynomial-time computable by a program B. Then, algorithm $A_{3.2}$ is a usually polynomial-time learning algorithm for F. The choice of various parameters within the algorithm will become clear shortly.

Learning Algorithm $A_{3.2}$
input: ε, δ, n;
begin
$\quad l = 1$;
$\quad$ **repeat forever**
$\qquad \gamma = \dfrac{\delta}{2l^2}$;
$\qquad$ let $m = \left\lceil \dfrac{4q(n, l)}{\varepsilon} \right\rceil^{\frac{1}{(1-\alpha)}}$;
$\qquad$ make m calls of EXAMPLE;
$\qquad$ let S be the set of examples seen;
$\qquad$ let $r = Q(S)$;
$\qquad$ let $m_1 = \dfrac{16}{\varepsilon^2 \gamma}$;
$\qquad$ make m_1 calls of EXAMPLE;
$\qquad$ let σ be the sequence of examples seen;
$\qquad$ using B, check that r is the name of a concept g
$\qquad\qquad$ consistent with a fraction of at least
$\qquad\qquad\quad \left\lceil 1 - \dfrac{3}{4}\varepsilon \right\rceil$ of the examples in σ;
$\qquad$ if so, output r and halt; else, $l = l+1$;
$\quad$ **end**
end

We begin with a brief overview of the algorithm: $A_{3.2}$ iterates over increasingly larger guesses l for $l_{\min}(f)$, where f is the target concept. At each iteration, it obtains a set S of examples for the target concept. It then runs the Occam fitting Q on S to identify a concept g that is consistent with S. Then, $A_{3.2}$ estimates $P(f\Delta g)$ by comparing f and g on some randomly chosen examples. If $P(f\Delta g)$ turns out to be small, $A_{3.2}$ identifies g in its output and halts. Else, $A_{3.2}$ increments its guess for $l_{\min}(f)$ and begins a new iteration. Now, if l were a sufficiently large guess, i.e., $l \geq l_{\min}(f)$, it is likely that $P(f\Delta g) \leq \varepsilon$. Thus, after $l_{\min}(f)$ iterations, $A_{3.2}$ is increasingly likely to halt with a good approximation for f. We first show that $A_{3.2}$ is correct. Let $\hat{P}$ be the probability distribution on $\Sigma^* \times \{0, 1\}$ defined as follows:

$$\hat{P}((x, y)) = \begin{cases} P(x) \text{ if } y = f(x) \\ 0 \text{ otherwise} \end{cases}.$$

For $g \in F$, by Chebyshev's inequality (see Appendix),

$$\mathbf{Pr}\left\{ |\hat{P}_{(m)}(\text{graph}(g)) - \hat{P}(\text{graph}(g))| \geq \frac{1}{4}\varepsilon \right\} \leq \frac{16}{\varepsilon^2 m}. \tag{3.1}$$

Notation: For a random variable q and distribution P, $P_{(m)}(q)$ is the average value of q on m observations chosen randomly according to P. Thus, if $q_1, q_2, \ldots, q_m$ are the m observations of q, then $P_{(m)}(q) = \sum_{i=1}^{m} q_i$. For a set S, $P_{(m)}(S) = P_{(m)}(I_S)$ is the fraction of the m observations that are members of S.

Now,

$$\hat{P}(\text{graph}(g)) = \sum_{y = g(x)} \hat{P}(x, y)$$

$$= \sum_{g(x) = f(x)} P(x) = 1 - P(f\Delta g). \tag{3.2}$$

Referring to $A_{3.2}$, let ν denote the fraction of examples in σ with which g is consistent. Since σ is a random sample drawn according to $\hat{P}$,

$$\nu = \hat{P}_{(m_1)}(\text{graph}(g)). \tag{3.3}$$

Substituting (3.3) and (3.2) in (3.1), we get

$$\mathbf{Pr}\left\{ |v - (1 - P(f\Delta g))| \geq \frac{1}{4}\varepsilon \right\} \leq \frac{16}{\varepsilon^2 m_1}.$$

Hence, if $m_1 \geq 16/(\varepsilon^2\gamma)$,

$$\mathbf{Pr}\left\{ |v - (1 - P(f\Delta g))| \geq \frac{1}{4}\varepsilon \right\} \leq \gamma,$$

which can be expanded as

$$\mathbf{Pr}\left\{ v \geq 1 - P(f\Delta g) + \frac{1}{4}\varepsilon \right\} + \mathbf{Pr}\left\{ v \leq 1 - P(f\Delta g) - \frac{1}{4}\varepsilon \right\} \leq \gamma. \qquad (3.4)$$

From (3.4) we have

$$\mathbf{Pr}\left\{ v \geq 1 - P(f\Delta g) + \frac{1}{4}\varepsilon \right\} \leq \gamma.$$

If g is such that $P(f\Delta g) > \varepsilon$, then surely

$$\mathbf{Pr}\left\{ v \geq 1 - \varepsilon + \frac{1}{4}\varepsilon \right\} \leq \gamma,$$

or

$$\mathbf{Pr}\left\{ v \geq 1 - \frac{3}{4}\varepsilon \right\} \leq \gamma.$$

Thus, at any particular value of l, the probability that $A_{3.2}$ will output the name of a concept g such that $P(f\Delta g) > \varepsilon$ is at most γ. Noting that $\gamma = \delta/(2l^2)$, the probability that A outputs the name of a concept g such that $P(f\Delta g) > \varepsilon$ at any value of l is at most

$$\sum_{l=1}^{\infty} \frac{\delta}{2l^2} \leq \delta.$$

It remains to bound the run time of $A_{3.2}$. Note that each iteration of the algorithm takes time polynomial in n, $1/\varepsilon$, $1/\delta$, and l, since both Q and B run in time polynomial in these parameters. Thus, it suffices for us to show that with probability at least $1/2$, l is bounded from above by a polynomial in $l_{\min}(f)$. This can be achieved by showing that the expected value of l is bounded by a polynomial in $l_{\min}(f)$.

For any particular value of l, let $F(l) \subseteq F$ denote the set of concepts in F that have names of length l or less, i.e.,

$$F(l) = \{f \in F \,|\, l_{\min}(f) \leq l\}.$$

Suppose that on a particular iteration of the main loop of $A_{3.2}$, Q identifies a concept g on input S. Then, since Q is Occam,

$$g \in F(q(n, l_{\min}(S))\,|S\,|^{\alpha}).$$

Since $l_{\min}(S) \leq l_{\min}(f)$ and $|S| \leq m$,

$$F(q(n, l_{\min}(S))\,|S\,|^{\alpha}) \subseteq F(q(n, l_{\min}(f))m^{\alpha}),$$

and, hence,

$$g \in F(q(n, l_{\min}(f))m^{\alpha}).$$

Now, the probability that any concept $g \in F(q(n, l_{\min}(f))m^{\alpha})$, such that $P(f \Delta g) \geq \varepsilon/2$, is consistent with all the examples of S is at most

$$|F(q(n, l_{\min}(f))m^{\alpha})| \left[1 - \frac{\varepsilon}{2}\right]^m.$$

This can be shown using the arguments of the proof of Theorem 2.1. We will pick m so that this probability is at most $1/2$, i.e.,

$$|F(q(n, l_{\min}(f))m^{\alpha})| \left[1 - \frac{\varepsilon}{2}\right]^m \leq \frac{1}{2}. \tag{3.5}$$

Surely,

$$|F(q(n, l_{\min}(f))m^{\alpha})| \leq 2^{q(n, l_{\min}(f))m^{\alpha}}.$$

By substituting the above, we can show that inequality (3.5) holds for

$$m = \left[\frac{4q(n, l_{\min}(f))}{\varepsilon}\right]^{\frac{1}{(1-\alpha)}}. \tag{3.6}$$

Now, $A_{3.2}$ picks m to be

$$m = \left[\frac{4q(n, l)}{\varepsilon}\right]^{\frac{1}{(1-\alpha)}},$$

so that when $l \geq l_{\min}(f)$, (3.6) will hold. This implies that when $l \geq l_{\min}(f)$, with probability at least $1/2$, the concept g identified by Q will be such that $P(f \Delta g) < \varepsilon/2$. Now, (3.4) implies that

$$\mathbf{Pr}\left\{ v \le 1 - P(f\Delta g) - \frac{1}{4}\varepsilon \right\} \le \gamma.$$

If $P(f\Delta g) < \varepsilon/2$, then surely

$$\mathbf{Pr}\left\{ v < 1 - \frac{\varepsilon}{2} - \frac{1}{4}\varepsilon \right\} \le \gamma.$$

Therefore,

$$\mathbf{Pr}\left\{ v < 1 - \frac{3}{4}\varepsilon \right\} \le \gamma,$$

and

$$\mathbf{Pr}\left\{ v \ge 1 - \frac{3}{4}\varepsilon \right\} = 1 - \mathbf{Pr}\left\{ v < 1 - \frac{3}{4}\varepsilon \right\} \ge (1 - \gamma).$$

Thus, at any iteration for which $l \ge l_{\min}(f)$, with probability at least 1/2, Q will identify a concept g such that $P(f\Delta g) < \varepsilon/2$. Then, with probability at least $(1 - \gamma)$, the concept g will be consistent with a fraction of at least $(1 - (3\varepsilon)/4)$ of the examples in σ and the algorithm will terminate. Hence, the probability of an iteration terminating is $1/2(1 - \gamma)$, which is at least 1/4 since $\gamma \le 1/2$ for all $l \ge 1$.

Let $\zeta(l_0)$ denote the event that $l = l_0$ at termination of the algorithm. Then, the expected value of l at the termination of the algorithm is given by

$$\sum_{l_0=0}^{\infty} l_0 \mathbf{Pr}\left\{ \zeta(l_0) \right\}.$$

Expanding,

$$\sum_{l_0=0}^{\infty} l_0 \mathbf{Pr}\left\{ \zeta(l_0) \right\} = \mathbf{Pr}\left\{ l_0 < l_{\min}(f) \right\} \sum_{l_0=0}^{l_{\min}(f)} l_0 \mathbf{Pr}\left\{ \zeta(l_0) \big/ l_0 < l_{\min}(f) \right\}$$

$$+ \mathbf{Pr}\left\{ l_0 \ge l_{\min}(f) \right\} \sum_{l_0=l_{\min}(f)}^{\infty} l_0 \mathbf{Pr}\left\{ \zeta(l_0) \big/ l_0 \ge l_{\min}(f) \right\}.$$

Notation: $\mathbf{Pr}\left\{ A \big/ B \right\}$ is the conditional probability of A given B.

Surely, we can take $\mathbf{Pr}\left\{ l < l_{\min}(f) \right\} = 0$ and $\mathbf{Pr}\left\{ l \ge l_{\min}(f) \right\} = 1$ and write

$$\sum_{l_0=0}^{\infty} l_0 \mathbf{Pr}\left\{ \zeta(l_0) \right\} \le \sum_{l_0=l_{\min}(f)}^{\infty} l_0 \mathbf{Pr}\left\{ \zeta(l_0) \big/ l_0 \ge l_{\min}(f) \right\}.$$

As shown earlier, the probability that the algorithm will terminate at any $l \geq l_{min}(f)$ is at least 1/4. Thus,

$$\sum_{l_0=0}^{\infty} l_0 \mathbf{Pr}\left\{\zeta(l_0)\right\} \leq \sum_{l_0=l_{min}(f)}^{\infty} l_0(1/4)(3/4)^{l_0-1-l_{min}(f)}$$

$$\leq \sum_{l_0=l_{min}(f)}^{\infty} l_0(3/4)^{l_0-l_{min}(f)}.$$

Setting $t = l_0 - l_{min}(f)$, we get

$$\sum_{l_0=l_{min}(f)}^{\infty} l_0(3/4)^{l_0-l_{min}(f)} = \sum_{t=0}^{\infty} \left[t + l_{min}(f)\right](3/4)^t$$

$$= \sum_{t=0}^{\infty} t(3/4)^t + l_{min}(f)\sum_{t=0}^{\infty}(3/4)^t.$$

The last two sums are independent of $l_{min}(f)$. Using the ratio test[3] these sums can be shown to be convergent. Hence, the expected value of l is $O(l_{min}(f))$.

This completes the proof.

□

As mentioned earlier, Occam's Razor states that the simplest explanation of the observed phenomenon is most likely to be the correct one. Indeed, algorithm $A_{3.2}$ uses the Occam fitting Q to find a short explanation to fit the observed data. As shown in the proof of Theorem 3.3, such an explanation is likely to be a good one.

Theorem 3.3 also has an interesting interpretation in the realm of data compression. An Occam fitting can be viewed as a data compression algorithm for sets of examples. Let F be a class containing concepts of infinite cardinality and let Q be an Occam fitting for F. Then, if $f \in F$ is of infinite cardinality, Q is a compression algorithm for graph(f). To see this, let q and α be the bounding polynomial and bounding exponent of Q, respectively. Now, $l_{min}(f)$ is finite and, hence, for sufficiently large m, $q(n, l_{min}(f))m^{\alpha} \leq m$. Thus, Q takes as input subsets of graph(f) and outputs asymptotically smaller descriptions of its input—Q is indeed a compression algorithm for graph(f). Hence, we may interpret Theorem 3.3 as saying "a class F may be learned efficiently if there exists a compression algorithm for sets of examples of the concepts in F."

---

3. Ratio test: the sum of an infinite series $a_1, a_2, \ldots, a_i, \ldots$ converges if

$$\lim_{i \to \infty} \frac{a_{i+1}}{a_i} < 1.$$

It is interesting to note that Occam's Razor has a relative called the minimum description length principle (MDLP). MDLP essentially states that the best hypothesis is most likely to be the one that requires the fewest number of bits to communicate the observed data. MDLP is often interpreted in terms of Bayes's theorem on conditional probabilities. Loosely speaking, we can view Theorem 3.3 as a restatement of MDLP in our setting, in that it only requires a hypothesis that is within a polynomial of the shortest encoding of the observed data.

Example 3.5   Consider a concept composed of the union of finitely many intervals on N. That is, the concept can be expressed as $[a_1, b_1] \cup [a_2, b_2] \cup \cdots \cup [a_k, b_k]$ for some finite k. Let Σ^* be the binary encoding of N and let F be the class of all such concepts on Σ^*. Clearly, F is not of polynomial dimension, since for every n, Σ^n is shattered by F.

As representation for F, let us pick the mapping R that maps each $f \in F$ to the set of interval representations for it. That is, for each $f \in F$, $R(f)$ is the set of all representations for f as the union of finitely many intervals. We now show that there exists a polynomial-time Occam fitting Q for F in R.

We begin with a brief overview of Q. Given a set of examples S, Q picks the smallest number of intervals that are consistent with the examples in S. Also, it ensures that the end points of the intervals are as small as possible. This ensures that the length of the name output by Q is no more than a constant away from $l_{min}(S)$. Thus, Q is an Occam fitting for F in R with a zero bounding exponent and a linear bounding polynomial.

Figure 3.1 depicts the intervals selected by Q, given the examples $(2, 0)$, $(4, 1), (5, 1), (7, 0), (8, 1), (9, 1)$ as input. In particular, Q outputs $[3, 5] \cup [8, 9]$. In the figure, positive examples are shown with filled-in circles, while negative examples are shown with empty circles.

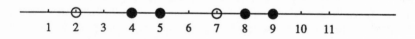

Figure 3.1 _____
The Occam fitting of Example 3.5 outputs $[3,5] \cup [8,9]$, given the examples $(2, 0), (4, 1), (5, 1), (7, 0), (8, 1),$ and $(9, 1)$ as input.

Fitting Q
input: S
begin
 let $S = \{(x_1, y_1),(x_2, y_2), \ldots, (x_k, y_k)\}$
  where the x_i are in increasing order;
 let $r = \varnothing$;
 while there exists $(x_i, 1)$ in S **do**
  let n be the greatest integer such that $y_n = 1$;
  let m be the greatest integer less than n
   such that $y_m = 0$;
  $r = r \cup [x_m+1, x_n]$;
  delete $(x_{m+1}, y_{m+1}), \ldots, (x_n, y_n)$ from S;
 end
 output r;
end

By Theorem 3.3, F is learnable in usually polynomial time.   ■

We now obtain a weak form of the converse of Theorem 3.3. Specifically, we will show that if a class is polynomial-time learnable in a representation, then it must possess an efficient Occam fitting. Our result holds only for a special family of classes and representations.

Let f be a concept and S a finite subset of Σ^*. Suppose we wish to treat the elements of S as exceptions to f, i.e., if $x \in S$ is not in f, then we shall accept x, and if x is in f, then we shall reject it. In essence, S is a finite list of *exceptions* to f, special elements whose membership status in f is to be reversed. Notice that $f \Delta S$ is the concept obtained by incorporating the exceptions of S into f.

A class F is said to be *closed under exception* if for all $f \in F$ and all finite $S \subseteq \Sigma^*$, incorporating the exceptions of S into f results in a concept that is also in F, i.e., for all $f \in F$ and finite $S \subseteq \Sigma^*$, $f \Delta S$ is in F.

The property of closure under exception is useful when it is efficiently computable. To capture this idea, we introduce the notion of strong closure. Essentially, a class F with representation R is strongly closed under exception if given a name for f and S, a short name for $f \Delta S$ can be efficiently computed. Formally, we have the following definition:

DEFINITION

Let F be closed under exception and let R be a representation for F. R is *strongly closed under exception* if there exists an algorithm C and constants c_1, c_2 such that

(a) C takes as input $r \in \Sigma^*$ and finite $S \subseteq \Sigma^*$. Let n be the length of the longest string in S and let $m = |S|$ be the cardinality of S.

(b)   If r is the name of some $f \in F$, C produces as output a name $r_1 \in R(f \Delta S)$, such that

$$|r_1| \leq c_1(|r| + nm)\log(|r| + nm) + c_2.$$

(c) C runs in time polynomial in the length of its input.

Many of the natural representations for familiar classes of concepts are strongly closed under exception.

Example 3.6   Recall that in Example 3.1 we defined the class of monotone monomial concepts and placed the representation of the monotone monomial formulae on it. Similarly, we have the class F of concepts generated by the set of all Boolean formulae and the representation R of the Boolean formulae for F. We will show that R is strongly closed under exception.

Let f be a Boolean formula and S be a finite subset of Σ^*. Let $S_0 = f \cap S$ and $S_1 = S - f$. For each x_i in S_1, construct the formula g_i for which x_i is the only satisfying assignment. The formula g_i is a conjunction of literals. Similarly, for each $x_i \in S_0$, construct the formula h_i for which x_i is the only satisfying assignment. Again, the formula h_i is a conjunction of literals. Let g be the formula

$$(f \vee g_1 \vee g_2 \vee \cdots) \wedge (\neg h_1) \wedge (\neg h_2) \wedge \cdots$$

Let $m = |S|$ and $n = \max \{|x| \mid (x, y) \in S\}$. Let r be the binary encoding of f. Now, f is defined on at most $|r|$ variables and, hence, g is defined on at most $\max \{|r|, n\} \leq |r| + n$ variables. Hence, the binary encoding of g is of length $O\left[(|r| + nm)\log(|r| + nm)\right]$. Also, g can be constructed in time polynomial in $|r|, n$, and m. It follows that R is strongly closed under exception.   ∎

A random polynomial-time fitting that is Occam is a *random polynomial-time Occam fitting*. Since this is a straightforward extension, we omit a formal definition here. With this notion, we can give the counterpart of Theorem 3.2 without the restriction of polynomial dimension.

THEOREM 3.4 ⎯⎯⎯⎯⎯⎯⎯⎯⎯⎯⎯⎯⎯⎯⎯⎯⎯⎯⎯⎯⎯

Let F be a class of concepts with a polynomial-time computable representation R. Suppose that R is strongly closed under exception. Then, F is polynomial-time learnable in R only if F has a random polynomial-time Occam fitting in R.

⎯⎯⎯⎯⎯⎯⎯⎯⎯⎯⎯⎯⎯⎯⎯⎯⎯⎯⎯⎯⎯⎯⎯⎯⎯⎯⎯⎯⎯⎯⎯⎯⎯⎯

Proof: Let A be a polynomial-time learning algorithm for F in R. Let R be polynomial-time computable by a program B and let C compute the strong closure of R.

The algorithm given below is a random polynomial-time Occam fitting for F in R, for a choice of ε that is to be determined shortly.

> **Occam Fitting Q**
> **input:** $S \subseteq \Sigma^* \times \{0, 1\}$;
> **begin**
>   let $n = \max \{|x| \mid (x, y) \in S\}$.
>   let $m = |S|$;
>   run A with input $\varepsilon, \delta = 1/4, n$;
>   **for** each call of EXAMPLE by A **do,**
>   give A a randomly chosen element of S;
>   let A output a name r for some $f \in F$;
>   using B, construct $E = \{x \mid (x, y) \in S, y \neq f(x)\}$;
>   **if** $|E| \leq \varepsilon m$, **then**
>   output $r_1 = C(r, E)$;
>   **else** fail;
> **end**

Since C computes the strong closure of R, there exist constants c_1 and c_2 such that

$$|r_1| \leq c_1(|r| + n|E|)\log(|r| + n|E|) + c_2.$$

Since $\delta = 1/4$, with probability at least $3/4$, A will identify $f \in F$ such that f is consistent with at least $(1 - \varepsilon)$ of the examples in S. In other words, with probability at least $3/4$, $|E| \leq \varepsilon m$. Hence, with probability at least $3/4$, Q will output a name r_1 that satisfies

$$|r_1| \leq c_1(|r| + n\varepsilon m)\log(|r| + n\varepsilon m) + c_2.$$

Since $\log(x)$ is $O(x^b)$ for arbitrarily small[4] $b > 0$, we can write

$$|r_1| \le c_3(|r| + n\varepsilon m)^{1+b} + c_4$$

for values of b, c_3, and c_4 that are to be determined shortly.

Since A is a polynomial-time algorithm, there exists fixed integer k such that $\left(\dfrac{nl}{\varepsilon\delta}\right)^k$ bounds the time complexity of A. Thus,

$$|r| \le \left[\frac{nl_{\min}(S)}{\varepsilon\delta}\right]^k.$$

Substituting this in the bound for $|r_1|$, we get

$$|r_1| \le c_3\left[\left[\frac{nl_{\min}(S)}{\varepsilon\delta}\right]^k + n\varepsilon m\right]^{1+b} + c_4.$$

Let us pick

$$\varepsilon = m^{\frac{-1}{k+1}}.$$

Hence, we can write our bound on $|r_1|$ as

$$|r_1| \le c_3\left[\left[\frac{nl_{\min}(S)m^{\frac{1}{k+1}}}{\delta}\right]^k + nm^{\frac{k}{k+1}}\right]^{1+b} + c_4.$$

Setting $\delta = 1/4$ and simplifying, we get

$$|r_1| \le c_3 m^{\frac{k(1+b)}{k+1}}\left[(4nl_{\min}(S))^k + n\right]^{1+b} + c_4.$$

We are free to pick b and will do so to ensure that

$$\frac{k(1+b)}{k+1} = \alpha < 1.$$

The choice of b will determine the values of c_3 and c_4.

---

4. This can be shown by evaluating $\displaystyle\lim_{x \to \infty} \frac{\log(x)}{x^b}$ using L'Hospital's rule.

Hence, there exist polynomial q and $\alpha < 1$ such that with probability at least 3/4,

$$|r_1| \le q(n, l_{min}(S))m^\alpha.$$

Since the run time of Q is clearly polynomial in the various parameters, we have shown that Q is a random polynomial-time Occam fitting for F in R.

□

3.4 One-Sided Error

In this section, we consider time complexity results for learning with one-sided error. Essentially, the results developed in the previous sections have natural analogs in this setting. We will discuss the analog of Theorem 3.1 and leave the others as exercises to the reader. First, we specify the form of the output in the definition of learning with one-sided error. This is a straightforward extension of our earlier definitions.

DEFINITION _____

Algorithm A learns F in R *with one-sided error* if (a) A is a PAC learning algorithm for F in R; and (b) the concept identified by F in its output is always a subset of the target concept.

_____

We also define the notion of a minimal fitting, wherein the concept identified by the fitting is the least concept consistent with the input.

DEFINITION _____

Q is a *minimal fitting* for F in R if:

(a) Q takes as input a set of examples $S \subseteq \Sigma^* \times \{0, 1\}$.

(b)   There exists $f \in F$ such that f is consistent with S, then Q outputs $r \in R(g)$ where g is the least concept in F consistent with S.

_____

In the above, if Q is deterministic and runs in time polynomial in the size of its input and in $l_{min}(g)$, we say Q is a polynomial-time minimal fitting.

Note that by definition, if there exists a minimal fitting for F in any representation, then F must be minimally consistent.

Under these definitions, we have:

THEOREM 3.5 _____

Let F be a class of polynomial dimension and let R be a representation for F. F is polynomial-time learnable in R with one-sided error if F has a polynomial-time minimal fitting.

_____

Proof: Let $\hat{Q}$ be a polynomial-time minimal fitting for F in R. Modify the algorithm $A_{3.1}$ of Theorem 3.1 by replacing Q with $\hat{Q}$. Then, combining the techniques of Theorem 2.2 and Theorem 3.1, it is easy to show that the algorithm learns with one-sided error and in polynomial time.

□

Example 3.7   Consider the fitting given in Example 3.4 for the class of axis-parallel rectangles. On input S, Q constructs the least axis-parallel rectangle that contains the positive examples in S. To see this, notice that any other axis-parallel rectangle must have its lower boundary below x_{min}, its upper boundary above x_{max}, and similarly along the y-axis. Thus, Q constructs the least axis-parallel rectangle consistent with S. Hence, Q is actually a polynomial-time minimal fitting for F and as argued in the proof of Theorem 3.4, algorithm A of Example 3.4 learns F with one-sided error.   ■

3.5 Hardness Results

In this section we show that there exist classes that are of polynomial dimension and, hence, polynomial-sample learnable, but are unlikely to be polynomial-time learnable. For such classes, the number of examples required for learning is small, but it is computationally intractable to process these examples. We assume that the reader is somewhat familiar with the complexity classes of *NP* and *RP*. Readers unfamiliar with these notions should consult the references listed in the Bibliographic Notes.

Recall that we defined a k-DNF formula in Exercise 2.3 to be a Boolean formula in disjunctive normal form, with no more than k conjuncts per term. We now define a k-term-DNF formula to be a Boolean formula consisting of a disjunction of at most k terms, each term being the conjunction of literals. For example, $(a \wedge b \wedge c) \vee (\neg c \wedge d)$ is in 2-term-DNF. We may view a k-term-DNF formula as a concept on Σ^* in the usual manner. The set of all k-term-DNF formulae will then define the class of k-term-DNF concepts on Σ^*.

On n variables, there are at most 2^{2nk} distinct k-term-DNF formulae. To see this, note that there are $2n$ literals, one for each variable and one for its negation. Thus, each term may be chosen in 2^{2n} ways. Since there are k terms, the number of distinct formulae possible is at most $(2^{2n})^k = 2^{2nk}$.

Let F be the class of k-term-DNF concepts on Σ^*, for some fixed k. Clearly, $|F^{[n]}|$ is bounded from above by the number of distinct k-term-DNF formulae on $n, n-1, n-2, \ldots, 1$ variables. Thus

$$|F^{[n]}| \leq 2^{2k} + 2^{4k} + \cdots + 2^{2nk} \leq n\, 2^{2nk}.$$

By Lemma 2.2 it follows that F is of polynomial dimension, and by Theorem 2.1 it follows that F is polynomial-sample learnable.

Fix the natural representation of the k-term-DNF formulae for F, i.e., for each $f \in F$, $R(f)$ is the set of k-term-DNF formulae for which f is the set of satisfying assignments. We now show that it is unlikely that F is polynomial-time learnable in R, i.e., it is unlikely that the k-term-DNF are polynomial-time learnable. To do so, we consider the following problem.

Consistency Problem:

input: A set of examples $S \subseteq \Sigma^* \times \{0, 1\}$.
output: Does there exist a k-term-DNF concept consistent with S?

THEOREM 3.6 ⎯⎯⎯⎯⎯⎯⎯⎯⎯⎯⎯⎯⎯⎯⎯⎯⎯⎯⎯⎯⎯⎯

For $k \geq 2$, the consistency problem above is NP-complete.

Proof: Omitted. A classic NP-completeness proof involving a reduction from the k-colorability of graphs. The interested reader may consult the reference in the Bibliographic Notes.

□

As a corollary to the above, we have the following.

COROLLARY 3.1 ⎯⎯⎯⎯⎯⎯⎯⎯⎯⎯⎯⎯⎯⎯⎯⎯⎯⎯⎯⎯⎯

If $NP \neq RP$ for $k \geq 2$, the k-term-DNF formulae are not polynomial-time learnable.

Proof: Let F be the class of k-term-DNF concepts with the representation R of the k-term-DNF formulae. Assume that the corollary is false. That is, $NP \neq RP$ and yet there exists a polynomial-time learning algorithm A for F in R. By Theorem 3.2, there exists a random polynomial-time fitting Q for F in R. We will now show that Q may be converted into a random polynomial-time algorithm Z for the consistency problem. This would place the consistency problem in RP. Since the consistency problem is NP-complete by Theorem 3.5, we will have $NP = RP$, a contradiction.

Algorithm Z is given below. On input S, Z runs Q on S. Let g denote the k-term-DNF concept identified by Q. Z checks to see whether g is consistent with S. If so, Z outputs "yes"; if not, Z outputs "no." Suppose there exists a k-term-DNF concept consistent with S. Since Q is a randomized algorithm, with probability greater than 1/2, g must be consistent with S. Hence, with probability greater than 1/2, Z will answer "yes." Alternatively, suppose there does not exist a k-term-DNF concept consistent with S. Then, g cannot be consistent with S and, hence, Z will always answer "no."

Algorithm Z
input: $S \subseteq \Sigma^* \times \{0, 1\}$;
begin
    run Q on input S;
    let g be the concept identified by Q;
    if for each $(x, y) \in S$, $y = g(x)$, **then**
        output "yes";
    else output "no";
end

We leave it as a simple exercise to the reader to show that Z runs in polynomial time.

□

3.6 Summary

We introduced the notion of a representation for a class of concepts and the notion of the time complexity of PAC learning. We then obtained theorems linking the time complexity of learning a class of concepts with the complexity of identifying (in the representation) a concept consistent with a given set of examples. These theorems were for classes of polynomial dimension. For classes not of polynomial dimension, we were able to obtain theorems linking the existence of efficient learning algorithms with the existence of Occam fittings. We also obtained analogs of the above results in the context of learning with one-sided error. Lastly, we presented some intractability results, showing that unless $NP = RP$, there exist classes of concepts that are polynomial-sample learnable but not polynomial-time learnable.

Additional readings on the topics of this chapter are suggested in the Bibliographic Notes.

3.7 Appendix

3.7.1 Randomized Algorithms

A probabilistic algorithm is one that tosses coins and uses the results of the tosses in its computations. Let A be a probabilistic algorithm. The function f computed by A is defined as follows:

$$f(x) = \begin{cases} y \text{ if } \mathbf{Pr}\ \{A(x)=y\} > 1/2 \\ \text{undefined otherwise.} \end{cases}$$

We say A is a randomized algorithm for f.

An interesting class of probabilistic algorithms accept the class of sets called RP. Specifically, let $S \subseteq \Sigma^*$. Consider a probabilistic algorithm A for accepting S such that A accepts each string in S with probability greater than $1/2$, but never accepts strings not in S. Thus, A makes only errors of omission. If A runs in time polynomial in the length of its input, we say S is in RP. For instance, the set of prime numbers (as well as the set of composites or nonprimes) is in RP.

Now, let F be a class of concepts and R be a representation for it. We consider a randomized fitting Q for F in R. Essentially, Q is a randomized algorithm that on any input would behave like a fitting with probability greater than $1/2$. We require that Q makes only errors of omission in that it will never output the name of a concept that is not consistent with the input. Specifically, Q is a randomized fitting for F in R if

(a) Q takes as input a set of examples $S \subseteq \Sigma^* \times \{0, 1\}$.

(b)   Suppose there exists $f \in F$ such that $S \subseteq \text{graph}(F)$. Then, with probability greater than $1/2$, Q outputs $r \in R(g)$, such that $g \in F$ and $S \subseteq \text{graph}(g)$. If Q fails to output such an i, Q outputs nothing.

The reader interested in additional information on the complexity class RP should refer to the Bibliographic Notes for an appropriate reference.

3.7.2 Chebyshev's Inequality

Let q be a random variable distributed according to a distribution P. Let $\mu = P(q)$ be the expectation of q. The variance v of q is the expectation of $(q - \mu)^2$. That is, $v = P((q - \mu)^2)$. $P_{(m)}(q)$ denotes the average value of q on m observations of q, randomly and independently drawn according to P. That is, if we have m random observations $q_1, q_2, \ldots, q_m$ of q,

$$P_{(m)}(q) = \frac{1}{m} \sum_{i=1}^{i=l} q_i .$$

For a set S, $P_{(m)}(S) = P_{(m)}(I_S)$ is the fraction of the m observations that are members of S.

Chebyshev's inequality bounds the probability that the observed mean $P_{(m)}(q)$ differs from the true mean $P(q)$ by more than ε.

Chebyshev's Inequality: If q has finite variance v,

$$\mathbf{Pr} \{ |P_{(m)}(q) - P(q)| \geq \varepsilon \} \leq \frac{v}{\varepsilon^2 m} .$$

Now let f and g be two concepts on Σ^* and let P be any probability distribution on Σ^*. Let $\hat{P}$ be the probability distribution on $\Sigma^* \times \{0, 1\}$ defined as follows:

$$\hat{P}((x, y)) = \begin{cases} P(x) \text{ if } y = f(x) \\ 0 \text{ otherwise} \end{cases} .$$

Now, $I_{\text{graph}}(g)$, the indicator function of graph(g), is $\{0, 1\}$ valued and, hence, has variance at most 1. Noting that we use graph(g) and $I_{\text{graph}}(g)$ interchangeably, we can invoke Chebyshev's inequality to get

$$\mathbf{Pr} \left\{ |\hat{P}_{(m)}(\text{graph}(g)) - \hat{P}(\text{graph}(g))| \geq \varepsilon \right\} \leq \frac{1}{\varepsilon^2 m} .$$

3.8 Exercises

3.1.   Show that the class of k-DNF formulae of Exercise 2.3 are polynomial-time learnable.

3.2.   Show that the k-CNF formulae of Exercise 2.6 are polynomial-time learnable. Also, show that they are polynomial-time learnable with one-sided error.

3.3.   Give examples of classes and representations that are strongly closed under exception.

3.4.   Suppose we generalize the definition of strong closure under exception as follows:

DEFINITION _____

Let F be closed under exception and let R be a representation for F. R is *strongly closed under exception* if there exists an algorithm C and polynomials p_1 and p_2 such that

(a) C takes as input $r \in \Sigma^*$ and finite $S \subseteq \Sigma^*$. Let n be the length of the longest string in S and let $m = |S|$ be the cardinality of S.

(b)   If r is the name of some $f \in F$, C produces as output a name $r_1 \in R(f \Delta S)$, such that

$$|r_1| \le p_1 \left[n, |r| \log(m) \right] + p_2 \left[n, \log(|r|), \log(m) \right] m$$

(c) C runs in time polynomial in the length of its input.

Show that Theorem 3.4 stands for this definition as well.

3.5.   Define the notion of a minimal Occam fitting, i.e., one that outputs a name of the least concept consistent with its input. Using this definition, state and prove the analogs of Theorems 3.2 and 3.3 for learning with one-sided error.

3.6.   A Manhattan curve is a piecewise linear curve composed of segments parallel to the coordinate axes. Let F be the class of all continuous Manhattan curves of finite length on $\mathbf{N}^2$ that do not intersect themselves. Place the representation R on F, such that for each $f \in F$, $R(f)$ is a list of points such that the line joining the points in order traces the curve f. Does F have a polynomial-time Occam fitting in R?

3.7.   Let F be the set of all finite subsets of Σ^*. Clearly, F is not of polynomial dimension. Place the representation R on F such that for each $f \in F, R(f)$ is all possible enumerations of the elements of f. That is, a name of f is simply a list of the elements of f in some order. Show that F has a polynomial-time Occam fitting in R and, hence, is learnable in usually polynomial time. This is simply rote learning. On the other hand, place the representation R_1 on F such that for each $f \in F, R_1(f)$ is the set of all Turing machines that accept f. Does there exist a polynomial-time Occam fitting for F in R? The above brings out an important aspect of our definition of polynomial-time learnability—the strong dependence on the representation chosen for the class of concepts.

3.8.   Give an appropriate definition of random polynomial-time learnability. Prove the following variant of Theorems 3.1 and 3.2: Let F be of polynomial dimension and let R be a polynomial-time computable representation for F. F is random polynomial-time learnable in R if and only if there exists a random polynomial-time fitting for F in R. Is the family of class/representation pairs that are random polynomial-time learnable distinct from the set of class/representation pairs that are polynomial-time learnable?

3.9.   Give an appropriate definition of random polynomial-time computability of a representation. Show that the variant of Theorem 3.2 in Exercise 3.8 stands if R were random polynomial-time computable instead of polynomial-time computable.

3.10.   Show that every k-term-DNF formula of length l can be expressed as a k-CNF formula of length $p(l)$, for a fixed polynomial $p(\ )$. Thus, the k-term-DNF concepts are a subset of the k-CNF concepts. Recall that Corollary 3.1 states that the k-term-DNF concepts are not polynomial-time learnable in the representation of k-term-DNF formulae unless $NP = RP$. Now, let A be a polynomial-time learning algorithm for the k-CNF concepts with the k-CNF formulae as representation. (See Exercise 3.2.) Suppose that the target concept f is a k-term-DNF concept. A will construct a k-CNF formula g that is a good approximation to f. However, g may not be expressible as a k-term-DNF concept. If we are willing to overlook this detail, we can use A as a learning algorithm for the k-term-DNF concepts. In this variant of learning, the learning algorithm constructs a good approximation to the target concept, but does not guarantee that the constructed approximation belongs to the target class.

3.11.   Recall that in the appendix of Chapter 2 we defined an alternate learning framework called Framework 2, in which the learning algorithm had to infer the length parameter n. We showed that the sample complexity results of that chapter held within this framework. Show that the results of this chapter would hold as well in Framework 2.

3.12.   Consider n Boolean variables $a_1, a_2, \ldots, a_n$. A decision list L on these variables is a program of the form:

input x;
begin
$\quad$ **if** $\phi_1(x)$ **then** b_1;
$\quad$ **if** $\phi_2(x)$ **then** b_2;
$\quad$ **if** $\phi_3(x)$ **then** b_3;
$\quad \cdots$
$\quad$ **else** $b_s(x)$;
end

$\qquad$ Each ϕ_i is the conjunction of k literals, for fixed $k \in \mathbf{N}$, and each $b_i \in \{0, 1\}$. We view L as a concept on Σ^* in the usual convention. That is, L denotes the set of all strings of length n such that $L(x) = 1$. Specifically, $L(x) = b_i$, where i is the least integer in $1, 2, \ldots, s - 1$ such that $\phi_i(x) = 1$. If no such integer exists, $L(x) = b_s$. Let F be the class of all such concepts.
$\qquad$ Place the natural representation R of the decision lists on F, where for each $f \in F$, $R(f)$ is the set of all decision lists that generate f. Show that the class F is polynomial-time learnable in R.

3.13.   Consider the class F of DNF concepts, with the natural representation R of the DNF formulae. Is F polynomial-time learnable in R?

3.14.   Revisit Exercise 2.13 and the class F of concepts generated by the sentential forms of an unambiguous context-free grammar Γ. Place the representation R of sentential forms on this class, and show that F is polynomial-time learnable in R with one-sided error.

3.9 Bibliographic Notes

The material in this chapter is adapted from Blumer, Ehrenfeucht, Haussler, and Warmuth (1990), Haussler, Kearns, Littlestone, and Warmuth (1988), Kearns, Li, Pitt, and Valiant (1987a, b), Natarajan (1991), and Pitt and Valiant (1988). Theorem 3.6 and Exercise 3.8 are from Pitt and Valiant (1988). Theorem 3.4 and Exercise 3.3 are from Board and Pitt (1990). Theorem 3.5 is from Natarajan (1991). A discussion of the minimum description length principle and its Bayesian interpretation can be found in Rissanen (1978, 1986), Quinlan and Rivest (1989), Li and Vitanyi (1989), and Gao and Li (1989). Interesting applications of Occam's Razor in the area of theoretical physics are discussed in layman's terms in Hawking (1986). A discussion of the equivalence of various models of polynomial-time learnability may be found in Haussler, Kearns, Littlestone, and Warmuth (1988). For more on Chebyshev's inequality, see Feller (1957), Vol. 1, pp. 233. An extensive treatment of the complexity class *NP* may be found in Garey and Johnson (1979) and in Hopcroft and Ullman (1979), Chapter 10. A discussion of randomized computation may be found in Gill (1977) and Johnson (1990). Solovay and Strassen (1977) show that the set of composite numbers is in RP, while Adleman and Huang (1987) sketch a proof that the set of prime numbers is in RP. Exercise 3.12 is from Rivest (1987) and Ehrenfeucht and Haussler (1988). Exercise 3.13 is from Valiant (1984) and is a significant open problem at this time.

4

Learning Concepts on Uncountable Domains

In the preceding chapters, we considered classes of concepts on Σ^*, the strings of the Boolean alphabet. It is easy to see that Σ^* may be replaced by any countable domain, such as the integers or the natural numbers, and the results developed would still hold. But it is not obvious that the results would hold if we were to consider an uncountable set, such as the real numbers, as the domain. In this chapter, we explore this issue further.

The motivation for this extension to the real numbers is largely theoretical. In a practical computer, floating-point numbers are of finite length and can be modeled by the countable domain of Chapters 2 and 3. However, it is often intuitively appealing to eliminate the length of the numerical representations from consideration and analyze the inherent complexity of the problem. Such analysis yields measures and results that are independent of the particular machine implementation, thereby leading to useful theoretical tools.

4.1 Preliminaries

We assume that $\mathbf{R}^k$ is the domain of interest for some fixed $k \in \mathbf{N}$. In the interest of concreteness, we pick $\mathbf{R}^k$, although the results of this chapter hold for any domain with an appropriate definition of probability measures.

A concept on $\mathbf{R}^k$ is a measurable subset $f \subseteq \mathbf{R}^k$. The restriction of measurability is necessary for technical reasons. Readers unfamiliar with this notion may refer to the Appendix, or they may rely on intuition and ignore this restriction altogether. A class of concepts on $\mathbf{R}^k$ is a set of concepts on $\mathbf{R}^k$. Once again, we must restrict our attention to classes that are well behaved, a notion that will be defined later in this chapter. The restriction will be satisfied by all but the most pathological of classes and will not pose a hindrance in the practical sense.

Example 4.1   We give two examples of classes of concepts on $\mathbf{R}^k$. As the first example, let F be the class of all closed intervals on $\mathbf{R}$. The concept $f = [0.0, 1.0]$ is in F.

As the second example, recall the class of G axis-parallel rectangles in $\mathbf{R}^2$ introduced in Example 2.2, i.e., the class of all rectangles with sides are parallel to the coordinate axes. Viewed another way, each concept in G is the product of two closed intervals on $\mathbf{R}$. That is, $G = \{f \times g \mid f, g \in F\}$.   ∎

In this setting of concepts on the reals, we retain most of the definitions that we gave in Chapter 2 with respect to concepts on Σ^*. However, we do need to make some changes in these definitions to reflect that the domain is not discrete. It is important to note that these changes are strictly technical and do not alter the spirit of the definitions themselves. The changes are discussed below.

Firstly, we drop the length parameter n from the discussion because encodings of real numbers can be of infinite length. Thus, the learning algorithm takes as input ε and δ only. In turn, its sample complexity is a function of these parameters.

Secondly, the probability distribution P is now on $\mathbf{R}^k$. A formal definition of a distribution on $\mathbf{R}^k$ is somewhat technical and is given in the Appendix. Readers not interested in the details may proceed without digression, retaining an intuitive notion of a probability distribution.

Thirdly, the definition of EXAMPLE is modified as follows: Intuitively speaking, EXAMPLE works as before, picking examples at random according to the distribution P. Technically, for any measurable $S \subseteq \mathbf{R}^k$, with probability $P(S)$, any call of EXAMPLE will result in (x, y) such that $x \in S$.

Lastly, we remind the reader that we use the term *algorithm* in the broader sense throughout this chapter, with no regard to feasibility on any particular machine model.

We now give appropriate definitions of a learning algorithm and its sample complexity.

DEFINITION _____

An algorithm A is a PAC learning algorithm for a class of concepts F on $\mathbf{R}^k$ if

(a) A takes as input ε and δ.

(b) A may call EXAMPLE, which returns examples for some $f \in F$. The examples are chosen randomly according to an arbitrary and unknown probability distribution P on $\mathbf{R}^k$.

(c) For all concepts $f \in F$ and all probability distributions P on $\mathbf{R}^k$, A outputs a concept $g \in F$, such that with probability at least $(1-\delta)$, $P(f\Delta g) \le \varepsilon$.

_____

The definition of sample complexity remains exactly the same in spirit, i.e., it is the number of examples sought by the algorithm as a function of its input parameters. Formally, we have the following definition:

DEFINITION _____

Let A be a learning algorithm for a concept class F on $\mathbf{R}^k$. The *sample complexity* of A is the function $s : \mathbf{R} \times \mathbf{R} \to \mathbf{N}$ such that $s(\varepsilon, \delta)$ is the maximum number of calls of EXAMPLE by A, the maximum being taken over all runs of A on input ε and δ, with the target concept f ranging over all $f \in F$ and the probability distribution P ranging over all distributions on $\mathbf{R}^k$. If no finite maximum exists, $s(\varepsilon, \delta) = \infty$.

_____

On the discrete domain of Σ^*, our definition of polynomial-sample learnability required that the sample complexity vary polynomially in its arguments. Here, we define the notion of uniform learnability, requiring the sample complexity of the learning algorithm to be uniformly bounded. By uniformly bounded we mean that the number of examples is bounded from above by a quantity that may depend on ε and δ, but not on the target concept or the probability distribution.

DEFINITION _____

A class F is said to be *uniformly learnable* if there exists a learning algorithm A for F with sample complexity $s(\varepsilon, \delta)$ such that for all ε and $\delta \in (0, 1]$, $s(\varepsilon, \delta)$ is finite.

_____

Finally, we note that the notion of the Vapnik-Chervonenkis dimension of a class carries over to this setting. In the absence of the length parameter, we do not require, and do not have, the notion of asymptotic dimension for a class F. Instead, we deal directly with $\mathbf{D}_{VC}(F)$.

Example 4.2   The class F of intervals introduced in Example 4.1 is of dimension 2. To see this, consider the set $\{1.0, 2.0\}$. The intervals $[-1.0, 0.0]$, $[0.0, 1.5]$, $[1.5, 2.5]$, and $[-1.0, 2.5]$ shatter $\{1.0, 2.0\}$. We now show that no set of three points can be shattered by F. Suppose the set $\{a, b, c\}$ is shattered by F. Without loss of generality, assume that $a > b > c$. Surely, any interval that contains a and c also contains b. Thus, F cannot shatter $\{a, b, c\}$.

The class G of the axis-parallel rectangles is of dimension 4. Specifically, there exists a set of four points in $\mathbf{R}^2$ that is shattered by G. This was depicted in Figure 2.2. We leave it as an exercise for the reader to prove that no set of 5 points is shattered by G.   ∎

4.2 Uniform Convergence and Learnability

We now work toward the analog of Theorem 2.1 in this setting. To do so, we introduce the following result from classical probability theory.

Let F be a class of concepts on $\mathbf{R}^k$. Let $g \in F$ and $m \in \mathbf{N}$. Using the distribution P on $\mathbf{R}^k$, let us draw at random m elements $x_1, x_2, \ldots, x_m$ of $\mathbf{R}^k$. Recall the notation introduced in Section 3.7.2 that $P_{(m)}(g)$ denotes the fraction of these m elements that are in g. That is,

$$P_{(m)}(g) = \frac{1}{m} \sum_{i=1}^{m} g(x_i).$$

We want to estimate the probability that $P_{(m)}(g)$ is within ε of $P(g)$. If we think of g as an event, $P(g)$ is the probability of g occurring and $P_{(m)}(g)$ is the frequency of occurrence of g in a random sample of size m. By the law of large numbers, with probability approaching unity, the frequency of occurrence of an event converges to its probability as the sample size is increased. Thus, we know that, for a fixed g, $P_{(m)}(g)$ will converge to $P(g)$ as m is increased, and for sufficiently large m, the two will differ by less than ε with high probability. In Chapter 3, Chebyshev's inequality was used to estimate the rate of this convergence. What if we want $P_{(m)}(g)$ to be within ε of $P(g)$ simultaneously for every $g \in F$? The rate of this simultaneous or *uniform* convergence is the subject of the following theorem. In a sense, it is a generalization of Chebyshev's inequality to a class of events.

THEOREM 4.1 _____

[Vapnik-Chervonenkis Theorem] Let F be a class of concepts on $\mathbf{R}^k$ such that $d = \mathbf{D}_{\mathrm{VC}}(F)$ is finite, let $m \in \mathbf{N}$, and let $\varepsilon \in (0, 1]$. Let ζ be the event given by

ζ: there exists $g \in F$ such that $|P_{(m)}(g) - P(g)| > \varepsilon$.

Then, for $m \geq \dfrac{2}{\varepsilon^2}$,

$$\mathbf{Pr}\,\{\zeta\} \leq 4\Phi(2m, d)e^{-\frac{\varepsilon^2 m}{8}}, \tag{4.1}$$

where

$$\Phi(2m, d) = \sum_{i=0}^{d} \binom{2m}{i}.$$

_____

Proof: The proof of this theorem is almost identical to the proof of Theorem 4.3. We will prove Theorem 4.3 in full, since it offers us tighter results. Also see Exercise 4.9.

□

We will now apply Theorem 4.1 toward obtaining the analog of Theorem 2.1 in this setting. First, we need the following lemma. Recall that in Section 2.3 we defined graph(f) to be the set of all examples for f. Analogously, we use graph(F) to denote the class of graph sets for all the concepts in F. That is, graph(F) = {graph(f) | $f \in F$}.

LEMMA 4.1 _____

For any class of concepts F,

$\mathbf{D}_{\mathrm{VC}}(F) = \mathbf{D}_{\mathrm{VC}}(\mathrm{graph}(F))$.

_____

Proof: We first show that $\mathbf{D}_{\mathrm{VC}}(\mathrm{graph}(F)) \geq \mathbf{D}_{\mathrm{VC}}(F)$. Suppose that F shatters a set S. We claim that graph(F) shatters the set $\hat{S} = S \times \{1\}$. To see this, simply note that if $f \cap S = S_1$, then graph(f) $\cap \hat{S} = S_1 \times \{1\}$. Hence, the claim. Thus, graph(F) shatters a set at least as large as any set shattered by F and consequently, $\mathbf{D}_{\mathrm{VC}}(\mathrm{graph}(F)) \geq \mathbf{D}_{\mathrm{VC}}(F)$.

Next, we show that $\mathbf{D}_{\mathrm{VC}}(F) \geq \mathbf{D}_{\mathrm{VC}}(\mathrm{graph}(F))$. Suppose that graph($F$) shatters a set $\hat{S}$. We claim that F shatters the set $S = \{x \,|\, (x, y) \in \hat{S}\}$. Take any subset S_1 of S. There exists $f \in F$ such that $f \cap S = S_1$. To see this, consider the set

$$\hat{S}_1 = \text{graph}(S_1) \cap \hat{S}$$
$$= \{(x, y) \in \hat{S} \mid x \in S_1 \text{ and } y = 1 \text{ or } x \in S - S_1 \text{ and } y = 0\}.$$

Since $\text{graph}(F)$ shatters $\hat{S}$, there exists $f \in F$ such that $\text{graph}(f) \cap \hat{S} = \hat{S}_1$. But then $f \cap S$ would be S_1 and, hence, the claim. Thus, $\mathbf{D}_{VC}(F) \geq \mathbf{D}_{VC}(\text{graph}(F))$. It follows that $\mathbf{D}_{VC}(F) = \mathbf{D}_{VC}(\text{graph}(F))$.

□

Using Theorem 4.1 and Lemma 4.1, we can prove the following.

THEOREM 4.2 _____

Let F be any class of concepts on $\mathbf{R}^k$ such that $d = \mathbf{D}_{VC}(F)$ is finite. Then, F is uniformly learnable by an algorithm of sample complexity

$$s(\varepsilon, \delta) = \frac{16}{\varepsilon^2} \left[8d\ln \left[\frac{128}{\varepsilon^2} \right] + \ln \left[\frac{4}{\delta} \right] \right]. \tag{4.2}$$

Proof: Consider algorithm $A_{4.1}$ below for a value of m that will be determined shortly.

> **Learning Algorithm** $A_{4.1}$
> **input:** ε, δ;
> **begin:**
>   make m calls of EXAMPLE;
>   let S be the set of examples seen;
>   pick a concept $g \in F$ consistent with S;
>   output g;
> **end**

We proceed as in the proof of Theorem 2.1. Let f denote the target concept. Let $\hat{F}$ be the class of all concepts in F that differ from f with probability greater than ε, i.e., $\hat{F} = \{g \in F \mid P(f \Delta g) > \varepsilon\}$. Let $\hat{P}$ be the distribution on $\mathbf{R}^{k+1}$ given by

$$\hat{P}((x, y)) = \begin{cases} P(x) \text{ if } y = f(x) \\ 0 \text{ otherwise} \end{cases},$$

where $x \in \mathbf{R}^k$ and $y \in \{0, 1\} \subseteq \mathbf{R}$.

Let $(x_1, y_1), (x_2, y_2), \ldots, (x_m, y_m)$ be the m examples obtained by $A_{4.1}$. Notice that the examples are elements of $\mathbf{R}^{k+1}$ drawn according to $\hat{P}$. Suppose there exists $g \in \hat{F}$ consistent with all these examples. Then, $\hat{P}_m(\text{graph}(g)) = 1$. But, since $g \in \hat{F}$, $\hat{P}(\text{graph}(g)) < 1 - \varepsilon$. Therefore,

$$|\hat{P}_m(\text{graph}(g)) - \hat{P}(\text{graph}(g))| \ge \varepsilon. \tag{4.3}$$

By Lemma 4.1, $\mathbf{D}_{VC}(\text{graph}(F)) = \mathbf{D}_{VC}(F) = d$. Hence, by Theorem 4.1 the probability that (4.3) holds for any $g \in F$ is at most $4\Phi(2m, d)e^{-\varepsilon^2 m/8}$. To be precise, this is true only for $m \ge 2/\varepsilon^2$, but we will see that this condition holds. Thus, the probability that algorithm $A_{4.1}$ will output a concept in $\hat{F}$ is at most $4\Phi(2m, d)e^{-\varepsilon^2 m/8}$. We wish to choose m so that this probability is smaller than δ. That is,

$$4\Phi(2m, d)e^{-\frac{\varepsilon^2 m}{8}} \le \delta. \tag{4.4}$$

By Exercise 2.9, $\Phi(n, d) \le \left[\dfrac{en}{d}\right]^{d+1}$. Hence, it suffices if

$$4\left[\frac{2em}{d}\right]^{d+1} e^{-\frac{\varepsilon^2 m}{8}} \le \delta.$$

Taking logarithms on both sides, we get

$$\frac{1}{8}\varepsilon^2 m - (d+1)\ln\left[\frac{2em}{d}\right] \ge \ln\left[\frac{4}{\delta}\right]. \tag{4.5}$$

We simplify (4.5) to obtain an explicit expression for m by decomposing (4.5) into the two inequalities (4.6) and (4.7) below.

$$\frac{1}{16}\varepsilon^2 m \ge \ln\left[\frac{4}{\delta}\right], \tag{4.6}$$

$$\frac{1}{16}\varepsilon^2 m \ge (d+1)\ln\left[\frac{2em}{d}\right]. \tag{4.7}$$

Solving for m from (4.6), we get

$$m \ge \frac{16}{\varepsilon^2}\ln\left[\frac{4}{\delta}\right]. \tag{4.8}$$

Now consider (4.9) below.

$$m = \frac{128d}{\varepsilon^2} \ln \left[\frac{128}{\varepsilon^2} \right] \tag{4.9}$$

By substitution, we can verify that (4.9) implies (4.7). Also, differentiating both sides of (4.7) with respect to m, we can show that the derivative of the left-hand side exceeds the right-hand side for values of m that exceed (4.9). Hence, combining (4.8) and (4.9), we see that it suffices for m to satisfy (4.10).

$$m = \frac{16}{\varepsilon^2} \left[8d\ln \left[\frac{128}{\varepsilon^2} \right] + \ln \left[\frac{4}{\delta} \right] \right]. \tag{4.10}$$

By definition, m is the sample complexity $s(\varepsilon, \delta)$ of the algorithm, and the theorem is proved.

□

Compare (4.2) with the estimate of Theorem 2.1. In (4.2), the sample complexity varies as ε^{-2}, while in Theorem 2.1, it varies as ε^{-1}. Is the quadratic dependence of (4.2) necessary? As we will see below, it is not.

The following theorem is a specialized version of Theorem 4.1. The theorem is a result in probability theory, and its proof may be skipped without affecting the learning results that rest on it.

THEOREM 4.3 _____

Let F be a class of concepts on $\mathbf{R}^k$ such that $d = \mathbf{D}_{\mathrm{VC}}(F)$ is finite, let $m \in \mathbf{N}$, and let $\varepsilon \in (0, 1]$. Let ζ be the event given by

ζ: there exists $g \in F$ such that $P(g) < (1 - \varepsilon)$ and $P_{(m)}(g) = 1$.

Then, for $m \geq \dfrac{8}{\varepsilon}$,

$$\Pr \{\zeta\} \leq 2\Phi(2m, d)2^{-\frac{\varepsilon m}{2}}$$

where

$$\Phi(2m, d) = \sum_{i=0}^{d} \begin{bmatrix} 2m \\ i \end{bmatrix}.$$

_____

Proof: We prove the theorem through two claims.

Let $D = \mathbf{R}^k$ and let P be a distribution on D. Let E denote the set of all $x^m \in D^m$ such that there exists $f \in F$, $P(f) < 1 - \varepsilon$ and every item of x^m is an element of f, i.e., $f \in F$, $P(f) < 1 - \varepsilon$, and $[x^m] \subseteq f$.

Also, let J denote the set of all $x^m y^m \in D^{2m}$ such that there exists $f \in F$, $P(f) < 1 - \varepsilon$, and (a) every item in x^m is an element of f; and (b) at most $m(1 - \varepsilon/2)$ items in y^m are elements of f.

Notation: We use $x^m y^m$ to denote the concatenation of x^m and y^m. Thus, for $x^m \in D^m$ and $y^m \in D^m$, $x^m y^m \in D^{2m}$. Also, for $m \in \mathbf{N}$, P^m denotes the $m$fold product distribution on D^m.

The following claim carries out a technical procedure called "symmetrization."

CLAIM 4.1 _____

For $\varepsilon \in (0, 1]$ and $m \geq \dfrac{8}{\varepsilon}$,

$$P^m(E) \leq 2P^{2m}(J).$$

_____

Proof: We will show that

$$P^{2m}(J) \geq \frac{1}{2} P^m(E).$$

Using the switch function θ of Section 2.3, we can write

$$P^{2m}(J) = \int_{x^m y^m \in D^{2m}} \theta(x^m y^m \in J) dP^{2m}$$

$$= \int_{x^m \in D^m} \int_{y^m \in D^m} \theta(x^m y^m \in J) dP^m dP^m.$$

Since $E \subset D^m$, we have

$$P^{2m}(J) \geq \int_{x^m \in E} \int_{y^m \in D^m} \theta(x^m y^m \in J) dP^m dP^m.$$

Let $\beta : E \to F$ such that for each $x^m \in E$, $\beta(x^m)$ is a concept $f \in F$ such that $P(f) < 1 - \varepsilon$ and $[x^m] \subseteq f$. By the definition of E, such f must exist for each $x^m \in E$.

Let K denote the set of all $x^m y^m \in D^{2m}$ such that $x^m \in E$ and elements of $\beta(x^m)$ occur at most $m(1 - \varepsilon/2)$ times in y^m.

Clearly, $K \subseteq J$. Hence,

$$P^{2m}(J) \geq \int_{x^m \in E} \int_{y^m \in D^m} \theta(x^m y^m \in K) dP^m dP^m.$$

For each $x^m \in E$, the inner integral is the probability that an event with probability of occurrence at most $(1 - \varepsilon)$, occurs at most $m(1 - \varepsilon/2)$ times in m trials. As discussed in the Appendix, such an event follows the binomial distribution, and, if p is the probability of occurrence of the event, and $r > mp$, the probability of at most r successes in m trials can be approximated as

$$\Pr\{T_m \le r\} \ge 1 - \frac{r(1-p)}{(r-mp)^2}.$$

By differentiating the above expression, we can show that this probability increases as p decreases. Thus, for $p < 1 - \varepsilon$,

$$\Pr\{T_m \le r\} \ge 1 - \frac{r(1-p)}{(r-mp)^2} \ge 1 - \frac{r(1-(1-\varepsilon))}{(r-m(1-\varepsilon))^2}.$$

Substituting $r = m(1 - \varepsilon/2)$ and simplifying, we get

$$\Pr\{T_m \le m(1-\varepsilon/2)\} \ge 1 - \frac{4(1-\varepsilon/2)}{m\varepsilon} \ge \frac{1}{2} \text{ for } m \ge \frac{8}{\varepsilon}.$$

Thus, for $m \ge 8/\varepsilon$,

$$P^{2m}(J) \ge \int_{x^m \in E} \frac{1}{2} dP^m \ge \frac{1}{2} P^m(E).$$

This completes the proof of the claim.

□

CLAIM 4.2 _____

For $\varepsilon \in (0, 1]$,

$$P^{2m}(J) \le \Phi(2m, d) 2^{-\frac{\varepsilon m}{2}} \text{ where } \Phi(2m, d) = \sum_{i=0}^{d} \binom{2m}{i}.$$

_____

Proof: For each j, $1 \le j \le (2m)!$, let π_j be a distinct permutation of the indices $1, 2, 3, \ldots, 2m$. Clearly,

$$P^{2m}(J) = \int_{x^m y^m \in D^{2m}} \theta(x^m y^m \in J) dP^{2m} = \int_{x^m y^m \in D^{2m}} \theta\left[\pi_j(x^m y^m) \in J\right] dP^{2m}.$$

Summing both sides of the above over all permutations π_j,

$$\sum_{j=1}^{(2m)!} P^{2m}(J) = \sum_{j=1}^{(2m)!} \int_{x^m y^m \in D^{2m}} \theta\left[\pi_j(x^m y^m) \in J\right] dP^{2m}.$$

Rewriting, we get

$$P^{2m}(J) = \int\limits_{x^m y^m \in D^{2m}} \frac{1}{(2m)!} \sum_{j=1}^{(2m)!} \theta \left[\pi_j(x^m y^m) \in J \right] dP^{2m}.$$

Consider a particular $x^m y^m \in D^{2m}$. If $x^m y^m \in J$, there exists $f \in F$, $P(f) < 1 - \varepsilon$, such that every item of x^m is an element of f and at most $m(1 - \varepsilon/2)$ items in y^m are elements of f. Let g be the set of distinct items of $x^m y^m$ that are not elements of f, i.e., $g = [x^m y^m] - f$. We say g is a "witness" that $x^m y^m \in J$. Let l be the number of occurrences of elements of g in y^m. By definition, $l \geq m\varepsilon/2$. We estimate the number of permutations π_j such that g is a witness that $\pi_j(x^m y^m) \in J$. For each such permutation, the elements of g must occur in only the second m items of the permuted sequence of $2m$ items. Now, the position of the l items from g in the second m items of the permuted sequence may be chosen in $\binom{m}{l}$ ways. There are $l!$ permutations of the items of g amongst these positions and $(2m - l)!$ permutations of the remaining items in the remaining positions. Thus, there are at most

$$\binom{m}{l} l!(2m - l)!$$

permutations π_j for which g is a witness that $\pi_j(x^m y^m) \in J$.

We will now estimate the number of distinct possibilities for g. Consider the class of concepts H on the domain $[x^m y^m]$ given by

$$H = \{f \cap [x^m y^m] \mid f \in F\}.$$

Now, $g = [x^m y^m] - h$ for some $h \in H$, and, hence, there are at most $|H|$ possibilities for g. We now estimate $|H|$.

Since F shatters sets of cardinality at most d, H shatters sets of cardinality at most d. Thus, $\mathbf{D}_{VC}(H) \leq d$. Surely, the cardinality of $[x^m y^m]$ is at most $2m$. By Exercise 2.9, we have

$$|H| \leq \Phi(2m, d).$$

Thus, there are at most $\Phi(2m, d)$ possibilities for g.

Combining the above estimates, we see that the total number of permutations π_j such that $\pi_j(x^m y^m) \in J$ is at most

$$\Phi(2m, d) \binom{m}{l} l!(2m - l)!$$

Hence,

$$\frac{1}{(2m)!} \sum_{j=1}^{(2m)!} \theta \left[\pi_j(x^m y^m) \in J \right] \le \frac{1}{(2m)!} \Phi(2m, d) \begin{bmatrix} m \\ l \end{bmatrix} l!(2m-l)!$$

$$\le \Phi(2m, d) \frac{\begin{bmatrix} m \\ l \end{bmatrix}}{\begin{bmatrix} 2m \\ l \end{bmatrix}} \le \Phi(2m, d)2^{-l} \le \Phi(2m, d)2^{-\frac{\varepsilon m}{2}}.$$

In the above, the third inequality is obtained by using Stirling's approximation for factorials. Returning to our estimate for $P^{2m}(J)$, we have

$$P^{2m}(J) = \int_{x^m y^m \in D^{2m}} \frac{1}{(2m)!} \sum_{j=1}^{(2m)!} \theta \left[\pi_j(x^m y^m) \in J \right] dP^{2m}$$

$$\le \int_{x^m y^m \in D^{2m}} \Phi(2m, d)2^{-\frac{\varepsilon m}{2}} dP^{2m} = \Phi(2m, d)2^{-\frac{\varepsilon m}{2}}.$$

This completes the proof of the claim.

Combining Claims 4.1 and 4.2, the theorem is proved.

□

Note that in order for Claims 4.1 and 4.2 to hold, the quantities $P^m(E)$ and $P^{2m}(J)$ must exist, i.e., the sets E and J must be measurable. We say that F is *well behaved* if E and J are measurable for all $m \in \mathbf{N}$, $\varepsilon \in (0, 1]$, and P on $\mathbf{R}^k$. Except for some pathological cases, most concept classes are well behaved, and henceforth we will deal only with well behaved classes. For more on well behaved classes, see the references listed in the Bibliographic Notes.

We now apply Theorem 4.3 to obtain an improved form of Theorem 4.1. Specifically, the leading term in the sample complexity of the learning algorithm constructed improves from $\frac{1}{\varepsilon^2}$ to $\frac{1}{\varepsilon}$.

THEOREM 4.4 _____

Let F be any class of concepts on $\mathbf{R}^k$ such that $d = \mathbf{D}_{\text{VC}}(F)$ is finite. Then, F is uniformly learnable by an algorithm of sample complexity

$$s(\varepsilon, \delta) = \frac{8}{\varepsilon} \left[4d\ln \left[\frac{32}{\varepsilon} \right] + \ln \left[\frac{2}{\delta} \right] \right].$$

Proof: Consider algorithm $A_{4.1}$ again. We will show that it suffices for $m = s(\varepsilon, \delta)$ to satisfy the above equation. We proceed as in the proof of Theorem 4.2. Let f denote the target concept. Let $\hat{F}$ be the class of all concepts in F that differ from f with probability greater than ε, i.e., $\hat{F} = \{g \in F \mid P(f \Delta g) > \varepsilon\}$. Let $\hat{P}$ be the distribution on $\mathbf{R}^{k+1}$ given by

$$\hat{P}((x, y)) = \begin{cases} P(x) \text{ if } y = f(x) \\ 0 \text{ otherwise} \end{cases}.$$

Let $(x_1, y_1), (x_2, y_2), \ldots, (x_m, y_m)$ be the m examples obtained by $A_{4.1}$. Suppose there exists $g \in \hat{F}$ consistent with all these examples. That is, each $(x_i, y_i) \in \text{graph}(g)$. Then, $\hat{P}_m(\text{graph}(g)) = 1$. But, since $g \in \hat{F}$, $\hat{P}(\text{graph}(g)) < 1 - \varepsilon$. Therefore,

$$\hat{P}_m(\text{graph}(g)) = 1 \text{ and } \hat{P}(\text{graph}(g)) < 1 - \varepsilon. \tag{4.11}$$

By Lemma 4.1, $\mathbf{D}_{VC}(\text{graph}(F)) = \mathbf{D}_{VC}(F) = d$. Using this, and invoking Theorem 4.3, we see that the probability that (4.11) holds for any $g \in F$ is at most $2\Phi(2m, d)2^{-\varepsilon m/2}$. To be precise, this is true only for $m \geq 8/\varepsilon$, but we will see that this condition holds. Thus, the probability that algorithm $A_{4.1}$ will output a concept in $\hat{F}$ is at most $2\Phi(2m, d)2^{-\varepsilon m/2}$. We wish to choose m so that this probability is at most δ, i.e.,

$$2\Phi(2m, d)2^{-\frac{\varepsilon m}{2}} \leq \delta.$$

By Exercise 2.9, $\Phi(2m, d) \leq \left[\dfrac{2em}{d}\right]^{d+1}$. Thus, it suffices if

$$2\left[\frac{2em}{d}\right]^{d+1} 2^{-\frac{\varepsilon m}{2}} \leq \delta.$$

Taking logarithms on both sides and rearranging, we get

$$\frac{\ln(2)}{2}\varepsilon m \geq (d+1)\ln\left[\frac{2em}{d}\right] + \ln\left[\frac{2}{\delta}\right]. \tag{4.12}$$

We simplify (4.12) to obtain an expression for m, by decomposing (4.12) into (4.13) and (4.14) below.

$$\frac{\ln(2)}{4}\varepsilon m \geq \ln\left[\frac{2}{\delta}\right]. \tag{4.13}$$

$$\frac{\ln(2)}{4}\varepsilon m \geq (d+1)\ln\left[\frac{2em}{d}\right].\tag{4.14}$$

Solving (4.13) for m and noting that $\ln(2) > 1/2$, we get

$$m \geq \frac{8}{\varepsilon}\ln\left[\frac{2}{\delta}\right].$$

Consider (4.15) below:

$$m = \frac{32d}{\varepsilon}\ln\left[\frac{32}{\varepsilon}\right].\tag{4.15}$$

By substitution, it is easy to verify that (4.15) implies (4.14). Also, by differentiating both sides of (4.14) with respect to m, we can show that the derivative of the left-hand side exceeds the right-hand side for values of m that exceed (4.15). Combining the last two inequalities, we get

$$m = \frac{8}{\varepsilon}\left[4d\ln\left[\frac{32}{\varepsilon}\right] + \ln\left[\frac{2}{\delta}\right]\right].\tag{4.16}$$

By definition, m as a function of ε and δ is the sample complexity $s(\varepsilon, \delta)$ of the algorithm, and the theorem is proved.

□

In the above, we assume that graph(F) is well behaved in that the measurability assumptions of Theorem 4.3 hold. It is easy to see that graph(F) is well behaved if and only if F is well behaved.

Example 4.3   Consider the class of concepts F composed of homogeneous half-spaces on $\mathbf{R}^2$. Specifically, each $f \in F$ is the set of all points $(u,v) \in \mathbf{R}^2$ that satisfy the equation $\alpha u + \beta v \geq 0$ for fixed $\alpha, \beta \in \mathbf{R}$. (If the right-hand side of the above equation were nonzero, the resulting half-space would not be called homogeneous.)

We claim that $\mathbf{D}_{VC}(F) = 2$. To see this, simply pick any two points a and b that are not collinear with the origin. Then, clearly the set $\{a, b\}$ is shattered by F and $\mathbf{D}_{VC}(F) \geq 2$.

We now show that $\mathbf{D}_{VC}(F) < 3$. Suppose a set $S = \{a, b, c\}$ is shattered. Let $a = (a_x, a_y)$ where a_x and a_y are the x and y coordinates, respectively, of a. Similarly for b and c. Since every concept in F contains the origin, none of the three points a, b, and c can be the origin. Suppose a is in the third or fourth quadrant. Then, a homogeneous half-space contains a if and only if it does not contain the point $\hat{a} = (-a_x, -b_x)$. Hence, S is shattered if and only if $\{\hat{a}, b, c\}$ is shattered. Repeating the argument for b and c, it follows that we can assume each of a, b, and c to be in the first two quadrants. Let θ_a be the angle made by the line joining the origin to a with the x-axis. Similarly, define θ_b and θ_c. If any pair of these angles are equal, say $\theta_a = \theta_b$, then every homogeneous half-space that contains a will also contain b and, hence, S cannot be shattered. Thus, the three angles must be distinct. Without loss of generality, let $\theta_a > \theta_b > \theta_c$. Now, every homogeneous half-space that contains b must contain at least one of a or c. Thus, S cannot be shattered and $\mathbf{D}_{VC}(F) < 3$.

From the above, $\mathbf{D}_{VC}(F) = 2$, and by Theorem 4.3, we have learning algorithm $A_{4.2}$ for F. In essence, the algorithm first transposes the examples as necessary so that they lie in the first two quadrants. Then, it picks a line through the origin that separates the positive and negative examples seen. The algorithm assumes that at least one positive example and one negative example will be obtained. We leave it as an exercise for the reader to modify the algorithm to cover the case when this assumption is violated. Figure 4.1 illustrates the algorithm.

Learning Algorithm $A_{4.2}$
input: ε, δ;
begin:

make $\dfrac{8}{\varepsilon}\left[16\ln\left[\dfrac{64}{\varepsilon}\right] + \ln\left[\dfrac{2}{\delta}\right]\right]$ calls of EXAMPLE;

let S be the set of examples seen;
transpose the examples in S as necessary so
    that all of them lie in the first two quadrants;
let
$\theta_{\max+}$ = max $\{\arctan(v_i/u_i) \,|\, ((u_i, v_i), 1) \in S\}$;
$\theta_{\min+}$ = min $\{\arctan(v_i/u_i) \,|\, ((u_i, v_i), 1) \in S\}$;
$\theta_{\max-}$ = max $\{\arctan(v_i/u_i) \,|\, ((u_i, v_i), 0) \in S\}$;
if $\theta_{\min+} > \theta_{\max-}$ then
    $\alpha = -\tan(\theta_{\min+})$;
    $\beta = 1$;
else
    $\alpha = \tan(\theta_{\max+})$;
    $\beta = -1$;
output the homogeneous half-space $\alpha u + \beta v \geq 0$;
end

■

We now establish a lower bound on the sample complexity of a learning algorithm for a class of concepts. Theorem 4.5 below is essentially a tighter form of Theorem 2.2, and its proof uses many of the techniques used in the proof of Theorem 2.2. The proof is somewhat complicated, and the reader may find it helpful to revisit Theorem 2.2 first.

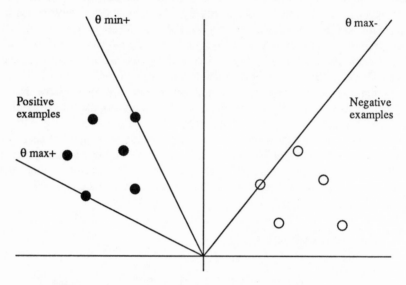

Figure 4.1
Learning half-spaces on $\mathbf{R}^2$.

Recall the definition of the learning operator Ψ corresponding to a learning algorithm A, as given in Section 2.3. In that definition, the operator Ψ took as input ε, δ, n and a sequence of examples σ, and then ran the learning algorithm A on inputs ε, δ, and n. Here, the learning operator takes as input ε, δ, and a sequence of examples σ, and then runs the learning algorithm A on inputs ε and δ. All else remains the same. Since this is a straightforward modification, we omit a formal definition.

THEOREM 4.5 _____

Let F be a class of concepts on $\mathbf{R}^k$ and let A be an admissible learning algorithm for F, with sample complexity $s(\varepsilon, \delta)$. If $\varepsilon \leq 1/4$, $\delta \leq 1/4$, and $\mathbf{D}_{VC}(F) \geq 16$,

$$s(\varepsilon, \delta) \geq \frac{\mathbf{D}_{VC}(F)}{16\varepsilon}.$$

Proof: Let $d = \mathbf{D}_{VC}(F)$ and $m = s(\varepsilon, \delta)$. By definition, F shatters a set S, $|S| = d$. Let $\{s_1, s_2, \ldots, s_d\}$ be the d elements of S and let x^m be an element of S^m.

For $\varepsilon \leq 1/4$, let P be the probability distribution defined as follows:

$$P(s_1) = 1 - 4\varepsilon \quad \text{and} \quad P(s_i) = \frac{4\varepsilon}{d-1}, \quad 2 \leq i \leq d.$$

Let Ψ be the learning operator corresponding to A. For $f \in F$, let $f(x^m)$ denote the sequence of examples obtained from x^m. That is, if $x^m = (x_1, x_2, x_3, \ldots, x_m)$, $f(x^m)$ is the sequence $(x_1, f(x_1)), (x_2, f(x_2)), \ldots, (x_m, f(x_m))$. Let $G \subseteq F$ be such that G shatters S and $|G| = 2^{|S|}$.

Let $A(\varepsilon, \delta)$ denote the output of A when run on input ε and δ, with f as the target concept. Since A is a PAC learning algorithm for F, for each $f \in G$, the probability that $P(f \Delta A(\varepsilon, \delta)) > \varepsilon$ is at most δ. That is,

$$\mathbf{Pr} \left\{ P(f \Delta A(\varepsilon, \delta)) > \varepsilon \right\} \leq \delta. \tag{4.17}$$

Using the learning operator Ψ of A, we can write

$$\mathbf{Pr} \left\{ P(f \Delta A(\varepsilon, \delta)) > \varepsilon \right\}$$

$$= \sum_{x^m \in S^m} \mathbf{Pr} \left\{ P(f \Delta \Psi(\varepsilon, \delta, f(x^m))) > \varepsilon \right\} \mathbf{Pr} \{f(x^m)\}. \tag{4.18}$$

In the above, $\mathbf{Pr} \{f(x^m)\}$ is the probability that $f(x^m)$ is the sequence of examples obtained in m calls of EXAMPLE.

Substituting (4.18) in (4.17) gives us,

$$\sum_{x^m \in S^m} \mathbf{Pr} \left\{ P(f \Delta \Psi(\varepsilon, \delta, f(x^m))) > \varepsilon \right\} \mathbf{Pr} \{f(x^m)\} \leq \delta.$$

Summing both sides of the above over all f in G, we get

$$\sum_{f \in G} \sum_{x^m \in S^m} \mathbf{Pr} \left\{ P(f \Delta \Psi(\varepsilon, \delta, f(x^m))) > \varepsilon \right\} \mathbf{Pr} \{f(x^m)\} \leq \sum_{f \in G} \delta.$$

Flipping the order of the sums in the above, we get

$$\sum_{x^m \in S^m} \sum_{f \in G} \mathbf{Pr} \left\{ P(f \Delta \Psi(\varepsilon, \delta, f(x^m))) > \varepsilon \right\} \mathbf{Pr} \{f(x^m)\} \leq \sum_{f \in G} \delta. \tag{4.19}$$

We will estimate the inner sum in (4.19):

$$\sum_{f \in G} \mathbf{Pr} \left\{ P(f \Delta \Psi(\varepsilon, \delta, f(x^m))) > \varepsilon \right\}. \tag{4.20}$$

Using the switch function θ, we can expand (4.20) as follows:

$$\sum_{f \in G} \sum_{h \in G} \theta \left[P(f \Delta h) > \varepsilon \right] \mathbf{Pr} \left\{ S \cap h = S \cap \Psi(\varepsilon, \delta, f(x^m)) \right\}. \tag{4.21}$$

The following inequality holds for any $\eta \in \mathbf{R}$:

$$\theta \left[P(f \Delta h) > \varepsilon \right] \geq \theta \left[P(f \Delta h) > \eta \right] \theta \left[\eta \geq \varepsilon \right].$$

Let $\zeta(f)$ denote the event $S \cap h = S \cap \Psi(\varepsilon, \delta, f(x^m))$. Using ζ and substituting the above inequality in (4.21) and noting that (4.21) was derived from (4.20), we get

$$\sum_{f \in G} \mathbf{Pr} \left\{ \theta(P(f \Delta \Psi(\varepsilon, \delta, f(x^m))) > \varepsilon) \right\}$$

$$\geq \sum_{f \in G} \sum_{h \in G} \theta \left[P(f \Delta h) > \eta \right] \theta \left[\eta \geq \varepsilon \right] \mathbf{Pr} \left\{ \zeta(f) \right\}. \tag{4.22}$$

Fix η as follows:

$$\eta = \frac{2 \varepsilon | S - [x^m] |}{d}.$$

Fix $x^m \in S^m$. We claim that for each $f \in G$, there exists $g \in G$ such that $g(x^m) = f(x^m)$ and for all $h \in G$, at least one of the following holds:

$$P(f \Delta h) > \eta, \quad P(g \Delta h) > \eta.$$

To see this, pick $g \in G$ such that g agrees with f on all of $[x^m]$ and disagrees with f on all of $S - [x^m]$. We note that such a choice of g is unique and denote it by pair(f). Clearly, $g(x^m) = f(x^m)$. Now, for any $h \in G$, $(f \Delta h) \cap (S - [x^m])$ and $(g \Delta h) \cap (S - [x^m])$ are mutually disjoint. Thus, at least one of the following inequalities holds:

$$P(f \Delta h) \geq \frac{P(S - [x^m])}{2}, \quad P(g \Delta h) \geq \frac{P(S - [x^m])}{2}.$$

By our choice of P,

$$P(S - [x^m]) \geq 4\varepsilon \frac{|S - [x^m]|}{d-1} > 4\varepsilon \frac{|S - [x^m]|}{d},$$

and, hence, the claim.

We now return to (4.22). Split G into disjoint sets G_1 and G_2 such that for each $f \in G_1$, $\text{pair}(f) \in G_2$ and vice versa. This split is not unique, but any such split will suffice. We can now write the right-hand side of (4.22) as

$$\sum_{f \in G_1} \sum_{h \in G} \theta \left[P(f \Delta h) > \eta \right] \theta(\eta \geq \varepsilon) \Pr \{\zeta(f)\}$$

$$+ \sum_{g \in G_2} \sum_{h \in G} \theta \left[P(g \Delta h) > \eta \right] \theta(\eta \geq \varepsilon) \Pr \{\zeta(g)\}. \tag{4.23}$$

If $g = \text{pair}(f)$, then $f(x^m) = g(x^m)$. Hence, $\zeta(f) = \zeta(g)$ and we can write (4.23) as

$$\sum_{f \in G_1} \sum_{h \in G} \left[\theta \left[P(f \Delta h) > \eta \right] + \theta \left[P(\text{pair}(f) \Delta h) > \eta \right] \right]$$

$$\times \theta \left[\eta \geq \varepsilon \right] \Pr \{\zeta(f)\}. \tag{4.24}$$

Since at least one of $P(f \Delta h) > \eta$, $P(\text{pair}(f) \Delta h) > \eta$ must hold, we have

$$\theta \left[P(f \Delta h) > \eta \right] + \theta \left[P(\text{pair}(f) \Delta h) > \eta \right] \geq 1.$$

Substituting the above in (4.24) and noting that (4.24) was derived from the right-hand side of (4.22), we get

$$\sum_{f \in G} \Pr \left\{ P(f \Delta \Psi(\varepsilon, \delta, f(x^m))) > \varepsilon \right\}$$

$$\geq \sum_{f \in G_1} \sum_{h \in G} \theta(\eta \geq \varepsilon) \Pr \{\zeta(f)\}. \tag{4.25}$$

But

$$\theta \left[\eta \geq \varepsilon \right] = \theta \left[\frac{2\varepsilon |S - [x^m]|}{d} \geq \varepsilon \right] = \theta \left[|[x^m]| \leq \frac{d}{2} \right].$$

Hence, the right-hand side of (4.25) can be written as

$$\sum_{f \in G_1} \sum_{h \in G} \theta \left[|[x^m]| \le \frac{d}{2} \right] \mathbf{Pr} \left\{ \zeta(f) \right\}$$

$$= \sum_{f \in G_1} \theta \left[|[x^m]| \le \frac{d}{2} \right] \sum_{h \in G} \mathbf{Pr} \left\{ S \cap h = S \cap \Psi(\epsilon, \delta, f(x^m)) \right\}$$

$$= \sum_{f \in G_1} \theta \left[|[x^m]| \le \frac{d}{2} \right] = 1/2 \sum_{f \in G} \theta \left[|[x^m]| \le \frac{d}{2} \right].$$

The last equality follows from the fact that $|G_1| = |G_2| = |G|/2$. Substituting the above in (4.19), we get

$$\sum_{x^m \in S^m} 1/2 \sum_{f \in G} \theta \left[|[x^m]| \le \frac{d}{2} \right] \mathbf{Pr} \left\{ f(x^m) \right\} \le \sum_{f \in G} \delta.$$

Flipping the order of the sums, we get

$$1/2 \sum_{f \in G} \sum_{x^m \in S^m} \theta \left[|[x^m]| \le \frac{d}{2} \right] \mathbf{Pr} \left\{ f(x^m) \right\} \le \sum_{f \in G} \delta. \tag{4.26}$$

We now estimate the inner sum in the above:

$$\sum_{x^m \in S^m} \theta \left[|[x^m]| \le \frac{d}{2} \right] \mathbf{Pr} \left\{ f(x^m) \right\}.$$

In essence, this sum is the probability that $|[x^m]|$ will be at most $d/2$. That is,

$$\sum_{x^m \in S^m} \theta \left[|[x^m]| \le \frac{d}{2} \right] \mathbf{Pr} \left\{ x^m \right\} = \mathbf{Pr} \left\{ |[x^m]| \le \frac{d}{2} \right\}$$

$$= 1 - \mathbf{Pr} \left\{ |[x^m]| > \frac{d}{2} \right\}, \tag{4.27}$$

and it suffices to estimate the latter probability. If $|[x^m]| > d/2$, then the items of x^m must lie in $S - \{s_1\}$ at least $d/2$ times. By our choice of P, the probability of picking an element in $S - \{s_1\}$ is 4ϵ. Thus, the probability of picking an element from $S - \{s_1\}$ at least $d/2$ times in l attempts follows the binomial distribution: the probability of achieving at least r successes in m trials, given that the probability of success at each trial is p. Let us call this probability $\mathbf{Pr} \left\{ T_m \ge r \right\}$. As given in the appendix, for $r > mp$,

$$\mathbf{Pr} \left\{ T_m \ge r \right\} \le \frac{r(1-p)}{(r - mp)^2}.$$

Noting that $p = 4\epsilon$ and $r = d/2$, and substituting the above in (4.27), we get

$$\sum_{x^m \in S^m} \theta \left[|[x^m]| \le \frac{d}{2} \right] \Pr \{x^m\} = 1 - \Pr \left\{ |[x^m]| > \frac{d}{2} \right\}$$

$$\ge 1 - \frac{r(1-p)}{(r-mp)^2}. \qquad (4.28)$$

Substituting (4.28) in (4.26), and solving for m, we get

$$m \ge \frac{r}{p} - \frac{1}{p} \left[\frac{r(1-p)}{(1-2\delta)} \right]^{1/2}.$$

Note that the above does not violate the assumption that $r > mp$ and, hence, is valid. Setting $r = d/2$ and $p = 4\varepsilon$, we see that

$$m \ge \frac{d}{8\varepsilon} - \left[\frac{d(1-4\varepsilon)}{2(1-2\delta)} \right]^{1/2}.$$

For $d \ge 16$, and $\delta \le 1/4$, the second term in the above equation is at most half the first term. Hence, for $d \ge 16$, and $\delta \le 1/4$,

$$m \ge \frac{d}{16\varepsilon} \ge \frac{\mathbf{D}_{VC}(F)}{16\varepsilon}.$$

This completes the proof.

□

As a corollary to Theorems 4.4 and 4.5, we have the following.

COROLLARY 4.1 ───────────────────────────────────

A class of concepts on $\mathbf{R}^k$ is uniformly learnable if and only if $\mathbf{D}_{VC}(F)$ is finite.

───

Example 4.4   Consider the class F of concepts on $\mathbf{R}$ such that each $f \in F$ is the union of finitely many closed intervals on $\mathbf{R}$. Clearly, $\mathbf{D}_{VC}(F)$ is not finite. By Theorem 4.4, F is not uniformly learnable.

Now let G be the class of concepts on $\mathbf{R}^2$ such that each $f \in G$ is a convex polygon. As follows from Exercise 4.2, $\mathbf{D}_{VC}(G)$ is not finite. Hence, by Theorem 4.4, G is not uniformly learnable. Also see Exercise 4.7.   ∎

4.3 Summary

We extended the paradigm of PAC learning to classes of concepts defined on uncountable domains, such as the reals. Using the Vapnik-Chervonenkis theorem on the uniform convergence of classes of events, we linked the uniform learnability of a class with its Vapnik-Chervonenkis dimension. We then obtained a variant of the Vapnik-Chervonenkis theorem more suitable for our purposes. Using this variant, we were able to improve the sample complexity of the learning algorithm obtained with the general form of the Vapnik-Chervonenkis theorem. Finally, we obtained a lower bound on the sample complexity of a learning algorithm, sharpening our previous lower bound of Theorem 2.2.

Additional readings on the topics of this chapter are suggested in the Bibliographic Notes.

4.4 Appendix

4.4.1 Measurability and Probability Distributions

We extend the familiar notion of an interval on $\mathbf{R}$ to $\mathbf{R}^k$. An interval on $\mathbf{R}^k$ is the box obtained by taking the Cartesian product of k intervals, one for each of the k coordinate axes. Each of the k intervals may be closed, open, or half-open.

Let F be a class of sets on $\mathbf{R}^k$ satisfying the following conditions:

(a) Every interval on $\mathbf{R}^k$ is in F.

(b) F is closed under complementation, i.e., for each $f \in F$, the complement $\mathbf{R} - f$ is also in F.

(c) F is closed under countable union, i.e., for every countable collection $f_1, f_2, \ldots, f_n, \ldots$ of sets in F, $\bigcup_{n=1}^{\infty} f_n$ is also in F.

The smallest class of sets F that satisfy the above properties is known as the class $\mathbf{B}$ of *Borel* sets on $\mathbf{R}^k$.

We say that a set $f \subseteq \mathbf{R}^k$ is *measurable* if f is a Borel set, i.e., $f \in \mathbf{B}$.

A probability distribution P on $\mathbf{R}^k$ is a function assigning a value $P(f) \geq 0$ to each $f \in \mathbf{B}$, such that

(a) $P(\mathbf{R}^k) = 1$.

(b) For every countable collection $f_1, f_2, \ldots, f_n, \ldots$ of sets in $\mathbf{B}$,

$$P\left[\bigcup_{n=1}^{\infty} f_n\right] = \sum_{n=1}^{\infty} P(f_n).$$

4.4.2 Bounds for the Binomial Distribution

Let T be an event with probability of occurrence p. Let T_m denote the number of occurrences of T in m random trials. Now, the probability that T will occur exactly r times in m trials is

$$\mathbf{Pr}\,\{T_m = r\} = \begin{bmatrix} m \\ r \end{bmatrix} p^r (1-p)^{m-r}.$$

And the probability that T will occur at least r times in m trials is

$$\mathbf{Pr}\,\{T_m \geq r\} = \sum_{i=r}^{i=m} \begin{bmatrix} m \\ i \end{bmatrix} p^i (1-p)^{m-i}.$$

T_m is said to be distributed according to the binomial distribution. It is well known that for $r > mp$,

$$\mathbf{Pr}\,\{T_m \geq r\} \leq \frac{r(1-p)}{(r-mp)^2}.$$

For further discussion on the above, please consult the appropriate references in the Bibliography.

4.5 Exercises

4.1.   Let G be the axis-parallel rectangles of Example 4.1. Show that no set of 5 points in $\mathbf{R}^2$ is shattered by G.

4.2.   Estimate $\mathbf{D}_{VC}(F)$ for the following: (a) let F be the class of all circles in $\mathbf{R}^2$; and (b) let F be the class of all convex polygons in $\mathbf{R}^2$ with k sides for fixed k.

4.3.   Let F and G be two classes of concepts on $\mathbf{R}^k$. Estimate (a) $\mathbf{D}_{VC}(F \times G)$; (b) $\mathbf{D}_{VC}(F \bigcup G)$; and (c) $\mathbf{D}_{VC}(F \bigcap G)$ in terms of $\mathbf{D}_{VC}(F)$ and $\mathbf{D}_{VC}(G)$.

4.4.   Compare the bounds of Theorems 4.4 and 2.1. Notice that the $(n+1)$ term of Theorem 2.1 has been replaced by a $\log(1/\varepsilon)$ term in Theorem 4.4. Can you use Theorem 4.4 to improve Theorem 2.1? If so, show how this may be done.

4.5.   Theorem 4.5 showed that

$$s(\varepsilon, \delta) \geq \frac{\mathbf{D}_{VC}(F)}{16\varepsilon}.$$

Show that the following inequality must hold as well.

$$s(\varepsilon, \delta) \geq \frac{1}{\varepsilon} \ln \left[\frac{1}{\delta} \right].$$

This inequality would make the lower bound on the sample complexity almost match the upper bound given in Theorem 4.4, in an asymptotic sense.

4.6.   Consider a computer on which each unit of memory is a real number and which can perform arithmetic operations on real numbers in unit time. Such a machine is called an infinite precision random-access machine, *real* RAM for short. A program for such a machine consists of two parts: (a) a "finite control" part, which is simply a string in Σ^*, such as a program for a Turing machine; and (b) a list of finitely many real constants, each of which may be of infinite precision. The length of such a program is the string length of the finite control plus the number of real constants in the program.

With respect to algorithms that run on such machines: For classes of concepts on $\mathbf{R}^k$, develop notions of polynomial-time learnability and usually polynomial-time learnability. These notions will be variants of those given in Chapter 3, and the results of Chapter 3 will carry over to them.

Show that the class of finitely many intervals on $\mathbf{R}$ possesses a polynomial-time Occam fitting and, hence, is learnable in usually polynomial time.

4.7.   Consider the class F of all half-spaces (not necessarily homogeneous) in $\mathbf{R}^k$ for fixed k. What is $\mathbf{D}_{VC}(F)$?

(a)   Give a detailed learning algorithm for this class, such as the one given in Example 4.3. Does your algorithm run in polynomial time on the RAM?

(b)   Can you extend your algorithm to unions of two half-spaces? What about unions of arbitrarily many half-spaces?

4.8.   Prove Theorem 4.1 along the lines of the proof of Theorem 4.3. Specifically, you will need to prove a variant of Claim 4.1 for the case when E denotes the set of all $x^m \in D^m$ such that there exists $f \in F$ for which the hit frequency of f differs from its hit probability by at least ε. That is, if m_1 elements of x^m are in f, then

$$\left| \frac{m_1}{m} - P(f) \right| > \varepsilon.$$

J denotes the set of all $x^m y^m \in D^{2m}$ such that there exists $f \in F$ for which the hit frequency of f in x^m and y^m differ by at least $\varepsilon/2$. That is, if m_1 elements of x^m are in f and m_2 elements of y^m are in f, then

$$\left| \frac{m_1}{m} - \frac{m_2}{m} \right| \geq \frac{\varepsilon}{2}.$$

4.6 Bibliographic Notes

Theorem 4.1 is from Vapnik and Chervonenkis (1971). Generalizations of the theorem may be found in Pollard (1986), Chapter 2. Theorems 4.3 and 4.4 are adapted from Blumer, Ehrenfeucht, Haussler, and Warmuth (1990). Theorem 4.5 is adapted from Ehrenfeucht, Haussler, Kearns, and Valiant (1989). The discussion on measurability and distributions is from Parzen (1960), page 150, and Feller (1957), Vol. 2, Chapter 4. Additional details on the measurability assumptions of Theorems 4.1 and 4.3 may be found in Blumer, Ehrenfeucht, Haussler, and Warmuth (1990). More on uniform and nonuniform models of learning may be found in Ben-David, Benedek, and Mansour (1989). The discussion on the binomial distribution is from Feller (1957), Vol. 1, pages 151–152. Exercise 4.6 is adapted from Blumer, Ehrenfeucht, Haussler, and Warmuth (1990). Exercise 4.7(b) is from Long and Warmuth (1990). For additional details on the real RAM, see Preparata and Shamos (1985).

5

Learning Functions

In the foregoing material, we considered the learnability of classes of concepts defined on the countable domain of Σ^* and the uncountable domain of $\mathbf{R}^k$. There are natural learning situations in which we learn functions rather than concepts. For instance, we learn to estimate a person's weight from his appearance, to estimate the ambient temperature from physical sensations, to predict stock market prices from some visible parameters, and so on. Hence, it is useful to generalize the learning model to classes of functions, functions from Σ^* to Σ^* and from $\mathbf{R}^k$ to $\mathbf{R}^k$. Such a generalization of the model is the subject of this chapter.

5.1 Learning Functions on Countable Domains

Let f be a function from a set X to a set Y. We say that X and Y are the *domain* and *range*, respectively, of f. The function f is said to be *total* if it is defined over all of its domain X.

In this section, we are concerned with total functions from Σ^* to Σ^*. A *class* F of functions from Σ^* to Σ^* is a set of total functions from Σ^* to Σ^*. An example for a function f is a pair $(x, f(x))$. A learning algorithm for a class of functions is an algorithm that attempts to infer an approximation to a function in F from examples for it. The learning algorithm has at its disposal a subroutine EXAMPLE, which at each call produces a randomly chosen example of the function to be learned. The function f for which examples are provided is the *target function*. The examples are chosen according to an arbitrary and unknown probability distribution P on Σ^* in that the probability that a particular example $(x, f(x))$ will be produced at any call is $P(x)$.

As in the case of concepts, we define the notion of a PAC learning algorithm. The definition involves the modification mentioned below.

To present the modification, it is convenient to have the following definition in hand.

DEFINITION _____

Let $f:\Sigma^* \to \Sigma^*$. For $n_1, n_2 \in \mathbb{N}$, the *projection* $f^{[n_1][n_2]}$ of f on $\Sigma^{[n_1]} \times \Sigma^{[n_2]}$ is

(a)   undefined if there exists $x \in \Sigma^{[n_1]}$ such that $f(x) \notin \Sigma^{[n_2]}$.

(b)   the   function $f^{[n_1][n_2]} : \Sigma^{[n_1]} \to \Sigma^{[n_2]}$ where   for   all $x \in \Sigma^{[n_1]}$, $f^{[n_1][n_2]}(x) = f(x)$.

The projection of a class of functions F is the class $F^{[n_1][n_2]}$ given by

$$F^{[n_1][n_2]} = \{ f^{[n_1][n_2]} \mid f \in F, f^{[n_1][n_2]} \text{ is defined} \}.$$

When learning concepts on Σ^*, the learning algorithm takes as input a length parameter n that bounds the portion of the domain that is relevant to the learner. Here, we will provide as input *two* length parameters n_1 and n_2. The parameter n_1 bounds the portion of the domain that is relevant, while the parameter n_2 bounds the portion of the range of the target function that is relevant. Specifically, the probability distribution P is zero on all strings of length greater than n, and the target function f is such that $f^{[n_1][n_2]}$ is defined.

DEFINITION _____

An algorithm A is a PAC learning algorithm for a class of functions F if

(a) A takes as input ε, δ, n_1, and n_2.

(b) A may call EXAMPLE, which returns examples for some $f \in F$. The examples are chosen randomly and independently according to an arbitrary and unknown probability distribution P on $\Sigma^{[n_1]}$.

(c)   For all $f \in F$ for which $f^{[n_1][n_2]}$ is defined, and all probability distributions P on $\Sigma^{[n_1]}$, A outputs a function $g \in F$, such that with probability at least $(1 - \delta), P(f \Delta g) \leq \varepsilon$.

Notation: For any two functions f and g, $f \Delta g = \{x \,|\, f(x) \neq g(x)\}$.

Recall the definition of the learning operator Ψ corresponding to a learning algorithm A, as given in Section 2.3. In that definition, the operator Ψ took as input ε, δ, n and a sequence of examples σ, and then ran the learning algorithm A on inputs ε, δ, and n. Here, we modify this definition so that the learning operator Ψ takes as input ε, δ, n_1, n_2, and a sequence of examples σ, and then runs the learning algorithm A on inputs ε, δ, n_1, and n_2. All else remains the same. Since this is a straightforward modification, we omit a formal definition. As in Chapter 2, we will restrict our attention to admissible learning algorithms, i.e., those algorithms whose learning operators compute random functions.

We now develop notions of sample complexity and polynomial-sample learnability in this setting. The intent and significance of these notions are identical to those introduced in Chapter 2. In particular, the sample complexity of a learning algorithm is the number of examples required by the algorithm as a function of the input parameters.

DEFINITION _____

Let A be a learning algorithm for a class of functions F. The *sample complexity* of A is the function $s : R \times R \times N \times N \rightarrow N$ such that $s(\varepsilon, \delta, n_1, n_2)$ is the maximum number of calls of EXAMPLE by A, the maximum being taken over all runs of A on inputs ε, δ, n_1, and n_2, with the target function f ranging over all $f \in F$ for which $f^{[n_1][n_2]}$ is defined, and the probability distribution P ranging over all distributions on $\Sigma^{[n_1]}$. If no finite maximum exists, $s(\varepsilon, \delta) = \infty$.

As before, a class of functions is said to be polynomial-sample learnable if there exists a learning algorithm for it with polynomial-sample complexity.

DEFINITION _____

A class of functions F is said to be *polynomial-sample learnable* if there exists a learning algorithm A for F with sample complexity $p(1/\varepsilon, 1/\delta, n_1, n_2)$, where p is a polynomial function of its arguments.

5.1.1 Dimension and Learnability

An important question to ask at this point is whether learning a class of functions F is equivalent to learning the concept class graph(F) consisting of the graph sets of the functions in F. If so, we could simply invoke the learnability results of the earlier chapters and move on to other topics. As it happens, such is not the case. To see this, notice that when learning F as a class of functions, for a particular target function f, EXAMPLE will never output elements of $\Sigma^* \times \Sigma^*$ that are not in graph(f). However, when learning graph(F) as a class of concepts on $\Sigma^* \times \Sigma^*$, EXAMPLE may output any element of $\Sigma^* \times \Sigma^*$, without regard to the target concept graph(f). Thus, learning F as a class of functions is somewhat more restricted than learning graph(F) as a class of concepts. That is, while the latter is sufficient for the former, it is certainly not necessary.

The Vapnik-Chervonenkis dimension of a class of concepts turned out to be an important measure in the study of the learnability of classes of concepts. Here, we generalize the Vapnik-Chervonenkis dimension to classes of functions and use this generalized dimension in the study of learnability.

We begin by generalizing the notion of shattering. In order to distinguish this notion of shattering from the one given in Section 2.3, we will refer to it as "generalized" shattering and to the earlier notion as "special" shattering.

DEFINITION _____

Let F be a class of functions from a set X to a set Y. We say F *shatters* $S \subseteq X$ if there exist two functions f, $g \in F$ such that

(a)   For all $x \in S, f(x) \neq g(x)$.

(b)   For all $S_1 \subseteq S$, there exists $h \in F$ such that h agrees with f on S_1 and with g on $S - S_1$. i.e.,
    for all $x \in S_1, h(x) = f(x)$
    for all $x \in S - S_1, h(x) = g(x)$.

_____

We illustrate this definition with the following example.

Example 5.1   Consider the class F of all polynomials of degree 3 on **R**. That is, each $f \in F$ is a cubic polynomial of one variable, mapping **R** to **R**. We claim that F shatters the set $S = \{0, 1, 2, 3\}$. To see this, consider the two polynomials $f = x$ and $g = x^2 + 1$. Now, for any subset S_1 of S, we can construct a cubic polynomial h that agrees with f on S_1 and with g elsewhere on S. For instance, let $S_1 = \{1, 3\}$. Then,

$$g = -\frac{5}{3}x^3 + 7x^2 - \frac{16}{3}x + 1$$

agrees with f on S_1 and with g on $S - S_1$. See Figure 5.1.

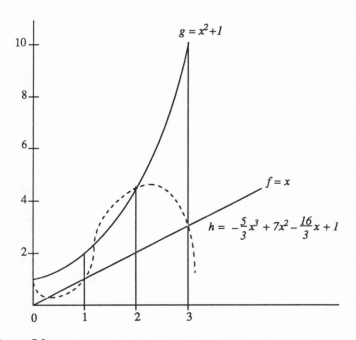

Figure 5.1 _____
Generalized shattering. The set $\{0, 1, 2, 3\}$ is shattered by the class of all cubic polynomials on **R**.

In fact, F shatters every set of four elements from **R**.   ∎

Suppose that G is a class of concepts on X. Let F be the class of indicator functions of G, which are functions from X to the set $\{0, 1\}$. That is, $F = \{I_g \mid g \in G\}$. Notice that F shatters a set S in the generalized sense if and only if G shatters S in the special sense. Thus, when considering classes of concepts, the notion of generalized shattering collapses smoothly to special shattering.

Akin to the definition of the dimension of class of concepts, we have the following:

DEFINITION _____

Let F be a class of functions from a set X to a set Y. The *generalized dimension* of F, denoted by $\mathbf{D}_G(F)$, is the greatest integer d such that there exists a set of cardinality d that is shattered by F.

_____

Note that the generalized dimension collapses to the Vapnik-Chervonenkis dimension for classes of concepts. Specifically, if F is a class of concepts and I_F is the class of indicator functions for F, then $\mathbf{D}_G(I_F) = \mathbf{D}_{VC}(G)$.

The following lemma is the analog of Lemma 2.1 and establishes a relationship between the cardinality of a class and its generalized dimension.

LEMMA 5.1 _____

Let X and Y be two finite sets and let F be a set of total functions from X to Y. If $d = \mathbf{D}_G(F)$, then,

$$2^d \leq |F| \leq |X|^d |Y|^{2d}.$$

_____

Proof: The first inequality is immediate from the definition of $\mathbf{D}_G(F)$ and the definition of shattering. The second inequality is proved by induction on $|X|$.

Basis: Clearly true for $|X| = 1$, for all $|Y|$. Also, we can assume $d \geq 1$ since the hypothesis holds trivially otherwise.

Induction: Assume true for $|X| = k$, $|Y| = l$ and prove true for $|X| = k+1$ and $Y = l$. Let $X = \{x_1, x_2, \ldots, x_{k+1}\}$ and $Y = \{y_1, y_2, \ldots, y_l\}$. Define the sets of functions $F_i \subseteq F$ as follows:

$$F_i = \{f \mid f \in F, f(x_1) = y_i\}.$$

Also, define the sets of functions F_{ij} and F_0 as follows: For $i \neq j$,

$$F_{ij} = \left\{ f \mid f \in F_i, \text{ there exists } g \in F_j \text{ such that } f = g \text{ on } X - \{x_1\} \right\}.$$

$$F_0 = F - \bigcup_{i \neq j} F_{ij}.$$

Now,

$$|F| = |F_0| + \left|\bigcup_{i \neq j} F_{ij}\right| \leq |F_0| + \sum_{i \neq j} |F_{ij}|.$$

We seek bounds on the quantities on the right-hand side of the last inequality. By definition, the functions in F_0 are all distinct on the k elements of $X - \{x_1\}$. Furthermore, the largest set shattered in F_0 must be of cardinality no greater than d. By the inductive hypothesis, we have

$$|F_0| \leq k^d l^{2d}.$$

Then, every F_{ij} shatters a set S of cardinality at most $(d-1)$. Otherwise, F would shatter $S \cup \{x_1\}$, which would be of cardinality greater than d. Also, since the functions in F_{ij} are all distinct on $X - \{x_1\}$, by the inductive hypothesis we have for $i \neq j$,

$$|F_{ij}| \leq k^{d-1} l^{2(d-1)}.$$

Combining the last three inequalities, we have

$$|F| \leq k^d l^{2d} + \sum_{i \neq j} k^{d-1} l^{2(d-1)}$$

$$\leq k^d l^{2d} + l^2 k^{d-1} l^{2(d-1)}$$

$$\leq k^d l^{2d} + k^{d-1} l^{2d} \leq (k+1)^d l^{2d}.$$

This completes the proof.

□

We now define an asymptotic variant of the generalized dimension.

DEFINITION _____

The *asymptotic dimension* of a class of functions F is the function $d : \mathbf{N} \times \mathbf{N} \rightarrow \mathbf{N}$ such that for all n_1, n_2, $\mathbf{D}_G(F^{[n_1][n_2]}) = d(n_1, n_2)$. We denote the asymptotic dimension of F by $\mathbf{D}(F)$.

_____

For simplicity, we drop the prefix "asymptotic," unless demanded by the context. Also, for the remainder of this chapter, we say "dimension" to mean generalized dimension, unless specified otherwise. If $\mathbf{D}(F)$ is $O(p(n_1, n_2))$ for some polynomial p, we say that F is of polynomial dimension.

The following lemma is the asymptotic corollary of Lemma 5.1.

LEMMA 5.2 _____

Let $F^{[n_1][n_2]}$ be of dimension d. Then,

$$2^d \le |F^{[n_1][n_2]}| \le 2^{d(n_1+2n_2+3)}.$$

_____

Proof: We only need to substitute $F^{[n_1][n_2]}$ for F, $\Sigma^{[n_1]}$ for X, and $\Sigma^{[n_2]}$ for Y in Lemma 5.1.

□

THEOREM 5.1 _____

Let F be a class of functions from Σ^* to Σ^*. Then, there exists a learning algorithm for F of sample complexity

$$s(\varepsilon, \delta, n_1, n_2) = \frac{1}{\varepsilon} \left[(n_1+n_2+3)\mathbf{D}_G(F^{[n_1][n_2]})\ln(2) + \ln\left[\frac{1}{\delta}\right] \right].$$

_____

Proof: We proceed as in the proofs of Theorems 2.1 and 4.2.
Consider algorithm $A_{5.1}$ below for a value of m that will be determined shortly.

> **Learning Algorithm** $A_{5.1}$
> **input:** $\varepsilon, \delta, n_1, n_2$;
> **begin:**
>   make m calls of EXAMPLE;
>   let S be the set of examples seen;
>   pick $g \in F$ consistent with S,
>   such that $g^{[n_1][n_2]}$ is defined.
>   output g;
> **end**

Let f be the target function. We require that with probability $(1-\delta)$, $A_{5.1}$ should output a function $g \in F$ such that the $P(f \Delta g) \le \varepsilon$.
Let $g^{[n_1][n_2]} \in F^{[n_1][n_2]}$ be such that $P(f^{[n_1][n_2]} \Delta g^{[n_1][n_2]}) > \varepsilon$. For a particular such $g^{[n_1][n_2]}$, the probability that any call of EXAMPLE will produce an example consistent with $g^{[n_1][n_2]}$ is at most $(1-\varepsilon)$. Hence, the probability

that m calls of EXAMPLE will produce examples all consistent with $g^{[n_1][n_2]}$ is at most $(1-\varepsilon)^m$. Now, there are at most $|F^{[n_1][n_2]}|$ choices for $g^{[n_1][n_2]}$. Therefore, the probability that m calls of EXAMPLE will produce examples all consistent with any such choice of $g^{[n_1][n_2]}$ is bounded by $|F^{[n_1][n_2]}|(1-\varepsilon)^m$. We will make m sufficiently large to bound this probability by δ. That is,

$$|F^{[n_1][n_2]}|(1-\varepsilon)^m \le \delta.$$

By Lemma 5.2,

$$|F^{[n_1][n_2]}| \le 2^{D_G(F^{[n_1][n_2]})(n_1+2n_2+3)}$$

Hence, it suffices if

$$2^{D_G(F^{[n_1][n_2]})(n_1+2n_2+3)}(1-\varepsilon)^m \le \delta.$$

Taking natural logarithms on both sides of the inequality, we get

$$D_G(F^{[n_1][n_2]})(n_1+2_2+3) + m\ln(1-\varepsilon) \le \ln(\delta).$$

Using the approximation $\ln(1+\alpha) \le \alpha$ and simplifying,

$$m \ge \frac{1}{\varepsilon}\left[(n_1+2_2+3)D_G(F^{[n_1][n_2]})\ln(2) + \ln\left(\frac{1}{\delta}\right)\right].$$

Hence, if m examples are drawn, with probability at least $(1-\delta)$, any function $g^{[n_1][n_2]} \in F^{[n_1][n_2]}$ consistent with the examples will be such that $P(f^{[n_1][n_2]} \Delta g^{[n_1][n_2]}) \le \varepsilon$. Since P is a distribution on $\Sigma^{[n_1]}$, $P(f\Delta g) = P(f^{[n_1][n_2]} \Delta g^{[n_1][n_2]})$. Also, all the examples seen will be of the form (x, y) where $x \in \Sigma^{[n_1]}$ and $y \in \Sigma^{[n_2]}$. Hence, $g^{[n_1][n_2]}$ is consistent with these examples if and only if g is consistent with them. It follows that any $g \in F$ that is consistent with all the examples seen and for which $g^{[n_1][n_2]}$ is defined will satisfy $P(f\Delta g) \le \varepsilon$ with probability at least $(1-\delta)$.

This completes the proof.

□

Example 5.2   Let π be a permutation on k items for some $k \in \mathbb{N}$. We define the function f_π from Σ^* to Σ^* as follows. Let $x \in \Sigma^*$. If x is of length k, $f_\pi(x) = y$, where y is the string obtained by applying the permutation π to the k bits of x; otherwise, $f_\pi(x) = x$. We call f_π a *permutation function*. Let F be the set of all permutation functions for all $k \in \mathbb{N}$.

We claim that F is of polynomial dimension. To see this, notice that for $n_2 \ge n_2$, $F^{[n_1][n_2]} = F^{[n_1][n_1]}$. But the number of distinct functions in $F^{[n_1][n_1]}$ is at most the number of distinct permutations on n_1 or fewer items. Thus,

$$|F^{[n_1][n_2]}| \leq |F^{[n_1][n_1]}| \leq \sum_{k \leq n_1} k! \leq n_1^{n_1+1}.$$

Invoking Lemma 5.2 on the above, we get $D_G(F^{[n_1][n_2]}) \leq (n_1+1)\log(n_1)$, which is polynomial in n_1 and n_2.

By Theorem 5.1, the permutation functions are polynomial-sample learnable.   ∎

Next, we will obtain a lower bound on the sample complexity of a learning algorithm for a class of functions. This result will be the analog of Theorem 2.2.

THEOREM 5.2 _____

Let F be a class of functions from Σ^* to Σ^* and let A be a learning algorithm for F, with sample complexity $s(\varepsilon, \delta, n_1, n_2)$. Then, for $\varepsilon \leq 1/8$ and $\delta < 1/4$, and all values of n_1 and n_2 for which $D_G(F^{[n_1][n_2]}) \geq 8$,

$$s(\varepsilon, \delta, n_1, n_2) \geq \frac{D_G(F^{[n_1][n_2]})}{16\varepsilon}.$$

Proof: The proof of this theorem is very similar to that of Theorem 4.5 and is left to the reader as an exercise.

□

Example 5.3   We examine another class of permutation functions. Let π be a permutation on the 2^k strings of Σ^k for some $k \in N$. The function f_π from Σ^* to Σ^* is defined as follows. Let $x \in \Sigma^*$. If x is of length k, $f_\pi(x) = x$; otherwise, $f_\pi(x) = y$, where y is the string obtained by applying the permutation π to x. Let F be the class of all such functions for all $k \in N$.

We claim that F is not of polynomial dimension. To see this, note that for $n_2 \geq n_1$, $F^{[n_1][n_2]} = F^{[n_1][n_1]}$. Then, since there are $(2^n)!$ permutations on the strings of Σ^n, we have

$$|F^{[n_1][n_1]}| = (2^{n_1})! \geq 2^{2^{n_1}}, \text{ for } n_1 \geq 2.$$

By Lemma 5.2,

$$\mathbf{D_G}(F^{[n_1][n_1]}) \geq \frac{\log|F^{[n_1][n_1]}|}{n_1 + 2n_1 + 3} \geq \frac{2^{n_1}}{3(n_1 + 1)},$$

which is not polynomial in n_1. By Theorem 5.2, the class F is not polynomial-sample learnable. ∎

5.1.2 Time Complexity of Function Learning

Analogous to our development of time complexity considerations for concept learning, we can obtain corresponding results for learning functions. To this end, we present the following analogs of the definitions given earlier in the context of concept learning.

The notion of a representation R for a class of functions F is identical to that given in Section 3.1 for a class of concepts. Also, for $f \in F$, $l_{min}(f)$ is the length of the shortest name for f. With these notions in hand, we now formally define an algorithm that learns a class of functions F in representation R.

DEFINITION _____

Algorithm A is a PAC learning algorithm for F in R if

(a) A takes as input ε, δ, n_1, and n_2.

(b) A may call EXAMPLE, which returns examples for some $f \in F$. The examples are chosen randomly according to an arbitrary and unknown probability distribution P on $\Sigma^{[n_1]}$.

(c) For all $f \in F$ for which $f^{[n_1][n_2]}$ is defined, and all probability distributions P on $\Sigma^{[n_1]}$, A outputs $r \in R(g)$ for some function $g \in F$, such that with probability at least $(1 - \delta), P(f \Delta g) \leq \varepsilon$.

_____

The time complexity of a learning algorithm is the run time of the algorithm as a function of the input parameters. In particular, we have the following definition.

DEFINITION _____

Let A be a learning algorithm for a class of functions F in R. The *time complexity* of A is the function $t : R \times R \times N \times N \times N \rightarrow N$ such that $t(\varepsilon, \delta, n_1, n_2, l)$ is the maximum number of computational time steps consumed by A, the maximum being taken over all runs of A in which the inputs are ε, δ, n_1, and n_2, with the target function f ranging over all $f \in F$ such that $f^{[n_1][n_2]}$ is defined and $l_{\min}(f) \le l$, and the probability distribution P ranging over all distributions on $\Sigma^{[n_1]}$. If no finite maximum exists, $s(\varepsilon, \delta) = \infty$.

As before, we say that a class of functions F is polynomial-time learnable in representation R if there exists a learning algorithm for F in R with time complexity polynomial in the various parameters. Formally, we have the following definition.

DEFINITION _____

F is *polynomial-time learnable* in R if there exists a deterministic learning algorithm A for F with time complexity $p(1/\varepsilon, 1/\delta, n_1, n_2, l)$, where p is a polynomial function of its arguments.

We are interested in identifying the family of pairs F and R such that F is polynomial-time learnable in R. To this end, we carry over the definitions of a fitting, a polynomial-time fitting, and a random polynomial-time fitting to this setting. Here, the input to a fitting is a subset of $\Sigma^* \times \Sigma^*$, rather than $\Sigma^* \times \{0, 1\}$ as in the case of concepts. This reflects the fact that a set of examples for a function is a subset of $\Sigma^* \times \Sigma^*$. We also need the following definitions.

DEFINITION _____

R is *polynomial-time computable* if there exists a deterministic algorithm B and fixed polynomial q such that

(a) B takes as input a pair of strings $r, x \in \Sigma^*$.

(b)   If $i \in R(f)$ for some $f \in F$, B halts in time $q\left[|x| + |r| + |f(x)| \right]$ and outputs $f(x)$.

We say that F is of *polynomial expansion* if there exists a polynomial $p : N \to N$ such that for all $f \in F$ and $x \in \Sigma^*$, $|f(x)| \leq p(|x|)$.

With these definitions in hand, we can state the following theorem.

THEOREM 5.3 _____

Let F be a class of functions from Σ^* to Σ^* and let R be a representation for F.

(a) F is polynomial-time learnable in R if all of the following hold: (1) F is of polynomial dimension; (2) F is of polynomial expansion; and (3) there exists a polynomial-time fitting for F in R.

(b) If F is polynomial-time learnable in R, and R is polynomial-time computable[1] then there exists a random polynomial-time fitting for F in R.

_____

Proof: The proof of (b) above is very similar to the proof of Theorem 3.2 and is left to the reader as an exercise. We prove (a) below.

Let p be a polynomial bound on the expansion of F, i.e., for all $g \in F$ and $x \in \Sigma^*$, $|g(x)| \leq p(|x|)$. Also, let Q be a polynomial-time fitting for F. We will show how algorithm $A_{5.1}$ of the proof of Theorem 5.1 may be modified to be a polynomial-time learning algorithm for F in representation R. Let f be the target function. Recall that $A_{5.1}$ calls EXAMPLE m times, where

$$m = \frac{1}{\varepsilon} \left[(n_1 + 2n_2 + 3) D_G(F^{[n_1][n_2]}) \ln(2) + \ln \left[\frac{1}{\delta} \right] \right].$$

Suppose the algorithm ignores the input value of n_2 and sets $n_2 = p(n_1)$. Then $g^{[n_1][n_2]}$ is defined for every $g \in F$. Thus, the algorithm can output any $g \in F$ that is consistent with the examples seen. Since $p(n)$ is polynomial in n_1, the total number of calls of EXAMPLE is polynomial in ε, δ, and n_1. Note that each call of EXAMPLE costs unit time by assumption.

It remains to show how to efficiently pick a function $g \in F$ that is consistent with S. More precisely, we need to compute a name in R of such a function g. The fitting Q can be used for this purpose. Given a set of examples S, Q outputs a name $r \in R(g)$ for a function $g \in F$ that is consistent with S. Furthermore, the run time of Q is polynomial in the length of its input and $l_{min}(S)$. Since each example in S is of length at most $n_1 + p(n_1)$, the length of Q's input is at most $|S|(n_1 + p(n_1))$, which is polynomial in ε, δ, and n_1. Also, $l_{min}(S) \leq l_{min}(f)$,

_____

1. The weaker condition that R is polynomial-time verifiable is sufficient. That is, there exists a polynomial-time program that accepts input (r, x, y) if and only if $y = f(x)$. Here, $f \in F$ is such that $r \in R(f)$. Notice that for concepts, verifiability and computability are equivalent.

where f is the target function. Thus, the run time of Q is polynomial in ε, δ, n_1, and $l_{\min}(f)$.

Algorithm $A_{5.2}$ is the appropriately modified form of $A_{5.1}$ and is a polynomial-time learning algorithm for F in R.

Learning Algorithm
input: ε, δ, n_1, n_2;
begin:

$$\text{let } m = \frac{1}{\varepsilon}\left[(n_1+2p(n_1)+3)\mathbf{D}_G(F^{[n_1][p(n_1)]})\ln(2) + \ln\left[\frac{1}{\delta}\right]\right];$$

make m calls of EXAMPLE;
let S be the set of examples seen;
output $Q(S)$;
end

□

Example 5.4   Consider the class F of permutation functions of Example 5.2. Clearly, F is of polynomial expansion, since for all $f \in F$ and $x \in \Sigma^*$, $|f(x)| = |x|$.

We use the following representation R for F: Let $f_\pi \in F$, where π is a permutation on k items. A name for f in R is a binary encoding of the map of π. Specifically, a name for f is the binary encoding of the bipartite graph $G = (U, V, E)$, where the vertex sets U and V each have k vertices, and the edge set E has an edge from vertex i in U to vertex $j \in V$, if π maps item i to item j.

We can also show that F has a polynomial-time fitting in R. Suppose we are given a set of examples S and are required to find a permutation function consistent with the examples. If $x = y$ for all $(x, y) \in S$, then we can simply output the identity permutation for some value of k. Otherwise, there must exist a value of k such that for every $(x, y) \in S$ for which $x \neq y$, $|x| = k$. Delete all $(x, y) \in S$ for which $|x| \neq k$. Construct a bipartite graph $G = (U, V, E)$, where the vertex sets U and V each have k vertices and the edge set E has an edge between every pair of vertices $u \in U$ and $v \in V$. Edges in G are denoted (i, j), $i \in U$, and $j \in V$.

We now delete each edge (i, j) from G, such that S contains an example (x, y) where the ith bit of x and the jth bit of y do not agree. Notice that any permutation that maps i to j cannot be consistent with such an example (x, y). This deletion process can be performed in $O(|S|k^2)$ time.

It is easy to see that any perfect matching of the resulting graph G is the map of a permutation that is consistent with S. (A perfect matching for the bipartite graph G is an assignment of a unique vertex $j \in V$ for each vertex $i \in U$, such that the edge (i, j) is an edge of G. Readers unfamiliar with this notion should consult the Bibliographic Notes.) Since perfect matchings of bipartite graphs can be computed in time polynomial in the size of the graph, we can conclude that F has a polynomial-time fitting in R.

By Theorem 5.3, F is polynomial-time learnable in R. ∎

5.2 Learning Functions on Uncountable Domains

In the preceding sections, we explored the learnability of classes of functions defined on countable domains such as the strings of a finite alphabet. In particular, we inquired into the number of examples needed for learning as an asymptotic function of the length parameters. We now consider the learnability of functions defined on uncountable domains such as the reals, and we inquire into the number of examples required for learning as a function of the error and confidence parameters only. The discussion is analogous to that of Chapter 4.

We consider functions from $\mathbf{R}^k$ to $\mathbf{R}^k$ for fixed $k \in \mathbf{N}$. We pick $\mathbf{R}^k$ for concreteness, although the results of this chapter will hold for any domain with an appropriate definition of probability measures.

A class of such functions is a set of functions from $\mathbf{R}^k$ to $\mathbf{R}^k$. For instance, the set of cubic polynomials of Example 5.1 is a class of functions from $\mathbf{R}$ to $\mathbf{R}$.

As with concepts on $\mathbf{R}^k$, we restrict the discussion to functions f such that graph(f) is measurable and to classes F such that graph(F) is well behaved.

In this setting of functions on $\mathbf{R}^k$, we define the notion of a PAC learning algorithm as follows:

DEFINITION _____

An algorithm A is a PAC learning algorithm for a class F of functions from $\mathbf{R}^k$ to $\mathbf{R}^k$ if

(a) A takes as input ε and δ.

(b) A may call EXAMPLE. EXAMPLE returns examples for some function f in F, where the examples are chosen randomly according to an arbitrary and unknown probability distribution P on $\mathbf{R}^k$.

(c)   For all probability distributions P and all functions f in F, A outputs a function $g \in F$, such that with probability at least $(1 - \delta)$, $P(f \Delta g) \leq \varepsilon$.

_____

We remind the reader of the technical differences between the above definition and the corresponding definition for functions on Σ^*. These differences arise because the distribution P is now on the uncountable domain of $\mathbf{R}^k$.

We can now establish the notions of sample complexity and uniform learnability in this setting. Since these notions are almost identical to those given in Chapter 4 for concepts on $\mathbf{R}^k$, they are not defined in full here.

With these definitions in hand, we have the following theorem on the conditions sufficient for uniform learnability of a class of functions on $\mathbf{R}^k$.

THEOREM 5.4

Let F be a class of functions from $\mathbf{R}^k$ to $\mathbf{R}^k$ such that $d = \mathbf{D}_{\mathrm{VC}}(\mathrm{graph}(F))$ is finite. Then, F is uniformly learnable by an algorithm of sample complexity

$$s(\varepsilon, \delta) = \frac{8}{\varepsilon}\left[8d\ln\left[\frac{64}{\varepsilon}\right] + \ln\left[\frac{2}{\delta}\right]\right]. \tag{5.1}$$

Proof: Consider the learning algorithm $A_{5.3}$ below. We will estimate m so that $A_{5.3}$ is a PAC learning algorithm for F.

Learning Algorithm
input: ε, δ;
begin:
    make m calls of EXAMPLE;
    let S be the set of examples seen;
    pick a function $g \in F$ consistent with S;
    output g;
end

We proceed as in the proof of Theorem 4.4. Consider the class of concepts $\mathrm{graph}(F)$ on $\mathbf{R}^k \times \mathbf{R}^k$. Let f denote the target function and let $\hat{F}$ be the class of all functions in F that differ from f with probability greater than ε. That is, $\hat{F} = \{g \in F \mid P(f \Delta g) > \varepsilon\}$. Let $\hat{P}$ be the distribution on $\mathbf{R}^{2k}$ given by

$$\hat{P}((x, y)) = \begin{cases} P(x) \text{ if } y = f(x) \\ 0 \text{ otherwise} \end{cases},$$

where $x \in \mathbf{R}^k$ and $y \in \mathbf{R}^k$. Let $(x_1, y_1), (x_2, y_2), \ldots, (x_m, y_m)$ be the m examples obtained by $A_{5.3}$. Suppose there exists $g \in \hat{F}$ consistent with all these examples. That is, each $(x_i, y_i) \in \mathrm{graph}(g)$. Then, $\hat{P}_m(\mathrm{graph}(g)) = 1$. But, since $g \in \hat{F}$, $\hat{P}(\mathrm{graph}(g)) < 1 - \varepsilon$. Therefore,

$$\hat{P}_m(\mathrm{graph}(g)) = 1 \text{ and } \hat{P}(\mathrm{graph}(g)) < 1 - \varepsilon. \tag{5.2}$$

Invoking Theorem 4.3, we see that the probability (5.1) holds for any $g \in \hat{F}$ is at most $2\Phi(2m, d)2^{-\varepsilon m/2}$. We wish to choose m so that this probability is at most δ. Proceeding as in the proof of Theorem 4.4, we see that it suffices for m to satisfy

$$m = \frac{8}{\varepsilon} \left[8d\ln \left(\frac{64}{\varepsilon} \right) + \ln \left(\frac{2}{\delta} \right) \right]. \tag{5.3}$$

By definition, this is the sample complexity of $A_{5.3}$, and the theorem is proved.

We note here that graph(F) should be well behaved as in the proof of Theorem 4.3.

□

Example 5.5   Let Z be a $k \times k$ matrix with entries from $\mathbf{R}$. Let $f_Z : \mathbf{R}^k \to \mathbf{R}^k$ be the function such that $f_Z(x) = Zx$, where Zx is the matrix-vector product of Z and x. Let F be the class of all such functions from $\mathbf{R}^k$ to $\mathbf{R}^k$. That is, F is the class of all *linear transformations* on $\mathbf{R}^k$.

We claim that $\mathbf{D}_{VC}(\text{graph}(F)) \le k$. Let $S \subseteq \mathbf{R}^k \times \mathbf{R}^k$ be a set of examples that is shattered by F. Specifically, let

$$S = \{(x_1, y_1), (x_2, y_2), \dots, (x_j, y_j)\}.$$

Let Z be a matrix such that f_Z is consistent with S. Since S is shattered by F, for each (x_i, y_i) in S there exists a matrix U such that f_U agrees with f_Z on all the examples in S, except for (x_i, y_i). Thus, $Zx = Ux$ for all $(x, y) \in S - \{(x_i, y_i)\}$ and $Zx_i \ne Ux_i$. This is possible only if each x_i is linearly independent of the remaining vectors $x_1, x_2, \dots, x_{i-1}, x_{i+1}, \dots, x_j$. Since there are at most k linearly independent vectors in $\mathbf{R}^k$, $j \le k$ must hold.

Since $\mathbf{D}_{VC}(\text{graph}(F))$ is finite, we can substitute $d = k$ in equation (5.3) and use algorithm $A_{5.3}$ above to learn the class F.

How do we pick a matrix Z such that f_Z is consistent with a given set of examples? Suppose we are given m examples $\{(x_i, y_i)\}$. Let X be the $k \times m$ matrix with the x_i as column vectors and let Y be the $k \times m$ matrix with the y_i as column vectors. If f_Z is to be consistent with these examples, we have

$$ZX = Y,$$

where Z is the unknown matrix. Taking transposes on both sides, we have

$$X^T Z^T = Y^T.$$

If Z_i and Y_i are the ith column of Z^T and Y^T respectively, we have k equations of the form

$$X^T Z_i = Y_i.$$

Note that X^T is an $m \times k$ matrix, Z_i is a k vector, and Y_i is a m vector. Using the Q-R decomposition method, we can solve these k equations for the k columns of Z. (Readers unfamiliar with the Q-R method should consult the Bibliographic Notes for references.)   ∎

We now establish a lower bound on the sample complexity of a learning algorithm for a class of functions from $\mathbf{R}^k$ to $\mathbf{R}^k$. Theorem 5.5 is essentially a restatement of Theorem 5.2.

THEOREM 5.5 _____

Let F be a class of functions from $\mathbf{R}^k$ to $\mathbf{R}^k$ and let A be a learning algorithm for F with sample complexity $s(\varepsilon, \delta)$. Then, if $\varepsilon \le 1/4$, $\delta < 1/4$, and $\mathbf{D}_G(F) \ge 16$,

$$s(\varepsilon, \delta) \ge \frac{\mathbf{D}_G(F)}{16\varepsilon}.$$

Proof: The proof follows that of Theorem 4.5, as in Theorem 5.2.

□

As a corollary to Theorems 5.4 and 5.5, we have the following.

COROLLARY 5.1 _____

A class of functions from $\mathbf{R}^k$ to $\mathbf{R}^k$ is uniformly learnable (a) if $\mathbf{D}_{VC}(\text{graph}(F))$ is finite; and (b) only if $\mathbf{D}_G(F)$ is finite.

Notice that if F is the class of indicator functions for a class of concepts G, then $\mathbf{D}_G(F) = \mathbf{D}_{VC}(G)$. Also, $\mathbf{D}_{VC}(\text{graph}(F)) = \mathbf{D}_{VC}(G)$ by Lemma 4.1. Thus, Corollary 5.1 can be rephrased as "the indicator functions of a class of concepts G on $\mathbf{R}^k$ is uniformly learnable if and only if $\mathbf{D}_{VC}(G)$ is finite." In essence, we have a restatement of Corollary 4.1. Thus, when considering classes of concepts, Corollary 5.1 collapses smoothly to Corollary 4.1.

An interesting question is whether Corollary 5.1 is tight, i.e., whether the necessary and sufficient conditions match. In the following, we give an example of a class of functions that lies in the gap between the necessary and sufficient conditions. Specifically, we exhibit a class of functions F such that

(a) $\mathbf{D}_G(F)$ is finite.

(b) $\mathbf{D}_{VC}(\text{graph}(F))$ is infinite.

(c) F is uniformly learnable.

Example 5.6   For $\alpha \in \mathbf{N}$, the ith bit of α is the ith bit in the binary representation of α, counting from the right. For instance, the second bit of 13 is 0 since the binary representation of 13 is 1101. Define the function $f_\alpha : \mathbf{R} \to \mathbf{R}$ as follows:

$$f_\alpha(x) = \begin{cases} \alpha \text{ if } x \in \mathbf{N} \text{ and the } x^{\text{th}} \text{ bit of } \alpha \text{ is 1} \\ 0 \text{ otherwise} \end{cases}.$$

In words, f_α essentially indicates which of the bits in the binary representation of α are 1 and which of them are 0. For instance, f_0 is 0 everywhere and $f_{13}(x) = 13$ for $x = 1, 3, 4$, and 0 elsewhere.

Define the class F as follows:

$$F = \{f_\alpha \mid \alpha \in \mathbf{N}\}.$$ ∎

CLAIM 5.1 _____

$\mathbf{D}_G(F) = 1$.

_____

Proof: Suppose F shatters a set of size greater than 1. Then F must shatter a set of size 2. Let $S = \{a, b\}$ be such a set. It follows from the definition of F that $a, b \in \mathbf{N}$. By the definition of shattering, there exist three functions f_α, f_β, and f_γ in F such that $f_\alpha(a) \neq f_\beta(a)$, $f_\alpha(b) \neq f_\beta(b)$, and $f_\gamma(a) = f_\alpha(a)$, $f_\gamma(b) = f_\beta(b)$. Since, $f_\alpha(a) \neq f_\beta(a)$, at least one of them must be nonzero. Without loss of generality, assume that $f_\alpha(a)$ is nonzero. Now, $f_\alpha(a) \neq 0$ implies that $f_\alpha(a) = \alpha$. Since $f_\gamma(a) = f_\alpha(a)$, $f_\gamma(a) = \alpha$. But then, $f_\gamma(a) \neq 0$ implies that $f_\gamma(a) = \gamma$. It follows that $\alpha = \gamma$, contradicting the assumption that $f_\gamma(b) = f_\beta(b) \neq f_\alpha(b)$. Hence, the claim.

□

CLAIM 5.2 _____

$\mathbf{D}_{VC}(\text{graph}(F))$ is infinite.

_____

Proof: Let S_1 be any arbitrarily large but finite subset of $\mathbf{N}$. Consider $S = S_1 \times \{0\}$. Now, graph(F) shatters S, since for any subset S_2 of S, there exists a set $f \in F$ such that $\text{graph}(f) \cap S = S_2$. To see this, let S_3 be such that $S - S_2 = S_3 \times \{0\}$. We can pick an integer $\alpha \in \mathbf{N}$ such that for all $x \in S_3$, the xth bit of α is 1, with all other bits in α being 0s. Thus, $f_\alpha(x) \neq 0$ if and only if $x \in S_3$. Hence, the claim.

□

CLAIM 5.3 _____

F is uniformly learnable.

_____

Proof: The algorithm $A_{5.4}$ below is a learning algorithm for F.

> **Learning Algorithm** $A_{5.4}$
> **input:** ε, δ;
> **begin**
>   make $\left\lceil \dfrac{1}{\varepsilon} \right\rceil \ln \left\lceil \dfrac{1}{\delta} \right\rceil$ calls of EXAMPLE;
>   **if** any of the examples seen is of the
>   form $(x, y), y \neq 0$,
>   **then** output f_y;
>   **else** output f_0;
> **end**

We now see that the probabilities work out for the above algorithm. Suppose the function to be learned were f_α for some $\alpha \neq 0$. Then, if $P(f_\alpha \Delta f_0) > \varepsilon$, with probability at least $(1-\delta)$, there must be an example of the form (x, α) produced in $(1/\varepsilon)\ln(1/\delta)$ calls of EXAMPLE. In this case, the algorithm will output f_α, implying that with probability $(1-\delta)$, the algorithm learns the unknown function exactly. Hence, the claim.

□

5.2.1 Learning with Respect to Metrics

In the foregoing, we examined the learnability of functions from $\mathbf{R}^k$ to $\mathbf{R}^k$, measuring the "distance" between two functions as the probabilistic weight of the points on which they differ. That is, the distance between two functions f and g is $P(f \Delta g) = \displaystyle\int_{f(x) \neq g(x)} dP$. In the more general setting, we could measure the distance between a pair of functions in some other metric and examine the learnability of classes of functions under these measures. Such a generalization is the subject of this section.

DEFINITION _____

A *metric* on $\mathbf{R}^k$ is a function $L : \mathbf{R}^k \times \mathbf{R}^k \to \mathbf{R}$ such that for any three x, y, and z in $\mathbf{R}^k$ (a) $L(x, y) \geq 0$;   (b) $L(x, x) = 0$;   (c) $L(x, y) = L(y, x)$;   and   (d) $L(x, y) + L(y, z) \geq L(x, z)$.

_____

For instance, consider the square or Euclidean metric L_2 on $\mathbf{R}^k$. For two points x and y in $\mathbf{R}^k$, $L_2(x, y)$ is the Euclidean distance between the two points. That is, if $x = (x_1, x_2, \ldots, x_k)$ and $y = (y_1, y_2, \ldots, y_k)$,

$$L_2(x, y) = \left[\sum_{i=1}^{k} |x_i - y_i|^2 \right]^{1/2}.$$

In general, for any $p \in \mathbf{N}$, the so-called L_p metric is given by

$$L_p(x, y) = \left[\sum_{i=1}^{k} |x_i - y_i|^p \right]^{1/p}.$$

Two limiting cases of the L_p metric are the discrete metric L_0 and the infinity metric L_∞:

$$L_0(x, y) = \begin{cases} 1 \text{ if } x \neq y \\ 0 \text{ otherwise} \end{cases},$$

$$L_\infty(x, y) = \max_i |x_i - y_i|.$$

We measure the distance between two functions f and g with respect to a metric L as

$$\int_{x \in \mathbf{R}^k} L(f(x), g(x)) dP.$$

In other words, the distance between two functions f and g is the expectation[2] of $L(f(x), g(x))$ taken over the probability distribution P.

For the case of the discrete metric,

$$\int_{x \in \mathbf{R}^k} L(f(x), g(x)) dP = \int_{f(x) \neq g(x)} dP = P(f \Delta g).$$

Thus, the results of the Section 5.4.1 were with respect to the discrete metric.

We now define the notion of PAC learning with respect to a metric.

---

2. Some authors define the L_p distance directly between two functions as

$$L_p(f, g) = \left\{ \int_{x \in \mathbf{R}^k} L(f(x), g(x))^p dP \right\}^{1/p}.$$

Although this definition is somewhat different from ours, the results of this section can be easily modified to hold under it.

DEFINITION _____

An algorithm A is a PAC learning algorithm for a class F of functions from $\mathbf{R}^k$ to $\mathbf{R}^k$, *with respect to a metric L,* if

(a) A takes as input ε and δ.

(b) A may call EXAMPLE, which returns examples for some function f in F. The examples are chosen randomly and independently according to an arbitrary and unknown probability distribution P on $\mathbf{R}^k$.

(c)   For all probability distributions P and all functions f in F, A outputs a function $g \in F$, such that with probability at least $(1-\delta)$,

$$\int_{x \in \mathbf{R}^k} L(f(x), g(x))dP \ \le \varepsilon.$$

_____

The definitions of sample complexity and uniform learnability stand as before.

We seek the analog of Theorem 5.4 for learning with respect to a metric. To this end, we define the notion of the diameter of a class of functions F with respect to a metric L. In words, the diameter of F with respect to L is the greatest value attained by $L(f(x), g(x))$ over every pair of functions $f, g \in F$ and every point $x \in \mathbf{R}^k$.

DEFINITION _____

Let F be a class of functions from $\mathbf{R}^k$ to $\mathbf{R}^k$ and let L be a metric on $\mathbf{R}^k$. The *diameter* $D_L(F)$ of F with respect to L is given by

$$D_L(F) = \sup_{x \in \mathbf{R}^k} \{L(f(x), g(x)) | f, g \in F\}.$$

_____

Notation: We use "sup" to denote the *supremum* of a set of reals, i.e., the least upper bound on the set. It is also meaningful to speak of the supremum of a function, which is the least upper bound on the value of the function.

We call $D_L(F)$ the diameter of F, since we can picture a "tube" of diameter $D_L(F)$ in $\mathbf{R}^k$ such that all the functions in F are contained within the tube.

THEOREM 5.6 _____

Let F be a class of functions from $\mathbf{R}^k$ to $\mathbf{R}^k$ and let L be a metric on $\mathbf{R}^k$. If $\rho = D_L(F)$ and $d = \mathbf{D}_{VC}(\text{graph}(F))$ are both finite, then F is uniformly learnable with respect to L by an algorithm of sample complexity

$$s(\varepsilon, \delta) = \frac{8\rho}{\varepsilon} \left[8d\ln\left[\frac{64\rho}{\varepsilon}\right] + \ln\left[\frac{2}{\delta}\right] \right].$$

_____

Proof: Consider algorithm $A_{5.3}$ again. We will estimate m so that $A_{5.3}$ is a PAC learning algorithm for F with respect to L.

For any two functions f, $g \in F$,

$$\int_{x \in \mathbf{R}^k} L(f(x), g(x))dP = \int_{f(x) \neq g(x)} L(f(x), g(x))dP \leq \int_{f(x) \neq g(x)} \rho\, dP$$

$$= \rho \left[\int_{f(x) \neq g(x)} dP \right] = \rho P(f \Delta g).$$

Thus, to satisfy

$$\int_{x \in \mathbf{R}^k} L(f(x), g(x))dP \leq \varepsilon,$$

we only need ensure $\rho P(f \Delta g) \leq \varepsilon$, or

$$P(f \Delta g) \leq \frac{\varepsilon}{\rho}. \tag{5.4}$$

As in the proof of Theorem 5.4, (5.4) will be satisfied with probability at least $(1 - \delta)$ if we replace ε with ε/ρ in equation (5.3). Specifically,

$$m = \frac{8\rho}{\varepsilon} \left[8d\ln\left[\frac{64\rho}{\varepsilon}\right] + \ln\left[\frac{2}{\delta}\right] \right].$$

Hence, the theorem is proved.

□

Note that for the discrete metric L_0, $\rho = 1$ and Theorem 5.6 collapses to Theorem 5.4.

Example 5.7   Let us modify the space of linear transforms of Example 5.5 as follows. Let Z be a $k \times k$ matrix with entries from the real interval $[-1, 1]$. Consider the function $f_Z : \mathbf{R}^k \to \mathbf{R}^k$, where $f(x) = Zx$ if x has all entries from $[-1, 1]$. If not, $f(x)$ is the zero vector. Since the entries of Z are from $[-1, 1]$, the entries of Zx are from $[-k, k]$.

Let F be the class of all such functions for fixed $k \in \mathbf{N}$. We inquire into the uniform learnability of F with respect to the infinity metric L_∞ given earlier. As in Example 5.5, we can show that $\mathbf{D}_{VC}(\mathrm{graph}(F)) \le k$. Hence, in order to apply Theorem 5.6, we only need to bound the diameter of F with respect to L_∞. Since Zx has entries from $[-k, k]$, it follows that for all $x \in \mathbf{R}^k$, $L_\infty(f(x), g(x)) \le 2k$. Thus, the diameter ρ of F satisfies

$$\rho = \sup_{x \in \mathbf{R}^k} \{L_\infty(f(x), g(x)) \mid f, g \in F\} \le 2k.$$

By Theorem 5.6, the class F is uniformly learnable with respect to the L_∞ metric.   ∎

5.3 Summary

We extended the notion of PAC learning to classes of functions defined on both countable and uncountable domains. We developed the notion of the generalized dimension of a class of functions, the analog of the Vapnik-Chervonenkis dimension. Using this notion, we obtained relatively tight bounds on the time and sample complexity of learning algorithms for classes of concepts on countable domains. For classes of concepts on uncountable domains, we gave upper and lower bounds on the sample complexity of a learning algorithm. The bounds were not tight in that the upper and lower bounds did not match. Finally, we explored the notion of learning with respect to a metric, wherein the "distance" between the target function and the output function was measured using the weighted integral of a given metric.

Additional readings on the topics of this chapter are suggested in the Bibliographic Notes.

5.4 Exercises

5.1.   Tighten Lemma 5.1 by showing that

$$|F| \le |Y|^{2d}\Phi(|X|, d)$$

where $\Phi(m, d) = \sum_{i=0}^{d} \begin{bmatrix} m \\ i \end{bmatrix}$.

5.2.   With respect to the RAM of Exercise 4.6: For classes of functions from $\mathbf{R}^k$ to $\mathbf{R}^k$, develop notions of polynomial-time learnability and usually polynomial-time learnability. Define an Occam fitting for classes of functions and give a theorem linking the existence of an Occam fitting to learnability in usually polynomial time.

5.3.   Analyze the time complexity of the algorithm of Example 5.5 for learning the matrix functions, with respect to the RAM.

5.4.   A bar graph on $\mathbf{R}$ is a piecewise linear function on the XY-plane composed of pieces parallel to the X-axis. Let F be the class of bar graphs, each composed of at most k bars for fixed $k \in \mathbf{N}$. Estimate $\mathbf{D}_{VC}(F)$ and $\mathbf{D}_G(F)$. Can you give a polynomial-time algorithm for learning F on the RAM? Pick a meaningful representation that you consider natural. For the case when k is not fixed, is there a learning algorithm for F running in usually polynomial time on the RAM?

5.5.   Consider the class F of piecewise linear functions from $\mathbf{R}$ to $\mathbf{R}$ composed of at most k pieces for fixed $k \in \mathbf{N}$. Estimate $\mathbf{D}_{VC}(\text{graph}(F))$ and $\mathbf{D}_G(F)$. Can F be learned efficiently on the RAM (a) for fixed k; and (b) for all k? Pick a meaningful representation that you consider natural.

5.6.   In Chapter 2, we showed that dropping the length parameter n from the input to the learning algorithm did not affect our results, since the learning algorithm could estimate a suitable value of n. Is the same true for the length parameters used in this chapter?

5.7.   In the context of learning functions on Σ^*, obtain analogs to the Occam's Razor results of Chapter 3.

5.8.   A certain investment banker has developed an uncanny method of picking profitable investments in the stock market. The banker examines nine market indices, each of which is an integer between 1 and 10, and based on these indices, recommends one of 400 major stocks. Suppose that a "knowledge engineer" wants to build an expert system that can imitate the banker. Estimate the number of samples needed as a function of the confidence and error allowed.

5.5 Bibliographic Notes

The PAC paradigm was extended to include functions by Natarajan and Tadepalli (1988). The material in this chapter is adapted from the above paper and from Natarajan (1989a, d), (1991). Additional results on the convergence of classes of functions may be found in Pollard (1986), Chapter 2, and Haussler

(1989). The latter's results are in terms of the *metric dimension* of a class of functions, which is a notion of dimension that is dependent on the metric of interest. Vapnik (1989) presents an interesting overview of convergence results and their application in statistical inference. Haussler and Long (1990) present some variants of Lemma 5.1. Perfect matchings on bipartite graphs are discussed in Tarjan (1983), Chapter 9. A discussion of the Q-R decomposition method for least-squares problems may be found in Golub and Van Loan (1983), page 147. An interesting open problem is to close the gap of Corollary 5.1. Kearns and Schapire (1990) explore the PAC learning of probabilistic concepts. Essentially, these are classes of functions that take on values in the range [0, 1], and the associated learning problem is related to the problem of learning probability distributions.

6

Finite Automata

The finite automaton, or finite state machine, has been studied extensively in many contexts. It is the simplest computational device and generates the lowest and best understood level of the computational hierarchy. On the one hand, electrical engineers, computer scientists, and mathematicians studied the finite automaton as an abstract model of circuits, logical devices, and mathematical problems. On the other hand, linguists interested in natural languages studied the class of syntactically described sets called the regular sets. As it happened, the class of sets accepted by the finite automaton is exactly the class of regular sets.

In this chapter, we examine the learnability of the regular sets in the representation of the finite automata. In doing so, we introduce a variant of the basic PAC model, in which the learning algorithm is permitted to ask questions, rather than passively receive random examples. As we will see, this added freedom increases the power of the learning algorithm.

6.1 Preliminaries

We assume that the reader is familiar with the notion of a finite automaton and will make only our notation precise.

We consider deterministic finite automata (DFA) on the binary alphabet Σ. A DFA M is denoted by a quadruple $(\mathbb{Q}, q_0, \mathbb{F}, \tau)$. $\mathbb{Q}$ is the finite set of states in the automaton, q_0 is the start state, $\mathbb{F} \subseteq \mathbb{Q}$ is the set of final or accepting states, and τ is the transition function. For any character $a \in \Sigma$, $\tau(q, a)$ is the state attained by M when started in state q with a as input. We extend τ to strings in Σ^* as well, in that for $x \in \Sigma^*$, $\tau(q, x)$ is the state attained by M when started in state q with x as input. The language $L(M)$ accepted by M is the set of all strings x such that M attains an accepting state when started in state q_0 with x as input. That is,

$$L(M) = \{x \mid \tau(q_0, x) \in \mathscr{F}\}.$$

It is well known that the regular sets are exactly those sets that are recognizable by the DFA. (See the Bibliographic Notes for an appropriate reference.) Let F be the class of all regular sets on Σ^* and let R be the representation of the DFA for F. Specifically, for each $f \in F$, the names in $R(f)$ are the DFA that accepts f. Strictly speaking, a name for f is the binary encoding of a DFA that accepts f. Note that a DFA with s states[1] on the binary alphabet can be encoded as a binary string of length $O(s\log(s))$ in a straightforward manner. Specifically, the transitions are encoded as triples of the form $(q_1, 0, q_2)$ and $(q_1, 1, q_2)$ to indicate the transitions from state q_1 to q_2 on 0 and 1, respectively. All of the states are encoded as integers, and the integers and the comma are encoded in binary as indicated in Example 3.1.

We are interested in the following question: Is the class F of regular sets polynomial-time learnable in the representation of the DFA? Rephrasing in our simplified notation: Are the DFA polynomial-time learnable?

Recall Theorems 3.1 and 3.3, our results on polynomial-time learnability. In Theorem 3.1 we showed that a class of concepts of polynomial dimension is polynomial-time learnable in a representation if there exists a polynomial-time fitting for the class in the representation. Unfortunately, Theorem 3.1 does not apply to the class of regular sets. As we reasoned in Example 2.6, every finite set is regular and, hence, the class of regular sets is not of polynomial dimension.

In an effort to examine the learnability of classes not of polynomial dimension, Theorem 3.3 specified conditions sufficient for usually polynomial-time learnability. In this case, it sufficed that the representation be polynomial-time computable and that there exists a polynomial-time Occam fitting for the class in the representation. We now examine whether the class of regular sets satisfy these conditions in the representation of the DFA.

Clearly, the representation of the DFA is polynomial-time computable. In particular, given the encoding of a DFA M and a string x, it is possible to verify in time polynomial in the length of the encoding and the length of x whether M accepts x.

We are now left with the following question: Does there exist an Occam fitting for the class of regular sets in the representation of the DFA? As it happens, the existence of an Occam fitting is a necessary condition for the polynomial-time learnability of the class of regular sets in the representation of

---

1. In this chapter, we use s to refer to the number of states in a DFA. Elsewhere in the book s will continue to denote the sample complexity of a learning algorithm.

the DFA. We show this by applying Theorem 3.4. But first, in order to satisfy the preconditions of Theorem 3.4, we must show that the representation of the DFA is strongly closed under exception.

LEMMA 6.1

The representation of the DFA for the regular sets is strongly closed under exception.

Proof: Given are a DFA M and a finite set of strings S. Let M have s states, let $n = \max\{|x| \mid (x, y) \in S\}$, and let $m = |S|$. Also, let $f = L(M)$. We will show how to construct a DFA $\hat{M}$ with at most $s + nm$ states such that $L(\hat{M}) = f\Delta S$.

Let $M = (\mathbb{Q}, q_0, \mathcal{F}, \tau)$ and let $\hat{M} = (\hat{\mathbb{Q}}, \hat{q}_0, \hat{\mathcal{F}}, \hat{\tau})$. The DFA $\hat{M}$ has the DFA M embedded in it. In addition, it has new states and transitions. These are described shortly.

Construct a binary tree as follows. First, take a single node, the root of the tree. Call this node z. Then, if there exists a string in S with prefix 0, add a new node z_0 with a directed edge labeled 0 from z to z_0. Similarly, if there exists a string in S with prefix 1, add a new node z_1, with a directed edge labeled 1 from z to z_1. If there exists a string in S with prefix 00, add a new node z_{00} with a directed edge labeled 0 from z_0 to z_{00}. And so on. Clearly, the tree has at most nm nodes. Figure 6.1 shows the tree for the case when $S = \{00, 01, 100\}$.

The tree described above represents the new states of $\hat{M}$. In particular, each node of the tree is a new state in $\hat{M}$, with the root being the start state $\hat{q}_0$. The labeled edges represent the transitions in $\hat{\tau}$ from these states on 0 and 1.

Some of the new states will not have transitions defined on both 0 and 1 at the conclusion of the above construction. Suppose that a new state q does not have a transition defined on 0. Let x be such that $q = \hat{\tau}(\hat{q}_0, x)$. Add a transition on 0 from q to the state $\tau(q_0, x)$ in M. That is, $\hat{\tau}(q, 0) = \tau(q_0, x)$. A state that does not have a transition defined on 1 is treated similarly.

It remains to specify the final states of $\hat{M}$. The final states of M are final states of $\hat{M}$ as well. Of the new states, suppose that for some string $x \in S$, $q = \hat{\tau}(\hat{q}_0, x)$. Since $x \in S$, q must be one of the new states. If $x \notin f$, make q a final state.

Let us now examine the behavior of $\hat{M}$, given any string x as input. If $x \in S$, $\hat{M}$ will halt in one of the new states, accepting x if and only if $x \notin f$. If $x \notin S$, $\hat{M}$ will halt in one of the states of M, accepting x if and only if M accepts. Hence, $\hat{M}$ accepts $(S - f) \cup (f - S)$, i.e., $L(\hat{M}) = f\Delta S$.

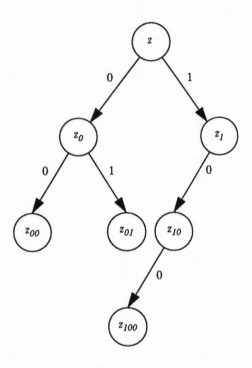

Figure 6.1 _____
The tree construction of Lemma 6.1.

As shown above, there are at most nm new states and, hence, $\hat{M}$ has at most $s + nm$ states. It follows that the binary encoding of $\hat{M}$ is of length $O\left[(s + nm)\log(s + nm)\right]$. Let i be the binary encoding of M and let j be the binary encoding of $\hat{M}$. Since M has s states, $|i| \geq s$. Hence, $|j|$ is $O\left[(s + nm)\log(s + nm)\right]$. Furthermore, it is clear that j can be computed in time polynomial in s, m, and n.

This completes the proof.

□

Since the representation of the DFA for the regular sets is strongly closed under exception, it follows from Theorem 3.4 that there must exist an Occam fitting for the regular sets in the representation of the DFA.

Now, an Occam fitting would do the following:

input: $S \subseteq \Sigma^* \times \{0, 1\}$.
output: Let $m = |S|$ and $n = \max \{|x| \,|\, (x, y) \in S\}$. Output the binary encoding r of a DFA M such that

$$|r| \leq p(n, l_{\min}(S))m^{\alpha} \tag{6.1}$$

for a fixed polynomial p and $0 \leq \alpha < 1$.

We explore the possibility that there exists an Occam fitting with $\alpha = 0$ and $p(n, l) = l$. Such a fitting would have to output the minimum DFA consistent with S, leading to the following problem.

Minimum DFA Problem[2]

   input: Finite set of examples, $S \subseteq \Sigma^* \times \{0, 1\}$.
   output: A DFA M consistent with S such that M has the fewest number of states.

Unfortunately, we have the following theorem.

THEOREM 6.1 _____

The minimum DFA problem is *NP*-hard.

_____

Proof: We omit the proof, which is a classical *NP*-hardness proof. The interested reader should consult the Bibliographic Notes for the appropriate reference.

□

In light of the above, we must liberalize our choices of α and p in (6.1). Specifically, we set $\alpha = 0$ and allow p to be any polynomial in l, leading to the following problem.

Small DFA Problem

   input: Finite set of examples, $S \subseteq \Sigma^* \times \{0, 1\}$.
   output: A DFA M consistent with S such that the number of states in M is at most $q(l_{\min}(S))$ for some fixed polynomial q.

As it happens, the small DFA problem is *NP*-hard as well.

_____

2. The reader should not confuse the minimum DFA problem with the problem of minimizing a given DFA, which can be solved efficiently.

THEOREM 6.2 _____
The small DFA problem is NP-hard.

_____

Proof: We omit the proof since it is technically rather difficult. The
interested reader should consult the Bibliographic Notes for the appropriate
reference.

□

Thus, we must relax the assumption that $\alpha = 0$. Rather than proceed with the
investigation at this point, we postpone the discussion to a later chapter, until
after we introduce the notion of predictability. Under the broader assumptions
of predictability, we will present evidence that the class of regular sets are not
polynomial-time learnable.

For the remainder of this section, we study the learnability of the regular
sets in a modified learning framework, wherein the learning algorithm is
provided with an additional teaching aid. The results here are positive in that
we have an efficient learning algorithm under the enhanced assumptions.

6.2 A Modified Framework

We permit the learning algorithm to make membership queries. That is, the
algorithm is provided with an additional subroutine MEMBER(), which can be
used to query the target concept on any string. That is, if f is the target concept,
for any $x \in \Sigma^*$, MEMBER(x) returns $f(x)$. We assume that each call of
MEMBER costs unit time. With this as the only modification, we let stand our
definition of polynomial-time learnability.

We now describe a polynomial-time learning algorithm for the regular sets,
within the modified framework.

First, we require some definitions and notation. The null string is denoted
by λ. If x and y are two strings, xy denotes the concatenation of the two strings.
We say a set $S \subseteq \Sigma^*$ is *suffix-closed* if for each $x \in S$, every suffix of x is also in
S. That is, if $x \in S$ and x is of the form yz, then $z \in S$. Similarly, we say $S \subseteq \Sigma^*$ is
prefix-closed if for each $x \in S$, every prefix of x is also in S. That is, if $x \in S$,
where x is of the form yz, then $y \in S$. If S and E are two subsets of Σ^*, we use
the notation

$$S \cdot E = \{xy \mid x \in S, y \in E\}.$$

Let f be the target concept and let $M_f = (\mathbb{Q}, q_0, \mathscr{F}, \tau)$ be the DFA with the
fewest states that accepts f.

The main idea behind the learning algorithm that we are about to present is the property of "right-invariance" that holds for every DFA. Readers unfamiliar with this property may consult the Bibliographic Notes for an appropriate reference. The right-invariance property states that for any two strings x and y, if there exists a string z such that M_f accepts xz but rejects, yz, then the states $\tau(q_0, x)$ and $\tau(q_0, y)$ must be distinct. The learning algorithm exploits this property to distinguish the states of the smallest DFA that represents the target concept.

At any stage, the learning algorithm has collected finitely many examples for the target concept. These examples are organized in an *observation table* that consists of three parts: (a) a nonempty suffix-closed set $S \subseteq \Sigma^*$; (b) a nonempty prefix-closed set $E \subseteq \Sigma^*$ of strings; and (c) a function T from $(S \cup S \cdot \Sigma) \cdot E$ to $\{0, 1\}$.

An observation table is best understood as a $\{0, 1\}$-valued matrix with rows labeled by elements of $S \cup S \cdot \Sigma$ and columns labeled by elements of E. The entry for row x and column z is $T(xz)$, and $T(xz) = 1$ if and only if $xz \in f$. Hence, if M_f accepts the string xz, $T(xz) = 1$ and if M_f rejects xz $T(xz) = 0$.

Let row(x) denote the entire row of entries labeled x. The learning algorithm uses these rows to disambiguate states of the automaton as follows: For two strings x and y in S, the algorithm can infer that the states $\tau(q_0, x)$ and $\tau(q_0, y)$ are distinct if there exists a string $z \in E$ such that $T(xz) \neq T(yz)$. The two states must be distinct because if $T(xz) \neq T(yz)$, then one of the strings xz, yz must be accepted by M_f, and the other must be rejected. Then, by virtue of the right-invariance property, the states $\tau(q_0, x)$ and $\tau(q_0, y)$ must be distinct. In short, $\tau(q_0, x) \neq \tau(q_0, y)$ if row(x) $\neq$ row(y).

Notice that the labels of the rows range over the elements of $S \cup S \cdot \Sigma$. Rows with labels from S stand for the states of the automaton. Rows with labels from $S \cdot \Sigma$ are used by the algorithm to determine the transition function τ of M_f. Let $y = xa$ be a string from $S \cdot \Sigma$, where $a \in \Sigma$. As noted in the previous paragraph, row(y) stands for the state $\tau(q_0, y)$. Notice that this is the same as the state $\tau(q_0, xa)$, the state attained by M_f upon reading the character a while in state $\tau(q_0, x)$. Thus, if row(x) stands for the state q_1 and row(y) stands for the state q_2, the learning algorithm can conclude that $\tau(q_1, a) = q_2$.

As the algorithm runs, it attempts to ensure that for each state q of M_f, there exists a string $y \in S$ such that row(y) corresponds to $q = \tau(q_0, y)$.

Suppose that $x \in S$ and $a \in \Sigma$. Hence, $xa \in S \cdot \Sigma$. If row(xa) is distinct from row(y) for all $y \in S$, then the state $\tau(q_0, xa)$ is not represented as row(y) for some $y \in S$. If such is the case, the algorithm seeks to "close" the table by adding xa to S and extending the observation table. Formally, we say that an observation table is *closed* if for each $xa \in S \cdot \Sigma$, there exists $y \in S$ such that row(y) = row(xa).

Suppose that at some stage in the execution of the algorithm, there exist two strings x, y in S such that row(x) = row(y). The algorithm would have no reason to distinguish the states $\tau(q_0, x)$ and $\tau(q_0, y)$ on the basis of the right-invariance property. Yet, if there exists $a \in \Sigma$ such that row$(xa) \neq$ row(ya), then the two states $\tau(q_0, x)$ and $\tau(q_0, y)$ must be distinct. In this case, the strings in $S \cdot \Sigma$ contain evidence that the states $\tau(q_0, x)$ and $\tau(q_0, y)$ are distinct, but this evidence is not reflected in the strings of S. To correct this, the algorithm seeks to make the table "self-consistent" by adding to E a string suitably chosen to make row(x) and row(y) distinct. Formally, we say that an observation table is *self-consistent* if for every pair of strings $x, y \in S$, if row$(x) =$ row(y), then for all $a \in \Sigma$, row$(xa) =$ row(ya).

A closed and self-consistent observation table (S, E, T) defines a DFA $M(S, E, T) = (\mathbb{Q}, q_0, \mathbb{F}, \tau)$ as follows:

$\mathbb{Q} = \{\text{row}(x) | x \in S\}$

$q_0 = \text{row}(\lambda)$

$\mathbb{F} = \{\text{row}(x) | x \in S \text{ and } T(x) = 1\}$

$\tau(row(x), a) = \text{row}(xa)..P$

We are now ready to present the learning algorithm. We begin with an overview of the algorithm in words. In essence, the algorithm constructs a plausible hypothesis (a DFA for the target concept) and then tests this hypothesis on randomly drawn examples to check its validity. The algorithm halts if the hypothesis is found to be valid with high probability. Otherwise, it uses the counterexample so found to construct a new and improved hypothesis.

The algorithm begins by setting $S = E = \{\lambda\}$. It then constructs the observation table for these settings by querying MEMBER. Afterward the algorithm enters its main loop, which is sketched below:

Main Loop:

1. Expand the table until it is closed and self-consistent.

2. Construct the DFA $M = M(S, E, T)$.

3. Test the hypothesis M against the target concept f by calling EXAMPLE. If a counterexample to M is found, add the counterexample to the table and repeat the main loop.

4. Exit loop: output M.

The algorithm is formally described as algorithm $A_{6.1}$ below.

Learning Algorithm $A_{6.1}$
input: ε, δ, n.
begin

   set $S = \{\lambda\}$ and $E = \{\lambda\}$;
   set $i = 1$;
   call MEMBER on λ and each $a \in \Sigma$;
   build the initial observation table (S, E, T);
   repeat forever
      while (S, E, T) is not closed or not self-consistent **do**
         if (S, E, T) is not self-consistent **then**
            find $x, y \in S, a \in \Sigma$, and $z \in E$ such that
               $\text{row}(x) = \text{row}(y)$ but $T(xaz) \neq T(yaz)$;
            $E = E \cup \{az\}$;
            extend T to $(S \cup S \cdot \Sigma) \cdot E$ by calling MEMBER;
         end
         if (S, E, T) is not closed **then**
            find $x \in S$ and $a \in \Sigma$ such that
               for all $y \in S, \text{row}(y) \neq \text{row}(xa)$;
            $S = S \cup \{xa\}$;
            extend T to $(S \cup S \cdot \Sigma) \cdot E$ by calling MEMBER;
         end
      end
      let $M = M(S, E, T)$;
      make $\dfrac{1}{\varepsilon} \left[2\ln(i+1) + \ln\left(\dfrac{1}{\delta}\right) \right]$ calls of EXAMPLE;
      let Z be the set of examples seen;
      if M is consistent with Z **then**
         output M and halt;
      else
         let (x, y) be an example in Z with which M is
            not consistent;
         add x and all prefixes of x to S;
         extend T to $(S \cup S \cdot \Sigma) \cdot E$ by calling MEMBER;
      end
      $i = i + 1$;
   end
end

Example 6.1   To understand the workings of $A_{6.1}$, consider the case when the target concept is the set of all strings that contain an even number of 0s and 1s. A DFA that accepts this language is given in Figure 6.2.

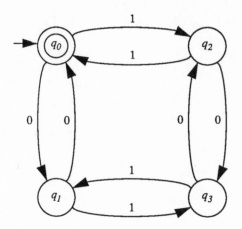

Figure 6.2 _____

The smallest DFA that accepts the set of all strings with an even number of 0s and 1s. States are depicted as circles and the final states as double circles. The start state has a free arrow entering it.

Figures 6.3, 6.4, and 6.5 show the observation tables constructed by $A_{6.1}$ as it converges towards the DFA of Figure 6.2.

Table (a) of Figure 6.3 is the initial observation table for $S = E = \{\lambda\}$. This table is not closed, since row($\lambda0$) = row(0) is distinct from row(y) for all $y \in S$. The string 0 is added to S, and the strings 00 and 01 are added to $S \cdot \Sigma$. The table is now closed and self-consistent. Hence, the algorithm constructs the DFA $M(S, E, T)$ as shown. Unfortunately, the counterexample (11, 1) is produced when EXAMPLE is called. So the algorithm adds 11 and its prefixes to S, suitably expands the table, and so on.

Notice that the DFA constructed by the algorithm in Figure 6.5(b) is the same as that of Figure 6.2. Thus, the algorithm halts.   ■

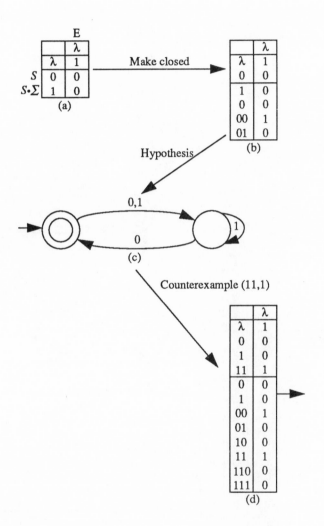

Figure 6.3 _____
The observation tables constructed by $A_{6.1}$.

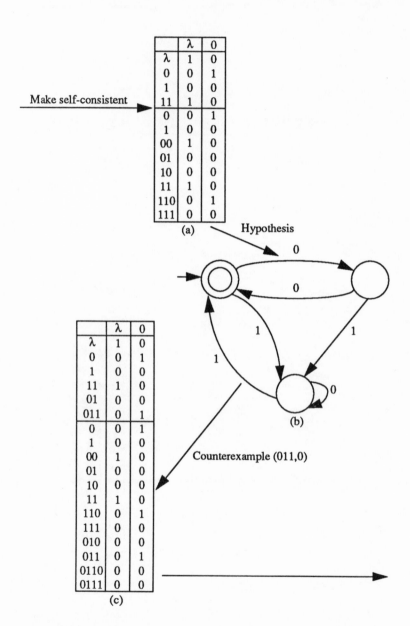

Make self-consistent

	λ	0
λ	1	0
0	0	1
1	0	0
11	1	0
0	0	1
1	0	0
00	1	0
01	0	0
10	0	0
11	1	0
110	0	1
111	0	0

(a)

Hypothesis

	λ	0
λ	1	0
0	0	1
1	0	0
11	1	0
01	0	0
011	0	1
0	0	1
1	0	0
00	1	0
01	0	0
10	0	0
11	1	0
110	0	1
111	0	0
010	0	0
011	0	1
0110	0	0
0111	0	0

(c)

Counterexample (011,0)

(b)

Figure 6.4 _____

The observation tables constructed by $A_{6.1}$ (contd.).

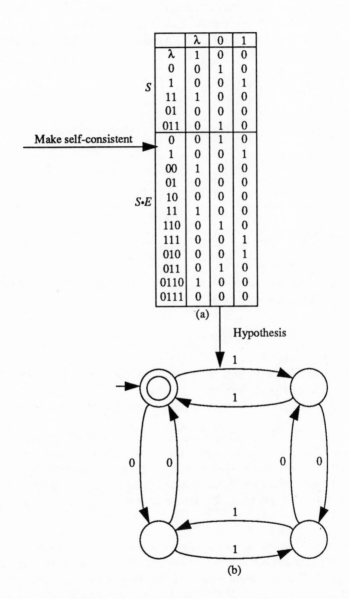

		λ	0	1
	λ	1	0	0
	0	0	1	0
S	1	0	0	1
	11	1	0	0
	01	0	0	0
	011	0	1	0
	0	0	1	0
	1	0	0	1
	00	1	0	0
	01	0	0	0
S·E	10	0	0	0
	11	1	0	0
	110	0	1	0
	111	0	0	1
	010	0	0	1
	011	0	1	0
	0110	1	0	0
	0111	0	0	0

Make self-consistent

(a)

Hypothesis

(b)

Figure 6.5
The observation tables constructed by $A_{6.1}$ (contd.).

We will now prove that algorithm $A_{6.1}$ is correct.

Suppose that the algorithm halted at the ith iteration to output a DFA M such that $P(f\Delta L(M)) \geq \varepsilon$. The probability that such M would agree with a randomly drawn example for f is at most $(1-\varepsilon)$. In order for the algorithm to halt, such an M must agree with

$$\frac{1}{\varepsilon}\left[2\ln(i+1) + \ln\left[\frac{1}{\delta}\right]\right]$$

randomly drawn examples. The probability of such is at most

$$(1-\varepsilon)^{\frac{1}{\varepsilon}\left[2\ln(i+1) + \ln\left[\frac{1}{\delta}\right]\right]}.$$

For $\varepsilon < 1$, the above is at most

$$e^{-\left[2\ln(i+1) + \ln\left[\frac{1}{\delta}\right]\right]} = \frac{\delta}{(i+1)^2}.$$

Thus, the probability that the algorithm will output a DFA M such that $P(f\Delta L(M)) \geq \varepsilon$ at any iteration is at most

$$\sum_{i=1}^{\infty} \frac{\delta}{(i+1)^2} \leq \int_{1}^{\infty} \frac{\delta}{x^2} dx \leq \delta.$$

It follows that if the algorithm halts, then with probability $(1-\delta)$ it will output a DFA M such that $P(f\Delta L(M)) \leq \varepsilon$.

It remains to bound the running time of the algorithm, and we will do so in the following.

Notice that an observation table is merely a way of organizing a set of examples. Thus, we can speak of a DFA being consistent with an observation table, in the previously established sense of the word. Specifically, we say that a DFA M_1 is consistent with an observation table (S, E, T) if for every pair of strings $x \in S \bigcup S \cdot \Sigma$ and $z \in E$, M_1 accepts xz if and only if $T(xz) = 1$.

THEOREM 6.3

If (S, E, T) is a closed and self-consistent observation table, then the DFA $M = M(S, E, T)$ is consistent with the table. Any other DFA consistent with the table but not isomorphic to M must have more states than M.

Proof: The proof proceeds through the following claims. Let
$M = (\mathbb{Q}, q_0, \mathcal{F}, \tau)$.

CLAIM 6.1 _____

Let (S, E, T) be closed and self-consistent. Then, for every $x \in S \cup S \cdot \Sigma$,
$\tau(q_0, x) = \text{row}(x)$.

_____

Proof: The proof proceeds by induction on the length of x.

Basis: $|x| = 0$, i.e., $x = \lambda$. The claim is clearly true if $x = \lambda$, since
$\tau(q_0, \lambda) = q_0 = \text{row}(\lambda)$.

Induction: Assume that the claim holds for all x of length k or less. Prove
true for x of length $k + 1$. Let $x \in S \cup S \cdot \Sigma$ be of length $k + 1$. Then, $x = ya$ for
$a \in \Sigma$ and y of length k. By the definition of the transition function τ,

$$\tau(q_0, x) = \tau(q_0, ya) = \tau(\tau(q_0, y), a).$$

If x was from $S \cdot \Sigma$, then $y \in S$. If x was from S, then $y \in S$ since y is a prefix of x
and S is prefix-closed. In either case, $y \in S \cup S \cdot \Sigma$, $|y| \leq k$ and by the inductive
hypothesis, $\tau(q_0, y) = \text{row}(y)$. Hence, we can write

$$\tau(q_0, x) = \tau(\tau(q_0, y), a) = \tau(\text{row}(y), a).$$

By the definition of τ for $M(S, E, T)$,

$$\tau(\text{row}(y), a) = \text{row}(ya).$$

But $ya = x$, and, hence, $\tau(q_0, x) = \text{row}(x)$ and the claim is proved.

□

CLAIM 6.2 _____

Let (S, E, T) be a closed and self-consistent table. Then $M = M(S, E, T)$ is
consistent with (S, E, T).

_____

Proof: We wish to show that for all $x \in S \cup S \cdot \Sigma$ and $z \in E$, M accepts xz if
and only if $T(xz) = 1$. The proof proceeds by induction on the length of z.

Basis: $|z| = 0$, i.e., $z = \lambda$. If $z = \lambda$, $\tau(q_0, xz) = \tau(q_0, x)$, which is row($x$) by Claim 6.1. If $x \in S$, by the definition of $\mathcal{F}$, row(x) $\in \mathcal{F}$ if and only if $T(x) = 1$. If $x \in S \cdot \Sigma$, since (S, E, T) is closed there exists x_1 in S such that row(x) = row(x_1). Now, row(x_1) $\in \mathcal{F}$ if and only if $T(x_1) = 1$. But since row(x) = row(x_1), $T(x_1) = T(x)$, and, hence, row(x) $\in \mathcal{F}$ if and only if $T(x) = 1$.

Induction: Assume true for $|z| = k$ and prove true for $|z| = k+1$. Let $z \in E$ be of length $k+1$. Write $z = az_1$ for $a \in \Sigma$ and $|z_1| = k$. Since E is suffix-closed, $z_1 \in E$. Let x be any string in $S \cup S \cdot \Sigma$. Now,

$$\tau(q_0, xz) = \tau(\tau(q_0, x), z).$$

By Claim 6.1, $\tau(q_0, x) = $ row(x) and, hence,

$$\tau(q_0, xz) = \tau(\text{row}(x), z).$$

Because (S, E, T) is closed, there exists a string $x_1 \in S$ such that row(x) = row(x_1). (The existence of x_1 is trivially true if $x \in S$.) Thus, we can write

$$\tau(q_0, xz) = \tau(\text{row}(x_1), z).$$

By Claim 6.1, row(x_1) = $\tau(q_0, x_1)$ and, hence,

$$\tau(q_0, xz) = \tau(\tau(q_0, x_1), z) = \tau(q_0, x_1 z).$$

Writing $z = az_1$, we get

$$\tau(q_0, xz) = \tau(q_0, x_1 az_1).$$

Now, $x_1 a \in S \cdot \Sigma$ and $|z_1| = k$. By the inductive hypothesis, $\tau(q_0, x_1 az_1) \in \mathcal{F}$ if and only if $T(x_1 az_1) = 1$. But $T(x_1 az_1)$ is the entry in column az_1 of row(x_1). Since row(x) = row(x_1), $T(x_1 az_1) = T(xaz_1)$. Noting that $z = az_1$, we get that $\tau(q_0, x_1 az_1) \in \mathcal{F}$ if and only if $T(xz) = 1$. Hence, $\tau(q_0, xz) \in \mathcal{F}$ if and only if $T(xz) = 1$, and the claim is proved.

□

CLAIM 6.3 _____

Let (S, E, T) be closed and self-consistent and let $M = M(S, E, T)$ have s states. If $\hat{M} = (\hat{\mathbb{Q}}, \hat{q}_0, \hat{\mathcal{F}}, \hat{\tau})$ is a DFA consistent with (S, E, T) and has at most s states, then $\hat{M}$ is isomorphic to M.

Proof: We exhibit an isomorphism between M and $\hat{M}$.

Consider the (possibly multivalued) mapping $\phi: \mathbb{Q} \to \hat{\mathbb{Q}}$ such that a state row$(x) \in \mathbb{Q}$ maps to $\hat{\tau}(\hat{q}_0, y)$ if there exists $y \in S \cup S \cdot \Sigma$ such that row$(y) = $ row(x). Note that ϕ could be multivalued in that each state in $\mathbb{Q}$ could potentially map to more than one state in Q.

We now show that ϕ is actually one-to-one and onto, i.e., ϕ is a bijection from $\mathbb{Q}$ to $\hat{\mathbb{Q}}$.

Let $x, y \in S \cup S \cdot A$ such that row$(x) \neq$ row(y). Then, there exists $z \in E$ such that $T(xz) \neq T(yz)$. Since $\hat{M}$ is consistent with (S, E, T), $\hat{M}$ must accept one of xz, yz and reject the other. Hence,

$$\hat{\tau}(\hat{q}_0, xz) \neq \hat{\tau}(\hat{q}_0, yz)$$

and

$$\hat{\tau}(\hat{q}_0, x) \neq \hat{\tau}(\hat{q}_0, y).$$

But then, $\phi(\text{row}(x)) = \hat{\tau}(\hat{q}_0, x)$ and $\phi(\text{row}(y)) = \hat{\tau}(\hat{q}_0, y)$. It follows that $\phi(\text{row}(x)) \neq \phi(\text{row}(y))$ and no two distinct states in $\mathbb{Q}$ can map to the same state in $\hat{\mathbb{Q}}$. Hence, ϕ is not many-to-one.

Since ϕ is not many-to-one, $\hat{M}$ must have at least as many states as M. But by assumption, M has at most s states and, hence, $\hat{M}$ has exactly s states. It follows that ϕ must map each state in Q to exactly one state in $\hat{Q}$ and, hence, is one-to-one and onto.

We now show that ϕ maps q_0 to $\hat{q}_0$. By definition,

$$\phi(q_0) = \phi(\text{row}(\lambda)) = \hat{\tau}(\hat{q}_0, \lambda) = \hat{q}_0.$$

Next, we show that ϕ preserves the transition function in that for every $q \in \mathbb{Q}$ and $a \in \Sigma$,

$$\phi(\tau(q, a)) = \hat{\tau}(\phi(q), a).$$

By the definition of $\mathbb{Q}$, there exists $x \in S$ such that $q = $ row(x). Thus, we only need show that

$$\phi(\tau(\text{row}(x), a)) = \hat{\tau}(\phi(\text{row}(x)), a).$$

By the definition of τ, $\tau(\text{row}(x), a) = $ row(xa). Hence,

$$\phi(\tau(\text{row}(x), a)) = \phi(\text{row}(xa)) = \hat{\tau}(\hat{q}_0, xa).$$

Also,

$$\hat{\tau}(\phi(\text{row}(x)), a) = \hat{\tau}(\hat{\tau}(\hat{q}_0, x), a) = \hat{\tau}(\hat{q}_0, xa).$$

Hence, $\phi(\tau(\text{row}(x), a)) = \hat{\tau}(\phi(\text{row}(x)), a)$ and the transition function is preserved.

Finally, we show that ϕ maps $\mathfrak{F}$ to $\hat{\mathfrak{F}}$. Suppose that $row(x) \in \mathfrak{F}$. By the definition of $\mathfrak{F}$, $T(x) = 1$. Now, $\phi(row(x)) = \hat{\tau}(\hat{q}_0, x)$. Since $\hat{M}$ is consistent with (S, E, T) and $T(x) = 1$, $\hat{\tau}(\hat{q}_0, x)$ must be in $\hat{\mathfrak{F}}$. Hence, if $row(x) \in \mathfrak{F}$, $\phi(row(x)) \in \hat{\mathfrak{F}}$. Conversely, let $x \in S$. Since ϕ is a bijection, as x ranges over S, $\phi(row(x))$ ranges over all of $\hat{\mathbb{Q}}$. Suppose that x is such that $\hat{\tau}(\hat{q}_0, x) \in \hat{\mathfrak{F}}$. Since $\hat{M}$ is consistent with (S, E, T), $T(x)$ must be 1. By the definition of $\mathfrak{F}$, $row(x) \in \mathfrak{F}$. But then, $\phi(row(x)) = \hat{\tau}(\hat{q}_0, x)$. Thus, if $\phi(row(x)) \in \hat{\mathfrak{F}}$, then $row(x) \in \mathfrak{F}$. Hence, $\mathfrak{F}$ is mapped to $\hat{\mathfrak{F}}$ and vice versa. This concludes the proof of the claim.

Returning to the proof of Theorem 6.3, Claim 6.2 showed that $M = M(S, E, T)$ is consistent with (S, E, T) and Claim 6.3 showed that any other DFA $\hat{M}$ consistent with (S, E, T) must have at least as many states as M or be isomorphic to M. Thus, M is the unique minimal DFA consistent with (S, E, T).

This completes the proof.

□

We need one more claim before we can estimate the run time of algorithm $A_{6.1}$. Unlike the previous claims, the following claim concerns any observation table, not just closed and self-consistent tables.

CLAIM 6.4

Let (S, E, T) be any observation table. Then, any DFA consistent with (S, E, T) must have at least as many states as the cardinality of the set $\{row(x) \mid x \in S\}$.

Proof: Let $M = (\mathbb{Q}, q_0, \mathfrak{F}, \tau)$ be a DFA consistent with (S, E, T). Let x and y be two strings in S such that $row(x)$ and $row(y)$ are distinct. Then, there must exist $z \in E$ such that $T(xz) \neq T(yz)$. Then, $\tau(q_0, xz)$ and $\tau(q_0, yz)$ must be distinct states and so must $\tau(q_0, x)$ and $\tau(q_0, y)$. Hence, M must have at least as many states as there are distinct values for $row(x)$.

□

As before, let M_f have s states and be the smallest DFA for the target concept.

Suppose that $A_{6.1}$ finds that the observation table is not self-consistent: It finds two strings x and y in S such that $row(x) = row(y)$ and adds a string az to E such that $T(xaz) \neq T(yaz)$. Such an addition would increase the cardinality of the set $\{row(x) \mid x \in S\}$ by at least one, since $row(x)$ and $row(y)$ will no longer be equal. By Claim 6.4, the cardinality of $\{row(x) \mid x \in S\}$ cannot increase more than s times. To see this, note that M_f is always consistent with the observation table and has s states. If the cardinality of $\{row(x) \mid x \in S\}$ were greater than s, then, by Claim 6.4, M_f would have more than s states, resulting in a contradiction.

Suppose that $A_{6.1}$ finds that the observation table is not closed: It adds a string xa to S such that row(xa) is distinct from row(y) for all $y \in S$. Such an addition would increase the cardinality of the set $\{\text{row}(x) | x \in S\}$ by at least one. As argued in the previous paragraph, this cannot happen more than s times.

Suppose that $A_{6.1}$ tests a hypothesis $M = M(S, E, T)$ and finds a random counterexample (x, y) to it. Now, $A_{6.1}$ includes the example (x, y) in the observation table and after some computation produces another hypothesis $\hat{M}$. $\hat{M}$ is consistent with (S, E, T) but is not isomorphic to M since, unlike M, $\hat{M}$ is consistent with (x, y). By Theorem 6.3, $\hat{M}$ must have more states than M. Thus, the number of states in the DFA tested by $A_{6.1}$ must increase monotonically with the iterations of the outer loop. By Theorem 6.3, $M(S, E, T)$ is either isomorphic to M_f or has fewer states. If $M(S, E, T)$ is isomorphic to M_f, the algorithm must halt as no counterexamples will be found. Thus, the number of states in $M(S, E, T)$ increases monotonically with the iterations of $A_{6.1}$ and is bounded from above by s. It follows that the outer loop of $A_{6.1}$ must terminate after s iterations.

Recall that $A_{6.1}$ takes as input n, ε, and δ, where n is such that the probability distribution P controlling EXAMPLE is on $\Sigma^{[n]}$. We will now show that $A_{6.1}$ runs in time polynomial in ε, δ, n, and s.

Initially the set E consists of the single string λ. As we argued earlier, the observation table can be found not to be self-consistent at most s times. Thus, E can have at most s strings. Referring to $A_{6.1}$, notice that each time a string is added to E, the maximum length of the strings in E increases by at most one. Hence, the length of the strings in E is at most s.

Initially the set S consists of the single string λ. Strings are added to S at two distinct points in $A_{6.1}$: when the table is found not to be closed and when a counterexample is found. As we argued earlier, the observation table can be found not to be closed at most s times, contributing at most s strings to S. Also, at most s hypotheses can be rejected because a counterexample is found. Each time a counterexample is found, $O(n)$ strings are added to S. (Recall that in order to keep S prefix-closed, the counterexample and all its prefixes are added to S.) So, at termination, S will contain at most $s + sn$ strings. What is the maximum length of these strings? The strings added as counterexamples are of length at most n. Each time a string is added to S because the table is not closed, the maximum length of the strings in S increases by at most one. Thus, the length of the strings in S is at most $n + s$.

The total number of entries in the table is $|S \cup S \cdot \Sigma| \times |E|$. Using our estimates above, this number is $O((s + sn)s) = O(ns^2)$. The length of the strings in the table is $O(n + s)$ and, hence, the entire table is of size $O(n^2s^2 + ns^3)$.

CLAIM 6.5 _____

The run time of $A_{6.1}$ is polynomial in ε, δ, n, and s.

_____

Proof: A precise estimate of the run time of $A_{6.1}$ is left to the reader as an exercise. Below, we sketch the steps involved in such an estimate.

Consider the various operations that need to be performed by the algorithm. Surely, checking whether the observation table is closed or self-consistent can be done in time polynomial in the size of the table. Similarly, extending the observation table when a new string is added to S or E takes time polynomial in the size of the table. The DFA $M(S, E, T)$ can be constructed in time polynomial in the size of the observation table. And finally, each of these operations is done at most s times as established earlier. The number of calls of EXAMPLE() is polynomial in ε, δ, n, and s, and each call takes unit time by assumption. The number of calls of MEMBER() is polynomial in the size of the observation table, and, again, each call takes unit time by assumption. Hence, the claim.

□

6.3 Summary

We examined the learnability of the class of regular sets in the representation of the deterministic finite automata. Based on the results of Chapter 3, we showed that if the class of regular sets were polynomial-time learnable in the representation of the DFA, there must exist an efficient Occam fitting for the class. However, we found substantial evidence against the existence of an efficient Occam fitting. To overcome this difficulty, we modified the learning paradigm, permitting the learning algorithm to make membership queries. In testimony to the increased power of the modified paradigm, we were able to obtain a learning algorithm for the class of regular sets in the representation of the DFA.

Additional readings on the topics of this chapter are suggested in the Bibliographic Notes.

6.4 Exercises

6.1.   Obtain a precise estimate for the run time of $A_{6.1}$.

6.2.   Implement $A_{6.1}$ on a computer and run it on some sample DFA.

6.3.   Suppose that $A_{6.1}$ could make equivalence queries, i.e., it had available an additional routine COUNTEREXAMPLE(M), which took as input a DFA M and produced as output a string in $f\Delta L(M)$, if $f\Delta L(M)$ was nonempty. Modify $A_{6.1}$ to take advantage of this additional routine. Is your modified algorithm guaranteed to converge to the smallest DFA for the target concept f?

6.4.   Consider a learning algorithm that can make only equivalence queries, i.e., it has access to COUNTEREXAMPLE, but not to EXAMPLE or MEMBER. Assume that each call of COUNTEREXAMPLE costs unit time, and let stand the definition of time complexity. Can such an algorithm learn the DFA in polynomial time?

6.5.   A Boolean formula in which each variable occurs at most once is called a read-once formula. Show that the read-once formulae are polynomial-time learnable by a learning algorithm that has access to both MEMBER and EXAMPLE.

6.6.   Within the modified framework of learning algorithms that have access to both MEMBER and EXAMPLE, can you give a general theorem identifying necessary and sufficient conditions for polynomial-time learnability?

6.7.   Place the representation of the nondeterministic finite automata (NFA) on the regular sets. Can you show that the NFA are polynomial-time learnable in the framework of this chapter?

6.5 Bibliographic Notes

A general introduction to finite automata and regular sets may be found in Hopcroft and Ullman (1979), Chapter 2. The above reference also discusses the right-invariance property and the Myhill-Nerode theorem. Lemma 6.1 is from Board and Pitt (1990). The same paper also explores the general case when the automaton is not limited to the Boolean alphabet. Theorem 6.1 is from Gold (1978). Theorem 6.2 is from Pitt and Warmuth (1989). The same paper also treats the more general case of nondeterministic finite automata. The results on the modified framework for learning DFA are from Angluin (1986b). See also the related papers of Angluin (1982) and Gold (1972). Rivest and Schapire

(1987) discuss a "diversity-based" approach to learning DFA. There are a number of papers in the inductive inference literature on the problem of inferring DFA's. See Angluin and Smith (1983) for an overview. Exercise 6.3 is from Angluin (1986b). Exercise 6.4 is from Angluin (1989), where a host of other classes are also analyzed with respect to equivalence queries. Exercise 6.5 is from Angluin, Hellerstein, and Karpinski (1989). The learnability of context-free grammars under the extended framework of this chapter is studied in Angluin (1986a, 1988) and Berman and Roos (1987). See also Angluin (1987), Ishizaka (1990), and Sakakibara (1988). The PAC learnability of probabilistic automata is studied by Abe and Warmuth (1990).

7

Neural Networks

In this chapter we examine the class of concepts and functions computable by the family of circuits called neural networks. These networks were born of efforts to model the structure and computational behavior of the human brain, which appears to be a large network of neurons. As is evident from the Bibliographic Notes, there is a vast body of literature on the subject. Our discussion will be limited to a rather narrow focus of interest.

7.1 Preliminaries

A neural network is a collection of computational *units* that are interconnected in some manner. The computational power of the network depends on the kind of devices used as the units. In our discussion, the units will be the relatively simple devices called *linear-threshold* units.

A linear-threshold unit consists of a number of Boolean inputs and one Boolean output. Let $x_1, x_2, \ldots, x_n$ be the n inputs to the unit and let y be the output. Associated with the unit is a set of n fixed, real-valued *weights* w_i and a fixed, real-valued *threshold* b. The unit weights the ith input by the weight w_i. If the weighted sum of the inputs exceeds the threshold b, the output of the unit is 1; otherwise it is 0. That is,

$$y = \begin{cases} 1 \text{ if } \sum_{i=1}^{n} w_i x_i > b \\ 0 \text{ otherwise} \end{cases} \tag{7.1}$$

A linear-threshold unit is shown pictorially in Figure 7.1.

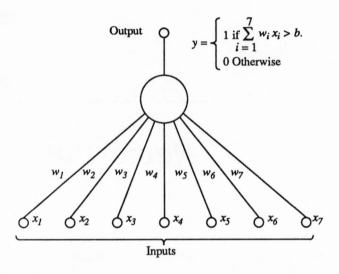

$$y = \begin{cases} 1 \text{ if } \sum_{i=1}^{7} w_i\, x_i > b. \\ 0 \text{ Otherwise} \end{cases}$$

Figure 7.1 _____

A linear-threshold unit.

A neural network consists of several units, a set of input terminals and a set of output terminals. The weights and thresholds of each unit in the network may be distinct from those of the others. The inputs of each unit may be connected to the input terminals or to the output of other units. The output of a unit may be connected to the inputs of other units or to an output terminal. The above connections are subject to the restriction that the outputs of two distinct units may not be connected to each other. See Figure 7.2. The interconnections between the units may be cyclic, and, hence, it is possible that the network oscillates without equilibrating on some inputs.

Suppose that a network N has n_1 inputs and n_2 outputs. Then, the network computes a partial function f from Σ^{n_1} to Σ^{n_2} as follows. The ith input to the network constitutes the ith bit of the input string, while the ith output of the network constitutes the ith bit of the output string. To evaluate the function f on a string $x \in \Sigma^{n_1}$, apply the bits of x as inputs to the network. The value of $f(x)$ is the string represented by the output bits of the network N if the output bits attain a steady state value. If a steady state is not reached, then $f(x)$ is undefined. For the case in which the network has exactly one output bit and computes a total function on Σ^{n_1}, the function computed by the network is simply the indicator function of a concept on Σ^{n_1}—we say that the concept is *accepted* by the network.

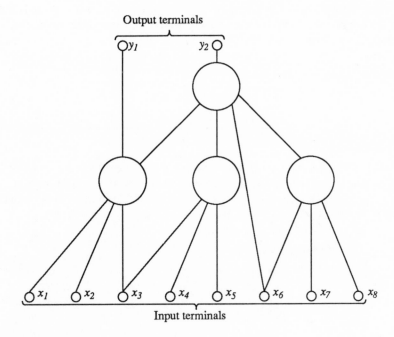

Figure 7.2 _____
A linear-threshold network.

7.2 Bounded-Precision Networks

In the foregoing, we permitted the weights and thresholds of a network to be arbitrary real numbers. Consider a network whose weights and thresholds are limited to some finite precision. We are interested in the relationship between the family of functions computable by these bounded-precision networks and the functions computed by the arbitrary precision networks.

In order to inquire into this issue further, we need the following lemma. (The Appendix at the end of the chapter presents a brief discussion of hyperplanes and half-spaces.)

LEMMA 7.1 _____

For $n \in \mathbf{N}$, consider a set of hyperplanes in $\mathbf{R}^n$ given by

$$\sum_{j=1}^{n} a_{i,j} x_j = b_i, \quad i \in S$$

for some finite set S. Let the $a_{i,j}$ and the b_i be integers such that $|a_{i,j}| \le k$ for fixed $k \in \mathbf{N}$. Then, the hyperplanes partition $\mathbf{R}^n$ into cells such that each nonempty n-dimensional cell is large enough to accommodate an n-dimensional sphere of radius

$$\frac{1}{n^{n+1}k^n}.$$

Proof: Pick a particular n-dimensional cell. Within this cell, we can inscribe an n-dimensional sphere that touches as many hyperplanes as possible. Let $(c_1, c_2, \ldots, c_n)$ be the coordinates of the center of this sphere. Then, for each of the hyperplanes touched by the sphere, we can write

$$\sum_{j=1}^{n} a_{i,j} c_j = \rho\eta_i + b_i, \qquad (7.2)$$

where

$$\eta_i = \left[\sum_{j=1}^{n} a_{ij}^2 \right]^{1/2}$$

and ρ is the radius of the sphere. In the above, η_i is the magnitude of the normal vector $(a_{i,1}, a_{i,2}, \ldots, a_{i,n})$ of the hyperplane.

Corresponding to the hyperplanes touched by the sphere, we can write a system of equations, each of the form (7.2). We can then solve the system for $(c_1, c_2, \ldots, c_n)$. Suppose that most l of the equations in the system are linearly independent. It suffices to focus on this linearly independent subset of l equations, as any solution of these equations will satisfy the entire system. We can write these l equations in matrix form:

$$\begin{bmatrix} a_{1,1} & a_{1,2} & \cdots & a_{1,n} & -\eta_1 \\ a_{2,1} & a_{2,2} & \cdots & a_{2,n} & -\eta_2 \\ \cdots & \cdots & \cdots & \cdots & \cdots \\ a_{l,1} & a_{l,2} & \cdots & a_{l,n} & -\eta_n \end{bmatrix} \begin{bmatrix} c_1 \\ c_2 \\ \cdots \\ \rho \end{bmatrix} = \begin{bmatrix} b_1 \\ b_2 \\ \cdots \\ b_l \end{bmatrix}$$

The rank of the matrix in the above is l. Surely, $(\eta_1, \eta_2, \ldots, \eta_l)$ is not the zero vector. Hence, it can form part of a basis for the space spanned by the columns of the matrix. Without loss of generality, say that the first $l-1$ columns of the matrix and $(\eta_1, \eta_2, \ldots, \eta_l)$ form a basis. Let z be the column vector given by

$$z = \begin{bmatrix} (b_1 - a_{1,l}c_l - a_{1,l+1}c_{l+1} - \cdots - a_{1,n}c_n) \\ (b_2 - a_{2,l}c_l - a_{2,l+1}c_{l+1} - \cdots - a_{2,n}c_n) \\ \cdots \\ (b_{l-1} - a_{l-1,l}c_l - a_{l-1,l+1}c_{l+1} - \cdots - a_{l-1,n}c_n) \\ (b_l - a_{l,l}c_l - a_{l,l+1}c_{l+1} - \cdots - a_{l,n}c_n) \end{bmatrix}.$$

We can write

$$\begin{bmatrix} a_{1,1} & a_{1,2} & \cdots & a_{1,l-1} & -\eta_1 \\ a_{2,1} & a_{2,2} & \cdots & a_{2,l-1} & -\eta_2 \\ \cdots & \cdots & \cdots & \cdots & \cdots \\ a_{l-1,1} & a_{l-1,2} & \cdots & a_{l-1,l-1} & -\eta_{l-1} \\ a_{l,1} & a_{l,2} & \cdots & a_{l,l-1} & -\eta_l \end{bmatrix} \begin{bmatrix} c_1 \\ c_2 \\ \cdots \\ c_{l-1} \\ \rho \end{bmatrix} = z.$$

Let D_1 be the matrix in the left-hand side of the above equation. Using Cramer's rule, we can solve for ρ as

$$\rho = \frac{\det(D_2)}{\det(D_1)},$$

where D_2 is the matrix

$$\begin{bmatrix} a_{1,1} & a_{1,2} & \cdots & a_{1,i-1} & (b_1 - a_{1,l}c_l - a_{1,l+1}c_{l+1} \cdots - a_{1,n}c_n) \\ a_{2,1} & a_{2,2} & \cdots & a_{2,i-1} & (b_2 - a_{2,l}c_l - a_{2,l+1}c_{l+1} \cdots - a_{2,n}c_n) \\ \cdots & \cdots & \cdots & \cdots & \cdots \\ a_{l,1} & a_{l,2} & \cdots & a_{l,i-1} & (b_l - a_{l,l}c_l - a_{l,l+1}c_{l+1} \cdots - a_{l,n}c_n) \end{bmatrix}.$$

Notation: $\det(D_1)$ denotes the determinant of D_1.

If we carry out a cofactor expansion of $\det(D_2)$ about the last column of D_2, we can write

$$\det(D_2) = \beta_l c_l + \beta_{l+1} c_{l+1} \cdots + \beta_n c_n + \beta_{n+1}$$

for some integers β_i. The β_i are integers since they are products of the $a_{i,j}$ and the $a_{i,j}$ are integers. We are free to pick the values of $c_l, c_{l+1}, \ldots, c_n$ in the above. Now, since we assumed that the cell was n-dimensional, $\rho > 0$ and, hence, it must be possible to pick $c_l, c_{l+1}, \ldots, c_n$ such that $\det(D_2)$ is a nonzero integer with the same sign as $\det(D_1)$. Let us make such a choice for $c_l, c_{l+1}, \ldots, c_n$, so that $|\det(D_2)| \geq 1$.

We now estimate $\det(D_1)$. Since $|a_{i,j}| \leq k$,

$$\eta_i = \left[\sum_{j=1}^{n} a_{i,j}^2 \right]^{1/2} \leq n^{1/2} k \leq nk.$$

Hence, we can show that $|\det(D_1)| \leq nl^l k^l$. (See Exercise 7.1.) Since $\det(D_2)$ has the same sign as $\det(D_1)$, and $|\det(D_2)| \geq 1$, it follows that

$$\rho = \frac{\det(D_2)}{\det(D_1)} \geq \frac{1}{nl^l k^l} \geq \frac{1}{n^{n+1}k^n}.$$

This completes the proof of the lemma.

□

Using Lemma 7.1, we can show that a linear-threshold unit with n inputs and arbitrary weights and threshold can be simulated by a linear-threshold unit that has weights and threshold limited to a precision of $O(n\log(n))$ bits.

THEOREM 7.1 _____

Let U be a linear-threshold unit with n inputs. Then, the weights and threshold of U can be replaced by finite precision numbers of $((n+3)\log(n+1)+1)$ bits each, preserving the function computed by U.

_____

Proof: Let $x_1, x_2, \ldots, x_n$ be the n inputs, let $w_1, w_2, \ldots, w_n$ be the n weights, and let b be the threshold of the unit U. The function computed by U is,

$$y = \begin{cases} 1 \text{ if } \sum_{i=1}^{n} w_i x_i > b \\ 0 \text{ otherwise} \end{cases}.$$

Consider the vectors

$$w = \begin{bmatrix} w_1 \\ w_2 \\ .. \\ w_n \\ b \end{bmatrix}, \quad x = \begin{bmatrix} x_1 \\ x_2 \\ .. \\ x_n \\ -1 \end{bmatrix}.$$

Both are vectors in $\mathbf{R}^{n+1}$. Now,

$$x^T w = \sum_{i=1}^{n} w_i x_i - b. \tag{7.3}$$

Notation: x^T is the transpose of x.

Thus, $x^T w > 0$ if and only if U outputs a 1 on input $x_1, x_2, \ldots, x_n$. For each possible value of x, write an inequality of the form $x^T w > 0$ if U outputs a 1 on input $x_1, x_2, \ldots, x_n$, and an inequality of the form $x^T w \leq 0$ if U outputs a 0. Notice that there are exactly 2^n distinct possible values for x, corresponding to the 2^n possibilities for the Boolean variables $x_1, x_2, \ldots, x_n$. Thus, we have a system of 2^n inequalities. Any choice of w that satisfies these inequalities will preserve the function computed by U.

Now,

$$\sum_{i=1}^{n} w_i x_i > b$$

if and only if for any $c > 0$

$$\sum_{i=1}^{n} \left[\frac{w_i}{c} \right] x_i > \frac{b}{c}.$$

We pick

$$c = \max\{ |w_1|, |w_2|, \ldots, |w_n|, |b| \}.$$

Hence, we can replace the weights of U by w_i/c and the threshold by b/c so that each is between -1 and 1, while preserving the function computed by U. Returning to our system of inequalities, we now know that there exists a choice of w with entries lying between -1 and 1. To limit the discussion to such a choice, we add $2n + 2$ inequalities of the following form to the system:

$$w_1 \leq 1$$
$$w_1 \geq -1$$
$$w_2 \leq 1$$
$$w_2 \geq -1$$
$$\ldots$$
$$w_n \leq 1$$
$$w_n \geq -1$$
$$b \leq 1$$
$$b \geq -1 \tag{7.4}$$

Now, each choice of w that satisfies all of the $(2^n + 2n + 2)$ inequalities in the system will preserve the function computed by U. We wish to show that there exists a choice of w that satisfies the system, with entries that can be represented exactly using a small number of bits. To investigate this choice, we now view w as a vector of variables rather than as fixed reals.

Notice that each of the inequalities constructed in (7.3) and (7.4) describes a half-space in $\mathbf{R}^{n+1}$. Specifically, the inequality $x^T w > 0$ describes the set of all points lying to one side of the hyperplane $x^T w = 0$. The inequality $x^T w \leq 0$ describes the set of all points lying on the other side of the hyperplane $x^T w = 0$. And similarly for the inequalities of (7.4). The intersection of the half-spaces defined by the inequalities is the space of all solutions to the system of inequalities. Thus, we only need to pick a point in the intersection of these half-spaces such that the coordinates of the point can be represented exactly in a small number of bits.

No two inequalities in the system correspond to the same hyperplane. To see this, notice that for each of these inequalities, the left-hand side determines the normal of the corresponding hyperplane, and the right-hand side determines the distance of the hyperplane from the origin. The 2^n inequalities of the form (7.3) correspond to mutually distinct hyperplanes since their left-hand sides range over the 2^n distinct possibilities for x. Similarly, the $2n+2$ inequalities of the form (7.4) correspond to mutually distinct hyperplanes since their left-hand sides are distinct. Finally, the hyperplanes corresponding to (7.3) are distinct from the hyperplanes of (7.4) since the former inequalities have right-hand sides of zero, while the latter have right-hand sides of unity.

Since the inequalities correspond to distinct hyperplanes, the intersection of the corresponding half-spaces must be either empty or a region of dimension $n+1$.

We can now invoke Lemma 7.1: We have a set of hyperplanes in $\mathbf{R}^{n+1}$ defining the half-spaces of the system of inequalities. The coefficients of the hyperplanes corresponding to (7.3) are the $(0, 1)$ entries of x. The coefficients of the hyperplanes corresponding to (7.4) are $(0, 1)$-valued by definition. Thus, the coefficients defining the hyperplanes are integers of absolute value bounded by unity. These hyperplanes partition $\mathbf{R}^{n+1}$ into some number of cells. The intersection of these half-spaces is one of these cells, and it is either empty or of dimension $\mathbf{R}^{n+1}$. By Lemma 7.1, if the cell is not empty, it must be possible to fit a sphere of radius $(n+1)^{-(n+2)}$ into it. We need to find a point within this sphere such that each coordinate of the sphere can be represented exactly in a small number of bits.

Let $(c_1, c_2, c_3, \ldots, c_{n+1})$ be the coordinates of the center of the sphere. By virtue of inequalities (7.4), each of the c_i must lie in the interval $[-1, 1]$. Thus, we can represent the magnitude of each c_i as a binary real in the form $0.e_1 e_2 \ldots$, where the e_i are binary bits. Truncate this number to the first $m = (n+3)\log(n+1)+1$ bits to obtain $\hat{c}_i$. That is, $\hat{c}_i = 0.e_1 e_2 \ldots e_m$. Now

$$|\hat{c}_i - c_i| \leq \sum_{j=m}^{\infty} 2^{-j} \leq (n+1)^{-(n+3)}.$$

Hence, the distance between the point with coordinates $(\hat{c}_1, \hat{c}_2, \ldots, \hat{c}_{n+1})$ and the center of the sphere is at most

$$\left[\sum_1^{n+1} ((n+1)^{-(n+3)})^2 \right]^{1/2} \leq (n+1)^{-(n+2)}.$$

Since the right-hand side of the above inequality is the radius of the sphere, the point $(\hat{c}_1, \hat{c}_2, \ldots, \hat{c}_{n+1})$ is also contained within the sphere.

Hence, we can pick $w_i = \hat{c}_i$ and $b = \hat{c}_{n+1}$ so that each is representable exactly by $((n+3)\log(n+1)+1)$ bits, preserving the function computed by U.

This completes the proof.

□

We can now apply Theorem 7.1 to show that the weights and thresholds in an entire network can be replaced by finite precision numbers, while preserving the function computed by the network.

THEOREM 7.2 _____

Let N be a network of linear-threshold units with n input terminals and u units. Then, the weights and thresholds of the units in N can be replaced by finite-precision numbers of $(n+u+3)\log(n+u+1)+1$ bits each, preserving the function computed by the network.

_____

Proof: Since there are n input terminals and u units, each unit in the network can have at most $n+u$ inputs. The theorem then follows from Theorem 7.1.

□

7.3 Efficiency Issues

In light of Theorem 7.2 we can restrict our discussion to those networks such that a network of n units has weights and thresholds of at most $(n+u+3)\log(n+u+1)+1$ bits each. Notice that each such network can be encoded by a binary string of length polynomial in n and u.

Let F be the class of all concepts that are accepted by the neural networks. Fix the natural representation R for F, where for each $f \in F, R(f)$ is the set of all networks that accept f. For simplicity, we view the names in $R(f)$ to be the networks themselves rather than their binary encodings.

The question of interest: Is F polynomial-time learnable in R? In our shorthand notation, we can ask: Are the neural networks polynomial-time learnable?

For any string $x \in \Sigma^*$, it is easy to show that there exists a network that accepts exactly that string and none other. See Exercise 7.2. Hence, for each n, every subset of Σ^n is accepted by some network. Specifically, such a network would accept the logical "or" of the networks accepting each string in the subset. It follows that F is not of polynomial dimension, and therefore, Theorem 3.1 does not apply.

We must turn then to Theorem 3.3 and ask whether there exists an Occam fitting for F in R and whether the neural networks are learnable in usually polynomial time. In fact, using Theorem 3.4, we can show that the existence of an Occam fitting is a necessary condition. To do so, we must first prove that the neural networks are strongly closed under exception. This is relatively straightforward and is left to the reader as Exercise 7.3. Here, we examine a simpler variant of the Occam fitting problem: Given a particular network and some examples, adjust the weights and thresholds in the network so that it is consistent with the examples. We show that even in the restricted case of a network with three units, this problem is NP-complete. This explains the computational complexity of algorithms for this problem, such as the gradient descent methods reported in the literature. Refer to the Bibliographic Notes for an appropriate reference.

In a departure from our established convention of omitting the proof of hardness results, we will prove in full the intractability of adjusting a network to be consistent with a given set of examples. This departure is because the problem of adjusting a network is of wide interest.

A three-unit network consists of three linear-threshold units connected as in Figure 7.3. Each unit in the lower layer is connected to all n input terminals. The unit in the upper layer has exactly two inputs, namely the output of the units in the lower layer.

Consider the following problem.

Three-Unit Training:

> **input:** A finite set of examples $\{(x, y)\}$ such that $x \in \Sigma^*$ and $y_i \in \{0, 1\}$.
> **output:** Does there exist a set of weights and thresholds for the units such that the network is consistent with the given examples?

We will show that the Three-Unit Training problem is NP-complete. To do so, we examine two other problems, the Set-Splitting problem and the Bilinear Confinement problem. We will define these problems shortly. The Set-Splitting problem is known to be NP-hard, as observed in the Bibliographic Notes. We will show that

1. Set-Splitting is polynomial-time reducible to Bilinear Confinement,

2. Bilinear Confinement is polynomial-time reducible to Three-Unit Training.

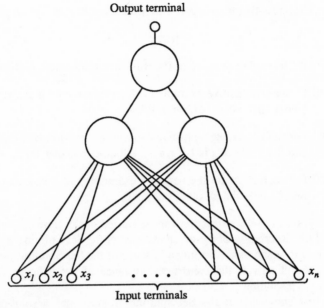

Output terminal

Input terminals

Figure 7.3 ——————————————————————————————
A three-unit network.

This will establish that Three-Unit Training is *NP*-hard. We then show that Three-Unit Training is in *NP*, thereby showing it to be *NP*-complete. (Before we proceed, the reader may choose to refer to the Appendix to gain some familiarity with the concept class of half-spaces.)

Set-splitting:

> **input:** A finite set $S = \{s_1, s_2, \ldots, s_n\}$ and a set of subsets of S, $C = \{c_1, c_2, \ldots, c_k\}, c_j \subseteq S$.
> **output:** Do there exist S_1, S_2 such that $S_1 \cup S_2 = S$ and for all c_j in C, $c_j \not\subseteq S_1$ and $c_j \not\subseteq S_2$?

Bilinear Confinement:

> **input:** A finite set of examples $\{(x, y)\}$ such that $x \in \Sigma^n$ and $y \in \{0, 1\}$. Each x is to be viewed as a point $(x_1, x_2, \ldots, x_n)$ in $\mathbf{R}^n$, where x_i is equal to the ith bit of x.
> **output:** Do there exist two open half-spaces Z_1 and Z_2 in $\mathbf{R}^n$ such that the intersection of the half-spaces is consistent with the given examples?

CLAIM 7.1 ——————————————————————————————

Set-splitting is polynomial-time reducible to Bilinear Confinement.

Proof: Suppose that we are given an instance of the Set-Splitting Problem:

$$S = \{s_1, s_2, \ldots, s_n\}, \quad C = \{c_1, c_2, \ldots, c_k\}.$$

Construct the following instance of the Bilinear Confinement problem:

(a) Create the positive example $(x, 1)$, where $x = 0^n$ is the string of n 0s. Notice that x is the origin in $\mathbf{R}^n$.

(b) For each c_j, create a positive example of the form $(x, 1)$, where $x \in \Sigma^n$ and the ith bit of x is 1 if $s_i \in c_j$. All other bits of x are 0.

(c) For each s_i create the negative example $(x, 0)$, where $x \in \Sigma^n$, the ith bit of x is 1, and all other bits are 0.

Surely, the above construction can be carried out in time polynomial in the length of the description of the given instance of the Set-Splitting problem.

It remains to show that the given instance of the Set-Splitting problem has a solution if and only if the constructed instance of the Bilinear Confinement problem has a solution.

We first show that if the Set-Splitting instance has a solution, then the Bilinear Confinement instance has a solution.

Suppose that S_1, S_2 is a solution to the Set-Splitting instance. Let Z_1 be the open half-space consisting of all points $x = (x_1, x_2, \ldots, x_n)$ that satisfy the equation

$$\sum_{l=1}^{n} a_l x_l > - 1/2,$$

where $a_l = -1$ if $s_l \in S_1$ and $a_l = n$ if $s_l \notin S_1$.

Consider the positive example $(0^n, 1)$ created in step (a) of the construction of the Bilinear Confinement instance. Clearly, $\sum_{l=1}^{n} a_l x_l = 0 > -1/2$. Hence, $x \in Z_1$.

For a particular c_j, consider the positive example $(x, 1)$ created in step (b) of the construction of the Bilinear Confinement instance. By definition S_1 is such that $c_j \not\subseteq S_1$. Thus, there exists $s_i \in c_j$ such that $s_i \notin S_1$. Since $s_i \in c_j$, $x_i = 1$. Also, since $s_i \notin S_1$, $a_i = n$. Note that the x_l take on values of 0 or 1 and the a_l take on values of -1 or n. Therefore, $\sum_{l=1}^{n} a_l x_l > -1/2$ and $x \in Z_1$.

It follows that for all the positive examples $(x, 1), x \in Z_1$.

For a particular s_j, consider the negative example $(x, 0)$ created in step (c) of the construction of the Bilinear Confinement instance. If $s_i \in S_1, x_i = 1$ and all the other x_l are 0. Also, $a_i = -1$. Hence, $\sum_{l=1}^{n} a_l x_l = -1 \le -1/2$. Therefore, if

$s_i \in S_1$ and $(x, 0)$ is the corresponding negative example constructed in step (c), then $x \notin Z_1$.

Now, construct the half-space Z_2 from S_2. By an argument similar to the above, $x \in Z_2$ for each positive example $(x, 1)$. Also, if $s_i \in S_2$ and $(x, 0)$ is the corresponding negative example constructed in step (c), then $x \notin Z_2$.

Since $S_1 \cup S_2 = S$, if $s_i \in S$ and $(x, 0)$ is the corresponding negative example constructed in step (c), then at least one of the following must hold: $x \notin Z_1$, $x \notin Z_2$. Also, $x \in Z_1$ and $x \in Z_2$ for each positive example $(x, 1)$. It follows that $Z_1 \cap Z_2$ is consistent with all the examples, and there exists a solution to the constructed instance of Bilinear Confinement.

We now show that if there exists a solution to the Bilinear Confinement instance, there exists a solution to the Set-Splitting instance. Suppose that a pair of open half-spaces Z_1, Z_2 is a solution to the Bilinear Confinement instance.

For each $s_i \in S$ let $(x, 0)$ be the corresponding negative example created in step (c). Let S_1 be those s_i such that $x \notin Z_1$, and let S_2 be those s_i such that $x \notin Z_2$. Since $(x, 0)$ is a negative example, $x \notin Z_1 \cap Z_2$. Hence, each s_i must be in at least one of S_1 or S_2. Thus, $S_1 \cup S_2 = S$.

It remains to show that for each $c_j \in C$, $c_j \nsubseteq S_1$ and $c_j \nsubseteq S_2$. Let Z_1 be given by

$$\sum_{l=1}^{n} a_{1,l} x_l > b_1$$

and Z_2 by

$$\sum_{l=1}^{n} a_{2,l} x_l > b_2.$$

Notice that the positive example $(0^n, 1)$ is one of the examples in the constructed instance of Bilinear Confinement. Thus, both Z_1 and Z_2 must contain the origin and, hence, $b_1 < 0$ and $b_2 < 0$.

Suppose there exists c_j such that $c_j \subseteq S_1$. By the definition of S_1, if $(x, 0)$ is the example constructed in step (c) for $s_i \in S_1$, then $x \notin Z_1$. But, for such x, all the x_l are zero except for x_i. Hence, if $s_i \in S_1$,

$$\sum_{l=1}^{n} a_{1,l} x_l = a_{1,i} \leq b_1. \tag{7.5}$$

Now, consider the positive example $(x, 1)$ constructed in step (b) corresponding to c_j. All the x_l are zero except for those x_i such that $s_i \in c_j$. Thus,

$$\sum_{l=1}^{n} a_{1,l} x_l = \sum_{s_i \in c_j} a_{1,i}. \tag{7.6}$$

Since we assumed that $c_j \subseteq S_1$, we can substitute (7.5) in (7.6) to get

$$\sum_{s_i \in c_j} a_{1,i} \le \sum_{s_i \in c_j} b_1 \le b_1.$$

The last inequality holds since $b_1 < 0$.

Thus, $x \notin Z_1$, a contradiction since Z_1, Z_2 is a solution to the Bilinear Confinement instance, and $x \in Z_1 \cap Z_2$ for each positive example $(x, 1)$.

By a similar argument, $c_j \not\subseteq S_2$ and, hence, S_1, S_2 is a solution to the Set-Splitting problem.

This completes the proof of the claim.

□

CLAIM 7.2 _____

Bilinear Confinement is polynomial-time reducible to Three-Unit Training.

_____

Proof: Given an instance B of Bilinear Confinement, we show how to construct an instance T of Three-Unit Training such that B has a solution if and only if T has a solution.

An instance B of Bilinear Confinement is a set of examples. We can assume that some of the examples are positive, since otherwise surely the instance has a solution. We can also assume that one of the given examples is of the form $(0^n, 1)$. If not, we can simply shift the origin of the coordinate system to coincide with the point x, where $(x, 1)$ is one of the positive examples given. Clearly, the shifted instance has a solution if and only if the original instance has a solution.

We now construct an instance T of Three-Unit Training as follows. The instance concerns a network with $n + 3$ inputs.

(a) For each of the given examples of the form (x, y), construct an example of the form $(x\,000, y)$.

(b) Create two additional positive examples $(0^n 101, 1)$ and $(0^n 011, 1)$.

(c) Create four additional negative examples $(0^n 100, 0)$, $(0^n 010, 0)$, $(0^n 001, 0)$ and $(0^n 111, 0)$.

Surely, the above construction can be carried out in time polynomial in the length of the encoding of the given instance of B. It remains to show that T has a solution if and only if B has a solution.

Suppose that there exist two open half-spaces Z_1 and Z_2 that form a solution to B. Let Z_1 be given by

$$\sum_{l=1}^{n} a_{1,l} x_l > b_1$$

and Z_2 by

$$\sum_{l=1}^{n} a_{2,l} x_l > b_2.$$

Recall that we forced the positive example $(0^n, 1)$ to be one of the examples in the instance B. Thus, both Z_1 and Z_2 must contain the origin and, hence, $b_1 < 0$ and $b_2 < 0$.

Consider the following three-unit network. The unit in the upper layer computes the logical AND of its two inputs x_1 and x_2 using the following linear-threshold function:

$$y = \begin{cases} 1 \text{ if } x_1 + x_2 > 3/2 \\ 0 \text{ otherwise} \end{cases}.$$

Each of the two units in the lower layer has $n+3$ inputs. One of the units has b_1 as its threshold and weights $\{a_{1,1}, a_{1,2}, \ldots, a_{1,n}, 1, 1, -1\}$. The other unit has threshold b_2 and weights $\{a_{2,1}, a_{2,2}, \ldots, a_{2,n}, -1, -1, 1\}$. It is easy to verify that this three-unit network is consistent with the examples of steps (a), (b), and (c). Hence, if B has a solution, then T has a solution.

It remains to show that if T has a solution, then B has a solution. Let a three-unit network N be a solution to T. Viewing each set of inputs to the network as a point in $\mathbf{R}^{n+3}$, it is not hard to see that one of the following must be true (Exercise 7.5):

1. There exists an open half-space Z such that the set of inputs accepted by N are exactly those that lie in the open half-space Z.

2. There exist two open half-spaces Z_1 and Z_2 such that the set of inputs accepted by N are exactly those that lie in the union of the half-spaces.

3. There exist two open half-spaces Z_1 and Z_2 such that the set of inputs accepted by N are exactly those that lie in the intersection of the half-spaces.

Suppose that we project all the examples created in steps (a), (b), and (c) onto the last three of the $n+3$ coordinate directions. We will get the following examples:

(000, 1), (101, 1), (011, 1),

(100, 0), (010, 0), (001, 0), (111, 0).

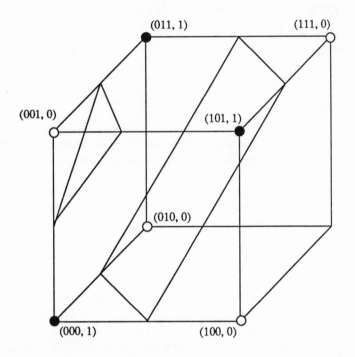

Figure 7.4 _____

The examples created in the reduction of Claim 6.2, as projected onto three dimensions. Also shown are two planes that separate the positive and negative examples.

These examples are depicted in Figure 7.4, where the positive examples are marked with filled-in circles and the negative examples with empty circles. With respect to the figure, we examine which of the cases (1), (2), and (3) are possible.

Clearly, there is no single half-space Z that contains all the filled-in circles and excludes all the empty ones. Hence, no single half-space can be consistent with all the examples of the instance T. Thus, case (1) is ruled out.

Also, there cannot be two half-spaces Z_1 and Z_2 such that the union of the two half-spaces includes all the filled-in circles and excludes all the empty circles. Thus, case (2) is ruled out.

Therefore, case (3) must hold. It follows that there exist two open half-spaces Z_1 and Z_2 consistent with all the examples of the instance T. (Figure 7.4 illustrates this with two planes such that the positive examples are sandwiched between them, while the negative examples lie outside. The region between the two planes is the intersection of two half-spaces corresponding to the two planes.) Let Z_1 be the half-space

$$\sum_{l=1}^{n+3} a_{1,l} x_l > b_1$$

and let Z_2 be

$$\sum_{l=1}^{n+3} a_{2,l} x_l > b_2.$$

Consider the half-spaces $\hat{Z}_1$,

$$\sum_{l=1}^{n} a_{1,l} x_l > b_1,$$

and $\hat{Z}_2$,

$$\sum_{l=1}^{n} a_{2,l} x_l > b_2.$$

It is easy to verify that $\hat{Z}_1$ and $\hat{Z}_2$ form a solution to B. To see this, suppose that $(x, 1)$ is a positive example in the instance B. By construction, $(x\,000, 1)$ is an example in T and, hence, $x\,000$ is contained in the half-space Z_1. Therefore, we have

$$\sum_{l=1}^{n+3} a_{1,l} x_l > b_1.$$

Since $x_{n+1} = x_{n+2} = x_{n+3} = 0$,

$$\sum_{l=1}^{n+3} a_{1,l} x_l = \sum_{l=1}^{n} a_{1,l} x_l > b_1.$$

It follows that x is contained in the half-space $\hat{Z}_1$. A similar argument holds for the negative examples, and with respect to $\hat{Z}_2$.

This completes the proof of the claim.

□

THEOREM 7.3 _____

Three-Unit Training is NP-complete.

Proof: By Claims 7.1 and 7.2, Three-Unit Training is NP-hard. It remains to show that the problem is in NP.

By Theorem 7.2, it suffices if the weights and thresholds in each of the three units are of length $O(n\log(n))$ bits each. There are $2n+2$ weights and 2 thresholds in all. These can be picked nondeterministically, and the resulting network can be run on the input examples to verify that it is consistent with them. Hence, the problem is in NP.

□

Thus, we have shown that a simplified version of the Occam fitting problem for the neural networks is NP-complete. Rather than proceed in this direction, we postpone our discussion until we introduce the notion of prediction in Chapter 8. Under the broader assumptions of predictability, we will present evidence that the neural networks are not polynomial-time learnable.

7.4 Summary

We examined the learnability of the class of concepts accepted by linear-threshold networks in the representation of the networks themselves. First, we showed that every network can be replaced by one wherein the parameters are small finite precision numbers. In light of this result, we restricted ourselves to networks with small finite precision parameters and showed that the polynomial-time learnability of such networks required the existence of efficient Occam fittings. However, we were able to show that even the problem of finding a network of three units consistent with a given set of examples is NP-complete. The last result lends sympathy to the difficulties encountered by algorithms such as "back-propagation." Given these negative results, as well as those that we will see in the next chapter, it appears that we must look for a different family of networks—a family that will be computationally tractable, but yet compute a broad enough class of functions so as to be of practical interest.

Additional readings on the topics of this chapter are suggested in the Bibliographic Notes.

7.5 Appendix

7.5.1 Hyperplanes and Half-Spaces

A hyperplane is the analog of a plane in higher dimensions. In $\mathbf{R}^n$, a hyperplane is the set of all points $(x_1, x_2, \ldots, x_n)$ that satisfy an equation of the form

$$\sum_{i=1}^{n} a_i x_i = b$$

for fixed reals a_i and b. The a_i and b are called the coefficients of the hyperplane. The vector $(a_1, a_2, \ldots, a_n)$ is the normal to the hyperplane, while

$$\frac{b}{\left[\sum_{i=1}^{n} a_i^2\right]^{1/2}}$$

is the distance of the hyperplane from the origin.

A half-space in $\mathbf{R}^n$ is all points that lie to one side of a hyperplane. A *closed* half-space includes the points on the hyperplane, while an *open* half-space excludes them. For instance, with respect to the above hyperplane, each of the following equations determines closed half-spaces:

$$\sum_{i=1}^{n} a_i x_i \geq b.$$

$$\sum_{i=1}^{n} a_i x_i \leq b.$$

With respect to the same hyperplane, each of the following equations determines open half-spaces:

$$\sum_{i=1}^{n} a_i x_i > b.$$

$$\sum_{i=1}^{n} a_i x_i < b.$$

Note that a half-space is a concept on $\mathbf{R}^n$ and we can speak of it being consistent with a set of examples.

7.6 Exercises

7.1. Let B be an $n \times n$ matrix with entries from $\mathbf{R}$. If the absolute value of each entry is at most k, show that $|\det(D_1)| \leq n^n k^n$.

7.2. Show that for any binary string, there exists a network consisting of a single linear-threshold unit that accepts that string and no other.

7.3.   Show that the neural networks are strongly closed under exception.

7.4.   Let F be the class of concepts accepted by linear-threshold networks with n input terminals and u units. Estimate $\mathbf{D}_{VC}(F)$.

7.5.   Let N be a three-unit network with n inputs. Viewing each set of inputs as a point in $\mathbf{R}^n$, show that one of the following must be true:

1.   There exists an open half-space Z such that the set of inputs accepted by N are exactly those that lie in the open half-space Z.

2.   There exist two open half-spaces Z_1 and Z_2 such that the set of inputs accepted by N are exactly those that lie in the union of the half-spaces.

3.   There exist two open half-spaces Z_1 and Z_2 such that the set of inputs accepted by N are exactly those that lie in the intersection of the half-spaces.

7.6.   An AND gate is a logical device with two Boolean inputs and one Boolean output. The output of the device is the logical AND of its inputs. Analogously, we have OR gates. A Boolean circuit is a network of AND gates and OR gates. Show that if f is a function computable by a Boolean circuit of n gates, there exists a linear-threshold network of $p(n)$ units that computes f for some fixed polynomial p. Prove the converse as well.

7.7 Bibliographic Notes

A general introduction to neural networks may be found in Minsky and Papert (1969), Nilsson (1990), and Rumelhart and McClelland (1986). Lemma 7.1 and Theorems 7.1 and 7.2 are from Hong (1988). The same results are also given in Raghavan (1988), using a slightly different proof technique. Theorem 7.3 and its proof are from Blum and Rivest (1988). Judd (1987), (1990) and Lin and Vitter (1989) present several related hardness results. The result that Set-Splitting is *NP*-complete is from Garey and Johnson (1979). The gradient descent algorithm for training networks is discussed in Rumelhart and McClelland (1986). Exercise 7.3 is from Board and Pitt (1990). Exercise 7.4 is from Natarajan (1989b) and Baum and Haussler (1989). Exercise 7.5 is from Blum and Rivest (1988), while Exercise 7.6 is from Hong (1988).

8

Generalizing the Learning Model

In the previous chapters, a learning algorithm for a class of concepts F was required to output a concept from F. We interpreted this to mean that the output concept is consistent with the prior information given. This is an artificial restriction that makes for technically simpler analysis of the learning model. However, in the more general setting, the algorithm should be permitted to output any concept, as long as it is probably a good approximation to the target concept. Such a relaxation is natural, since the role of the prior information should be to help the learning algorithm, not to hinder it by restricting the form of its output. This chapter explores progressive generalizations of the learning model along these lines.

8.1 Preliminaries

We begin the discussion through the following example:

Example 8.1   Recall that in Section 3.4 we showed that if $NP \neq RP$, the k-term-DNF concepts are not learnable in the representation of k-term-DNF formulae. Specifically, we showed that fitting a k-term-DNF formula to a given set of examples is NP-hard. Since the k-term-DNF concepts are of polynomial dimension, Theorem 3.5 requires that if $NP \neq RP$, the k-term-DNF concepts are not polynomial-time learnable in the representation of the k-term-DNF formula. Yet, in Exercise 3.10 we saw that the k-term-DNF concepts can be learned in polynomial time, in a weaker sense. Since this weaker form of learning is the topic of this section, we elaborate on the solution of Exercise 3.10 here.

Consider Boolean formulae on n variables $a_1, a_2, \ldots, a_n$. We claim that for each k-term-DNF formula on these variables, there exists a logically equivalent k-CNF formula on the same variables. Let $f = T_1 \lor T_2 \lor \cdots \lor T_k$ be a k-term-DNF formula, where the T_i are conjunctive terms of the form $x_1 \land x_2 \cdots$. Consider the k-CNF formula $g = C_1 \land C_2, \ldots$, where the C_i are disjunctive clauses of k literals constructed as follows: $C_i = y_1 \lor y_2 \lor y_3 \lor \cdots \lor y_k$, with y_1 being a literal from T_1, y_2 from T_2 and so on.

Let z be an assignment to the a_i. If z does not satisfy f, then for each of the T_i, there must exist at least one x_j that is false. This implies that there exists a clause $y_1 \lor y_2 \lor \cdots \lor y_k$ in g such that $y_1, y_2, \ldots, y_k$ all evaluate to false. Hence, z does not satisfy g. Conversely, suppose that z does not satisfy g. Then, there exists a clause $y_1 \lor y_2 \lor \cdots \lor y_k$ in g where $y_1, y_2, \ldots, y_k$ all evaluate to false. Since y_i was drawn from T_i, each term T_i of f must evaluate to false, and z does not satisfy f as well.

Suppose that the binary encoding of f is of length l. Then the standard form of f is of length $O(l)$ and f is defined on at most l variables. Now, g has at most $\binom{l}{k} \leq l^k$ clauses of k literals each. Hence, the standard form of g is of length $O(kl^k)$ and the binary encoding is of length $O(kl^k \log(l))$. In short, for every k-term-DNF formula with binary encoding of length l, there exists a logically equivalent k-CNF formula with binary encoding of length $O(kl^k \log(l))$.

In Exercise 3.2 we showed that the k-CNF concepts are learnable in the representation of k-CNF formulae. Let A be such a learning algorithm. Suppose that the target concept for A is a k-term-DNF concept f. As argued above, there exists a k-CNF-concept that is equivalent to f. Hence, as far as A is concerned, the target concept is a k-CNF concept and A will identify a k-CNF concept g that is probably a good approximation to f. In short, A constructs a probably good k-CNF approximation g to the k-term-DNF target concept f. Note that g may not have an equivalent k-term-DNF concept, and, hence, it is not as if A learns the k-term-DNF concepts in the representation of k-CNF formulae.

Algorithm A will run in time polynomial in the input parameters and in the length of the encoding of the shortest k-CNF formula for the target concept. As shown above, if l is the length of the encoding of a k-term-DNF formula, there exists an equivalent k-CNF formula with an encoding of length $O(kl^k \log(l))$. It follows that A runs in time polynomial in the input parameters and in the length of the encoding of the shortest k-term-DNF formula for the target concept.

In essence, A is an algorithm that learns the k-term-DNF concepts, producing output approximations that are k-CNF concepts expressed in the representation of the k-CNF formulae. We say that A learns the k-term-DNF in terms of the k-CNF. The run time of A is polynomial in the input parameters, as well as in the length of the shortest k-term-DNF formula representing the target concept.   ∎

From the foregoing, we see that there exists a class of concepts that is not tractably learnable, but possesses an efficient algorithm that learns the class in terms of another class of concepts. This leads us to inquire into the conditions under which such is possible, under both sample complexity and time complexity measures. Toward this goal, we construct a framework to formalize the notions of Example 8.1. Throughout this section, we deal only with concepts on Σ^*, and leave it to the reader to construct the analogs for concepts on uncountable domains.

Let F and G be two classes of concepts on Σ^*.

DEFINITION _____

An algorithm A is a PAC learning algorithm for F *in terms of G* if

(a) A takes as input ε, δ, and n.

(b) A may call EXAMPLE, which returns examples for some $f \in F$. The examples are chosen randomly according to an arbitrary and unknown probability distribution P on $\Sigma^{[n]}$.

(c) For all concepts $f \in F$ and all probability distributions P on $\Sigma^{[n]}$, A outputs a concept $g \in G$, such that with probability at least $(1-\delta)$, $P(f \Delta g) \le \varepsilon$.

In the above, we say that F is the *target class* and G is the *hypothesis class*. The above definition differs from that of Chapter 2 only in that the output concept is to be drawn from the hypothesis class G rather than from the target class F. If the target class and the hypothesis class are identical, the definition collapses to the earlier definition. Thus, we may speak of "learning a class in terms of itself" to refer to learning in the unextended PAC model of the earlier chapters.

We now study the sample complexity of learning in the generalized model.

8.2 Sample Complexity

We retain the supporting definitions of sample complexity, learning operators, and admissibility as given in Chapter 2.

The following results establish a relationship between the sample complexity of learning a class in terms of another and certain properties of the two classes.

THEOREM 8.1 _____

Let F and G be classes of concepts on Σ^* and let A be an admissible learning algorithm for F in terms of G, with sample complexity $s(\varepsilon, \delta, n)$. Then, for $\varepsilon \leq 1/4$, $\delta \leq 1/4$, and $\mathbf{D}_{VC}(F^{[n]}) \geq 16$,

$$s(\varepsilon, \delta, n) \geq \frac{\mathbf{D}_{VC}(F^{[n]})}{16\varepsilon}.$$

Proof: As that of Theorem 4.5.

□

We carry over from Chapter 2 the definition of polynomial-sample learnability. Specifically, a class F is said to be *polynomial-sample learnable* in terms of a class G if there exists a learning algorithm for F in terms of G with sample complexity $p(1/\varepsilon, 1/\delta, n)$, where p is a polynomial function of its arguments.

THEOREM 8.2 _____

Let F be a class of concepts. F is polynomial-sample learnable in terms of some class G by an admissible learning algorithm if and only if F is of polynomial dimension.

Proof: If F is of polynomial dimension, F is polynomial-sample learnable by Theorem 2.1. Simply pick $G = F$, and the theorem holds. Conversely, if F is not of polynomial dimension, the theorem follows from Theorem 8.1.

□

From Theorem 8.2 and Theorem 2.3, we can conclude that a class of concepts is polynomial-sample learnable in terms of some other class if and only if it is polynomial-sample learnable in terms of itself. Thus, allowing the target class to be different from the hypothesis class does not enlarge the family of concept classes that can be learned with polynomial-sample complexity.

Next, we examine the time complexity of learning a class in terms of another. The results below should be compared to those on the time complexity of learning a class in terms of itself, as given in Chapter 3.

8.3 Time Complexity

Let F and G be classes of concepts in Σ^*, and let R_G be a representation for G.

DEFINITION _____

An algorithm A is a PAC learning algorithm for F *in terms of R_G* if

(a) A takes as input ε, δ, and n.

(b) A may call EXAMPLE, which returns examples for some $f \in F$. The examples are chosen randomly according to an arbitrary and unknown probability distribution P on $\Sigma^{[n]}$.

(c) For all concepts $f \in F$ and all probability distributions P on $\Sigma^{[n]}$, A outputs $r \in R_G(g)$ for some $g \in G$, such that with probability at least $(1-\delta)$, $P(f \Delta g) \le \varepsilon$.

_____

Recall that in Section 3.1 we defined that for $f \in F$, $l_{\min}(f, R_F)$ denotes the length of the shortest name for f in R_F. Often, we simply wrote $l_{\min}(f)$ when R_F was clear from the context.

DEFINITION _____

Let A be a learning algorithm for F in terms of R_G. With respect to R_F, the *time complexity* of A is the function $t : \mathbf{R} \times \mathbf{R} \times \mathbf{N} \times \mathbf{N} \to \mathbf{N}$ such that $t(\varepsilon, \delta, n, l)$ is the maximum number of computational steps consumed by A, the maximum being taken over all runs of A in which the inputs are ε, δ, and n, with the target concept f ranging over all $f \in F$ such that $l_{\min}(f, R_F) \le l$, and the probability distribution P ranging over all distributions on $\Sigma^{[n]}$. If no finite maximum exists, $t(\varepsilon, \delta, n, l) = \infty$.

_____

DEFINITION _____

With respect to R_F, F is *polynomial-time learnable in terms of R_G* if there exists a deterministic learning algorithm for F in terms of R_G, with time complexity $p(1/\varepsilon, 1/\delta, n, l)$, where p is a polynomial function of its arguments.

_____

In each of the above definitions, when the concept classes and their representations are naturally associated, we can use our shorthand convention. For instance, in Example 8.1 F and R_F were the k-term-DNF concepts and k-term-DNF formulae, while G and R_G were the k-CNF concepts and the k-CNF formulae. Taking advantage of this natural association between concept class and representation, we simply say that the k-term-DNF formulae are polynomial-time learnable in terms of the k-CNF formulae.

The following theorem gives a sufficient condition for the learnability of the target class F as a function of (a) the learnability of the hypothesis class G; (b) the relationship between F and G; and (c) the relationship between their representations R_F and R_G. In words, the theorem states that if G is polynomial-time learnable in R_G, and F can be embedded in G with a polynomially-tight coupling between R_F and R_G, then F is polynomial-time learnable in terms of R_G.

THEOREM 8.3 _____

Let F and G be two classes of concepts with representations R_F and R_G, respectively. With respect to R_F, F is polynomial-time learnable in terms of R_G if (a) G is polynomial-time learnable in R_G; and (b) there exists a fixed polynomial q such that for all $f \in F$, and every finite $S \subseteq \text{graph}(f)$, $l_{\min}(S, R_G) \le q(l_{\min}(S, R_F))$.

_____

Proof: Let A be a polynomial-time learning algorithm for G in R_G. We claim that, with respect to R_F, A is a polynomial-time learning algorithm for F in terms of R_G.

Consider condition (b) of the statement of the theorem. Since $S \subseteq \text{graph}(f)$ for some $f \in F$, $l_{\min}(S, R_F)$ is defined and finite. By condition (b), $l_{\min}(S, R_G)$ is also defined and finite, implying that there exists a concept in G that is consistent with S. Hence, condition (b) implicitly requires that for each $f \in F$ and every finite set S of examples for it, there exists a concept in G that is consistent with S. It follows that for all $n \in \mathbf{N}$, $F^{[n]} \subseteq G^{[n]}$.

Let ε, δ, and n be the inputs to A. Suppose that $f \in F$ is the target concept. There exists $g \in G$ such that $g^{[n]} = f^{[n]}$. As far as A is concerned, g is the target concept, and with probability at least $(1 - \delta)$, A will identify a concept $\hat{g}$ such that $P(g \Delta \hat{g}) \le \varepsilon$. But since P is nonzero only on $\Sigma^{[n]}$, $P(g \Delta \hat{g}) = P(f \Delta \hat{g})$, and, hence, with probability at least $(1 - \delta)$, $P(f \Delta \hat{g}) \le \varepsilon$.

Let the time complexity of A be bounded by a polynomial $p(1/\varepsilon, 1/\delta, n, l)$. Suppose that on a certain run of A, S was the set of examples seen by it. Since the target concept could have been any concept in G consistent with S, the time consumed by A on that run must be at most $p(1/\varepsilon, 1/\delta, n, l_{\min}(S, R_G))$. But, by condition (b),

$$l_{\min}(S, R_G) \le q(l_{\min}(S, R_F)) \le q(l_{\min}(f, R_F)).$$

Hence, the time consumed by A is at most $p(1/\varepsilon, 1/\delta, n, q(l_{\min}(f, R_F)))$, and A is a polynomial-time algorithm for F in terms of R_G.

$\square$

To illustrate Theorem 8.3, we return to our example of k-term-DNF and k-CNF.

Example 8.2   We apply Theorem 8.3 to Example 8.1.

Let F be the k-term-DNF concepts and G the k-CNF-concepts. Also, let R_F be the representation of the k-term-DNF formulae and let R_G be the representation of k-CNF formulae.

As we know, the class of k-CNF concepts G is polynomial-time learnable in the k-CNF formulae and condition (a) of the theorem is satisfied. It remains to show that condition (b) is satisfied. Let S be a finite set of examples for some concept in F. Pick $f \in F$ such that $l_{\min}(f, R_F) = l_{\min}(S, R_F)$. As shown in Example 8.1, there exists a k-CNF concept g that is logically equivalent to f, i.e., there exists $g \in G$ such that $g = f$. Furthermore, we showed that the length of the binary encoding of g is bounded polynomially in the length of the binary encoding of f, i.e., there exists a polynomial q such that

$$l_{\min}(g, R_G) \le q\left[l_{\min}(f, R_F)\right] = q\left[l_{\min}(S, R_F)\right].$$

But $l_{\min}(S, R_G) \le l_{\min}(g, R_G)$ and, hence,

$$l_{\min}(S, R_G) \le q\left[l_{\min}(S, R_F)\right].$$

Thus, we have shown that condition (b) of Theorem 8.3 is satisfied as well, thereby confirming that the k-term DNF formulae are polynomial-time learnable in terms of the k-CNF formulae.   ∎

In the above, we related the polynomial-time learnability of the target class to the polynomial-time learnability of the hypothesis class. Recall that in Theorem 3.3 we obtained the Occam's Razor condition for learnability in usually polynomial time. To take advantage of this result, we present a result relating the usually polynomial-time learnability of the target class to the usually polynomial-time learnability of the hypothesis class. First, we formalize the notion of usually polynomial-time learnability in the present setting.

DEFINITION _____

With respect to R_F, F is learnable in terms of R_G *in usually polynomial time* if there exists a deterministic learning algorithm for F in terms of R_G, such that on every set of inputs ε, δ, and n, for every target concept $f \in F$ and probability distribution P on $\Sigma^{[n]}$, with probability at least $1/2$, the algorithm halts in time $p(1/\varepsilon, 1/\delta, l_{min}(f), n)$, where p is a polynomial function of its arguments.

THEOREM 8.4 _____

Let F and G be two classes of concepts with representations R_F and R_G, respectively. F is learnable in usually polynomial time in terms of R_G, if (a) G is learnable in R_G in usually polynomial time; and (b) there exists a fixed polynomial q such that for all $f \in F$, and each finite set S of examples for f, $l_{min}(S, R_G) \le q(l_{min}(S, R_F))$.

Proof: Similar to that of Theorem 8.3.

                                                                        □

Theorems 8.1 through 8.4 seek to relate the learnability of the target class with the learnability of the hypothesis class. Below, we give a result relating the learnability of the target class directly with the existence of an Occam fitting. The result is the analog of Theorem 3.3 in this setting.

DEFINITION _____

Algorithm Q is said to be a *generalized Occam fitting* for F in R_G if there exists a fixed polynomial q and fixed $0 \le \alpha < 1$ such that

(a) Q takes as input a set of examples $S \subseteq \Sigma^* \times \{0, 1\}$. Let $n = \max \{ |x| \,|\, (x, y) \in S \}$ and let $m = |S|$.

(b) Suppose that there exists a concept in F that is consistent with S. Then, Q outputs a name $r \in R_G(g)$ for a concept $g \in G$ that is consistent with S, such that $|r| \le q(n, l_{min}(S, R_G))m^\alpha$.

Unless required by the context, we drop the term *generalized* and simply say that Q is an Occam fitting for F in R_G. With respect to R_F, Q is said to be a polynomial-time Occam fitting if Q is deterministic and runs in time polynomial in the length of its input and $l_{min}(S, R_F)$.

THEOREM 8.5

Let F and G be two classes of concepts with representations R_F and R_G, respectively. With respect to R_F, F is learnable in terms of R_G in usually polynomial time if (a) there exists a polynomial-time Occam fitting for F in R_G; and (b) R_G is polynomial-time computable.

Proof: Similar to that of Theorem 3.3.

□

8.4 Prediction

In this section we examine a further generalization of the PAC learning model. This model is called "prediction" since it can be viewed as the traditional model of statistical prediction. Loosely speaking, statistical prediction is the process by which an algorithm takes a collection of randomly chosen examples for a function and then predicts the value of the function on any fresh point that may be presented to it. We call such an algorithm a "prediction strategy." (We use the term *prediction algorithm* in a more formal context later.)

We now argue that a prediction strategy is equivalent to a learning algorithm for a class in terms of another class. In the interest of technical simplicity, we consider only deterministic prediction strategies. Also, rather than specify input parameters for a prediction strategy, we proceed informally.

Let A be a learning algorithm for a class F in terms of a class G. We convert A into a prediction strategy as follows:

> run A.
> let A output a concept g.
> to predict the target concept
>> on a fresh instance x, simply output $g(x)$.

Conversely, given a prediction strategy A for a class F, we can convert it into a learning algorithm.

> run A.
>> to provide A with a collection of random examples,
>> call EXAMPLE sufficiently many times.
> when A is ready to predict,
>> let g be the set of all strings that A would predict as being in f.
> output g.

In the above, since the prediction strategy A is deterministic, the set g is well defined. The constructed algorithm learns F in the hypothesis class G, where G consists of all concepts g that it could possibly output when faced with a target concept from F.

Notice that when a prediction strategy is converted into a learning algorithm, there is no *a priori* restriction on the hypothesis class G. This is most natural and is the essence of prediction in that the prior information defines the target class to help the learner, but does not seek to confine the learner to a particular form of the output concept.

Thus, the notion of statistical prediction is equivalent to learning a target class in terms of an arbitrary hypothesis class. Since we are familiar with the definitions and machinery involved in the latter form, we will examine prediction entirely in that setting.

There is one restriction we would like to place on the hypothesis class. To understand the idea behind this restriction, notice that when we converted a learning algorithm into a prediction strategy, the concept g output by the learning algorithm needed to be evaluated on fresh strings in Σ^*. In order for this evaluation to be done effectively, it must be possible to compute membership in g effectively. Hence, we place the restriction that the hypothesis class G consist of the recursively enumerable sets. In other words, we restrict our interest to learning algorithms with the hypothesis class consisting of the sets recognizable by the Turing machines.

To complete the picture, we must specify a representation for the hypothesis class. In particular, we choose the natural representation R_T of the Turing machines for the hypothesis class of the computable sets. For each computable f, $R_T(f)$ is the set of binary encodings of the Turing machines that recognize f. A Turing machine may be encoded in binary just as we encoded finite automata in binary in Chapter 6. (Readers unfamiliar with such encoding should consult the Bibliographic Notes for an appropriate reference.)

DEFINITION _____

Let A be a learning algorithm that learns a target class F in terms of R_T. A is a *prediction algorithm* for F.

_____

The above definition of a prediction algorithm is rather broad and ignores efficiency issues. It would be desirable to have a notion that considers such issues, a notion of a "polynomial-time prediction" algorithm. Note that efficiency considerations enter at two points: (a) the time complexity of the prediction algorithm; and (b) the time complexity of the Turing machine output by the prediction algorithm. In order for us to declare the prediction efficient, both of these time complexities must be small.

Let $p(n)$ be a function of the variable n. We say that a Turing machine M may be simulated in $p(n)$ time if for all strings x, on input (x,M), the universal Turing machine M_U halts in time $p(|M|+|x|)$. Let $T(p(n))$ denote the class of concepts accepted by the Turing machines that can be simulated in $p(n)$ time. As representation for this class, we use $R_{T(p(n))}$, which is the representation composed of the binary encodings of the Turing machines. Specifically, for each concept $f \in T$, a name in $R_{T(p(n))}$ is the binary encoding of a Turing machine M that accepts f, where M can be simulated in $p(n)$ time.

DEFINITION _____

Let F be a class of concepts with representation R_F. With respect to R_F, F is *polynomial-time predictable* if there exists a polynomial $p(n)$ such that F is polynomial-time learnable in terms of $R_{T(p(n))}$.

_____

In keeping with our shorthand notation, when F and R_F are naturally associated, we take advantage of this association. For instance, we can simply say that "the k-term-DNF are polynomial-time predictable," a fact that will follow easily from Theorem 8.6.

An interesting feature of polynomial-time predictability is that it is a limiting case of polynomial-time learnability. Specifically, if a class is polynomial-time learnable in terms of any polynomial-time computable representation, then the class is polynomial-time predictable. Formally, we have the following.

THEOREM 8.6 _____

Let F and G be two classes of concepts with representations R_F and R_G, respectively, such that R_G is polynomial-time computable. With respect to R_F, if F is polynomial-time learnable in terms of R_G, then F is polynomial-time predictable.

_____

Proof: Straightforward and left to the reader as an exercise.

□

Next, we give a theorem identifying conditions necessary for polynomial-time predictability. By Theorem 8.6, these conditions are also necessary for polynomial-time learnability in terms of any polynomial-time computable representation. The theorem is the analog of Theorem 8.4 in this setting in that it is stated in terms of the existence of a generalized Occam fitting.

THEOREM 8.7

Let F be a class of concepts with representation R_F. With respect to R_F, F is polynomial-time predictable only if there exists a polynomial $p(n)$ such that F has a random polynomial-time Occam fitting in $R_{T(p(n))}$.

Proof: First, note that for any polynomial $p(n)$, $R_{T(p(n))}$ is strongly closed under exception. Then the claim follows as in Theorem 3.4. The details are left to the reader as an exercise.

$\square$

8.4.1 Hardness Results

Akin to the hardness results that we examined in Chapter 3, we have hardness results for prediction. The nature of these results is slightly different in that they rely on the existence of the so-called trapdoor functions rather than on the postulate that $P \ne NP$.

A trapdoor function is a one-to-one function $\mathfrak{T}: \Sigma^* \to \Sigma^*$ such that

(a) Both $\mathfrak{T}$ and its inverse $\mathfrak{T}^{-1}$ are easy to evaluate.

(b) Given $\mathfrak{T}$, it is difficult to construct the inverse function $\mathfrak{T}^{-1}$.

It is not known whether the existence of trapdoor functions follows from the assumption that $P \ne NP$. On the other hand, it is known that assuming their existence implies $P \ne NP$.

Trapdoor functions can be used for the cryptographic encoding of messages. To see this, suppose that a certain Mr. A wishes to have all messages sent to him cryptographically encoded so that only he can decode and understand the messages. Mr. A selects a trapdoor function $\mathfrak{T}$ for which he knows the inverse $\mathfrak{T}^{-1}$. He then publishes $\mathfrak{T}$, saying that all messages sent to him must be encoded using $\mathfrak{T}$. Note that $\mathfrak{T}$ is easy to evaluate, i.e., for any string x, $\mathfrak{T}(x)$ is easy to compute. In order to send Mr. A a message x, one simply computes $y = \mathfrak{T}(x)$ and mails y to Mr. A. Mr. A applies $\mathfrak{T}^{-1}$ to y. He would than have $\mathfrak{T}^{-1}(\mathfrak{T}(x)) = x$, which is the original message. Notice that it is computationally difficult for anyone eavesdropping on Mr. A's message to decode it: The inverse function $\mathfrak{T}^{-1}$ is not readily available to the eavesdropper and since $\mathfrak{T}$ is a trapdoor function, it is difficult for the eavesdropper to construct $\mathfrak{T}^{-1}$.

There are several functions that are generally believed to be trapdoor functions. We emphasize that these functions have not been proven to be trapdoor functions, but there is strong evidence that they are. Amongst these is the class called the Rivest-Shamir-Adleman public-key functions, a class of functions widely used for cryptographic encoding. The details of these functions are beyond the scope of this book, and the interested reader should refer to the appropriate references in the Bibliographic Notes.

Here, we will merely state a theorem establishing the intractability of predicting some important classes of concepts, under the assumption that the Rivest-Shamir-Adleman functions are trapdoor functions.

THEOREM 8.8 _____

Assuming that the Rivest-Shamir-Adleman public-key functions are trapdoor functions:

(a) Let F be the regular sets and let R_F be the representation of DFA for F. With respect to R_F, F is not polynomial-time predictable, i.e., the DFA are not polynomial-time predictable.

(b) Let F be the class of concepts representable as linear-threshold networks and let R_F be the representation of linear-threshold networks for F. With respect to R_F, F is not polynomial-time predictable, i.e., the linear-threshold networks are not polynomial-time predictable.

(c) Let F be the class of concepts representable as Boolean formulae and let R_F be the representation of the binary encodings of the Boolean formulae for F. With respect to R_F, F is not polynomial-time predictable, i.e., the Boolean formulae are not polynomial-time predictable.

_____

Proof: Outside the scope of this book. The reader should refer to the Bibliographic Notes for appropriate references.

□

In light of Theorem 8.6 and Theorem 8.8, we have that the DFA, the linear-threshold networks, and the Boolean formulae are not polynomial-time learnable in terms of any polynomial-time computable representation, under the assumption that the Rivest-Shamir-Adleman functions are indeed trapdoor functions. This is a significant negative result.

8.5 Boosting

In this section we consider the problem of boosting the confidence and precision of a prediction algorithm. Specifically, given an algorithm that predicts to a precision of 55% and a confidence of, say, 60%, we show how to construct a prediction algorithm that works for arbitrarily high precision and confidence. This is significant, since it implies that it is possible to construct improved algorithms by bootstrapping coarse building blocks.

A curious interpretation of such boosting is the following. Suppose that one had three doctors, each capable of diagnosis to an accuracy of 70%. In Claim 8.3, we show how to use these three doctors in combination to diagnose to an accuracy of 78%. (To be honest, it is necessary that these doctors be able to adapt to new diseases and symptoms, preserving their accuracy of 70%.) If we had additional doctors, we could improve this accuracy even further. While the claim seems rather powerful, there is another view of it that is somewhat deflating. Specifically, if any of these doctors knew of the construction of Claim 8.3, he or she might have been accurate to 78% in the first place! We could apply the same argument to weathermen instead of doctors. But perhaps the weather is more of a random phenomenon than human diseases and, hence, our assumption of concepts being well-defined sets may not hold.

The confidence boosting result that we present preserves the hypothesis class of the given algorithm through the boosting process. That is, the hypothesis class of the given algorithm and the boosted algorithm are the same. Thus, this result is suitable for boosting all learning algorithms, thereby including prediction algorithms. On the other hand, the precision boosting results do not preserve the hypothesis class in general and, hence, are suitable only for prediction algorithms.

8.5.1 Confidence Boosting

Consider a learning algorithm A that works only for a fixed value δ_0 of the confidence parameter δ. That is, the algorithm ignores the input value of δ and behaves as though $\delta = \delta_0$. We consider the problem of boosting the confidence of the algorithm. Specifically, using A, we would like to construct an algorithm $\hat{A}$ that is successful for arbitrarily small δ.

CLAIM 8.1 _____

Given a learning algorithm A that works for a fixed value of $\delta = \delta_0$, we can construct a learning algorithm $\hat{A}$ that works for arbitrary values of δ, and such that the hypothesis class of A and $\hat{A}$ are identical.

_____

Proof: Given A, we construct $\hat{A}$ as follows. In words, $\hat{A}$ uses A to repeatedly generate hypotheses, and then it tests these hypotheses. $\hat{A}$ halts when a suitable hypothesis is found. In essence, $\hat{A}$ is a variant of the "generate and test" algorithm of Exercise 2.10.

Prediction Algorithm $\hat{A}$
input: $\varepsilon, \delta, n;$
begin
    $i = 1;$
    while $i \leq \dfrac{\ln(\delta)}{\ln(\delta_0)}$ do
        run $A(\varepsilon, \delta_0, n)$ to obtain a concept $g;$
        let $m = \dfrac{1}{\varepsilon} \ln \left\lceil \dfrac{(i+1)^2}{\delta} \right\rceil;$
        make m calls of EXAMPLE;
        let S be the set of examples seen;
        if g is consistent with S, then
            abort and output $g;$
        $i = i + 1;$
    end
    output $g;$
end

Let f be the target concept. We estimate the probability that $\hat{A}$ outputs a concept g such that $P(f \Delta g) > \varepsilon$, conditional on its aborting during an iteration. At the ith iteration, the algorithm tests the output of A with $m = \dfrac{1}{\varepsilon} \ln \left\lceil \dfrac{(i+1)^2}{\delta} \right\rceil$ examples. The probability that a concept g such that $P(f \Delta g) > \varepsilon$ will be consistent with all these examples is at most

$$(1 - \varepsilon)^m \leq \frac{\delta}{(i+1)^2}.$$

Thus, the probability that the algorithm will abort with a concept g such that $P(f \Delta g) > \varepsilon$ at any iteration is at most

$$\sum_{i=1}^{\infty} \frac{\delta}{(i+1)^2} \leq \delta.$$

Next, we estimate the probability that $\hat{A}$ will output a concept g such that $P(f \Delta g) > \varepsilon$, conditional on its running to completion. At any particular iteration, the probability that $A(\varepsilon, \delta_0, n)$ will fail to output a concept g such that $P(f \Delta g) \leq \varepsilon$ is at most δ_0. Hence, the probability that $A(\varepsilon, \delta_0, n)$ will fail to output a concept g such that $P(f \Delta g) \leq \varepsilon$ in i iterations is at most δ_0^i. We pick i so that $\delta_0^i \leq \delta$. Solving, we see that it suffices for i to satisfy

$$i = \frac{\ln(\delta)}{\ln(\delta_0)}.$$

Thus, we have the bound on the number of iterations used in algorithm $\hat{A}$.

We now have the following: (a) If $\hat{A}$ aborts, then with probability at most δ, $P(f\Delta g) > \varepsilon$. (b) If $\hat{A}$ runs to completion, then with probability at most δ, $P(f\Delta g) > \varepsilon$.

Hence, whether $\hat{A}$ aborts or runs to completion, the probability that $P(f\Delta g) \leq \varepsilon$ is at least $(1 - \delta)$.

Clearly, A and $\hat{A}$ have the same hypothesis class.

This completes the proof.

□

In the above, the time and sample complexities of A and $\hat{A}$ are related by small polynomials in the input parameters. We leave it as an exercise to the reader to estimate the precise nature of these relationships.

8.5.2 Precision Boosting

Consider a prediction algorithm A that is successful for arbitrary values of the confidence parameter δ, but only for a fixed value ε_0 of the error parameter ε. That is, the algorithm ignores the input value of ε and behaves as though $\varepsilon = \varepsilon_0$. We consider the problem of boosting the precision of the algorithm. Specifically, using A, we would like to construct an algorithm $\hat{A}$ that is successful for arbitrarily small ε.

First, we consider a special case of the problem. Specifically, we consider the case in which A is a prediction algorithm with one-sided error, i.e., the output concept is always a subset of the target concept.

CLAIM 8.2 _____

Given a prediction algorithm A with one-sided error that works for a fixed value of $\varepsilon = \varepsilon_0$, we can construct a prediction algorithm $\hat{A}$ that works for arbitrary values of ε.

_____

Proof: Let A be the given algorithm for a class of concepts F, with sample complexity $s(\varepsilon_0, \delta, n)$. Consider algorithm $\hat{A}$ below.

Prediction Algorithm $\hat{A}$
input: ε, δ, n;
begin
   $i = 1$;
   $g = \varnothing$;
   $k = \dfrac{\ln(\varepsilon)}{\ln(\varepsilon_0)}$;
   while $i \le k$ do
      run $A\left[\varepsilon_0, \dfrac{\delta}{k}, n\right]$;
        each time A calls for an example **do**
          let $m = \dfrac{1}{\varepsilon}\ln\left[\dfrac{ks(\varepsilon_0, \delta/k, n)}{\delta}\right]$;
          make m calls of EXAMPLE;
          let S be the set of EXAMPLES seen;
          if there exists $(x, y) \in S$ such that
             $y \ne g(x)$ then
             give (x, y) as example to A;
          else abort and output g;
        end
      let h be the concept output by A;
      $g = g \cup h$;
      $i = i + 1$;
   end
   output g.
end

We begin with a brief overview of the algorithm. As $\hat{A}$ iterates over its "while" loop, it refines its approximation g to the target concept f. To do so, at each iteration, $\hat{A}$ runs A on a carefully chosen source of examples. Specifically, $\hat{A}$ filters the examples output by EXAMPLE, passing only examples not consistent with g. At the first iteration, g is the empty set. So A sees only positive examples for f. Since A boasts one-sided error, it constructs an approximation h such that $h \subseteq f$. $\hat{A}$ sets $g = g \cup h$ as its new approximation to f and starts the second iteration. In this iteration, A will see only positive examples for $(f - g)$ and will construct another approximation h. Since $g \cup h$ is a better approximation to f than is g, $\hat{A}$ sets $g = g \cup h$ and so on. Notice that the approximation g of $\hat{A}$ is always a subset of the target concept. In short, $\hat{A}$ starts with the empty set g and expands it iteratively until it is a sufficiently good approximation to f.

Now for the details: In order to obtain a filtered example from EXAMPLE, $\hat{A}$ calls EXAMPLE a certain number of times and picks a suitable example from amongst those produced. If none of the examples is suitable, then $\hat{A}$ aborts and outputs its current approximation g. We estimate the probability that $\hat{A}$ outputs a concept g such that $P(f\Delta g) > \varepsilon$, conditional on its aborting during an iteration.

Suppose that $P(f\Delta g) > \varepsilon$. Then, the probability that g will be consistent with the example produced by a particular call of EXAMPLE is at most $(1 - \varepsilon)$. If EXAMPLE is called m times, where

$$m = \frac{1}{\varepsilon}\ln\left[\frac{ks(\varepsilon_0, \delta/k, n)}{\delta}\right],$$

the probability that g will be consistent with all the examples so produced is at most

$$(1 - \varepsilon)^m = \frac{\delta}{ks(\varepsilon_0, \delta/k, n)}.$$

Since A calls for at most $s(\varepsilon_0, \delta/k, n)$ examples in a run, the probability of aborting a particular iteration with a concept g such that $P(f\Delta g) > \varepsilon$ is at most

$$\frac{\delta}{ks(\varepsilon_0, \delta/k, n)}s(\varepsilon_0, \delta/k, n) = \frac{\delta}{k}.$$

Since there are k iterations in all, the probability of aborting during any iteration with a concept g such that $P(f\Delta g) > \varepsilon$ is at most

$$\frac{\delta}{k}k = \delta.$$

We now estimate the probability that $\hat{A}$ will output a poor approximation to f, conditional on its running to completion after k iterations.

Let g_i denote the concept g at the end of the ith iteration and let h_i be the concept h constructed in the ith iteration. Thus, $g_0 = \varnothing$ and $g_i = g_i \cup h_i$. Note that A boasts one-sided error, and, hence, $g_i \subseteq f$ and $f\Delta g_i = f - g_i$.

Let P_i denote the probability distribution according to which A receives examples in the ith iteration. By construction, P_i is the natural distribution P of EXAMPLE, made conditional over $f - g_i$, i.e.,

$$P_i(x) = \begin{cases} P\dfrac{(x)}{P(f - g_i)} & \text{if } x \in f - g_i \\ 0 & \text{otherwise} \end{cases}.$$

Referring to Figure 8.1, we can write

$$P(f - g_i) = P\left[f - (g_i \cup h_i)\right] \leq P(f - g_i) - P(h_i - g_i).$$

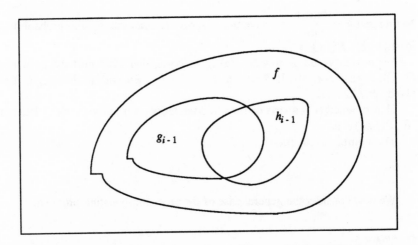

Figure 8.1 _____
The concepts constructed in the precision boosting algorithm of Claim 8.2.

By the definition of P_i,

$$P_i(h_i) = \frac{1}{P(f-g_i)}P(h_i-g_i).$$

Substituting the above in the previous equation, we get

$$P(f-g_i) \leq P(f-g_i) - P(f-g_i)P_i(h_i).$$

Now, since A is a prediction algorithm, with probability at least $(1-\delta/k)$, we have that $P_i(f\Delta h_i) \leq \varepsilon_0$. Referring to Figure 8.1, since P_i is nonzero only on $f-g_i$, it follows that $P_i(h_i) \geq 1-\varepsilon_0$. Hence, with probability at least $(1-\delta/k)$, we have

$$P(f-g_i) \leq P(f-g_i) - P(f-g_i)(1-\varepsilon_0) = P(f-g_i)\varepsilon_0.$$

Noting that $P(f-g_0) \leq 1$, we can solve the above recursion. We then have that if $\hat{A}$ runs to completion, then with probability $(1-\delta/k)^k$,

$$P(f-g_k) \leq \varepsilon_0^k.$$

Noting that $k = \dfrac{\ln(\varepsilon_0)}{\ln(\varepsilon)}$, we have that if $\hat{A}$ runs to completion, with probability at least $(1-\delta)$, $P(f - g_k) \le \varepsilon$.

We now have the following. (a) If $\hat{A}$ aborts, then with probability at least $(1-\delta)$, $P(f\Delta g) \le \varepsilon$. (b) If $\hat{A}$ runs to completion, then with probability at least $(1-\delta)$, $P(f\Delta g) \le \varepsilon$.

Hence, whether $\hat{A}$ aborts or runs to completion, with probability at least $(1-\delta)$, $P(f\Delta g) \le \varepsilon$.

This completes the proof.

□

We now consider the general case of the precision-boosting problem.

CLAIM 8.3 _____

Given a prediction algorithm A that works for a fixed value of $\varepsilon = \varepsilon_0 < 1/2$, we can construct a prediction algorithm $\hat{A}$ that works for arbitrary values of ε.

Proof: Algorithm $\hat{A}$ is given below. In the interest of clarity, we include the source of examples as an argument to $\hat{A}$ and A. Specifically, we write $\hat{A}(\varepsilon, \delta, n : \text{EX})$ to indicate that $\hat{A}$ is being called on inputs ε, δ, and n, with EX as the source of random examples.

In words, $\hat{A}(\varepsilon, \delta, n : \text{EX})$ does the following. If $\varepsilon \ge \varepsilon_0$, $\hat{A}$ invokes A; else, $\hat{A}$ calls itself recursively. On the first call, $\hat{A}$ calls $\hat{A}(\zeta, \delta/4, n : \text{EX})$ to obtain a concept h_1, where ζ satisfies $\varepsilon = 3\zeta^2 - 2\zeta^3$. $\hat{A}$ checks whether perchance h_1 is within ε of the target concept f. If so, $\hat{A}$ returns h_1. If not, $\hat{A}$ seeks to refine h_1 by calling $\hat{A}(\zeta, \delta/4, n : \text{EX2})$ to obtain a concept h_2. Here, EX2 is the source of examples that can be described thus: EX2 tosses a fair coin. If the toss comes up "heads," then EX2 picks an example for f according to the distribution P made conditional over those instances on which f and h_1 agree. If the toss comes up "tails," then EX2 picks an example for f according to the distribution P made conditional over those instances on which f and h_1 disagree. Then, $\hat{A}$ calls itself a third time, $\hat{A}(\zeta, \delta/4, n : \text{EX3})$, to obtain a concept h_3. EX3 picks examples according to P made conditional over those instances on which h_1 and h_2 disagree. $\hat{A}$ then combines the three concepts h_1, h_2, and h_3 to form a composite "majority" concept h_4. In essence, $h_4(x)$ is the majority vote among $h_1(x), h_2(x)$, and $h_3(x)$.

Prediction Algorithm $\hat{A}$
input: ε, δ, n;
example source: EX;
begin

if $\varepsilon \geq \varepsilon_0$ then return $A(\varepsilon_0, \delta, n : \text{EX})$;
let ζ satisfy $\varepsilon = 3\zeta^2 - 2\zeta^3$;
$h_1 = \hat{A}(\zeta, \delta/4, n : \text{EX})$;
make $\dfrac{16}{\varepsilon^2 \delta}$ calls of EX;
if h_1 agrees with a fraction of at least
    $(1 - \varepsilon/2)$ of these examples, **then return** h_1;
$h_2 = \hat{A}(\zeta, \delta/4, n : \text{EX2})$;
for each call of EX2 by $\hat{A}$, **do**
        toss a fair coin;
        if "heads" **then**
                call EX until an example (x, y) is found such
                that $y = h_1(x)$; give (x, y) to $\hat{A}$;
        else
                call EX until an example (x, y) is found such
                that $y \neq h_1(x)$; give (x, y) to $\hat{A}$;
end
$h_3 = \hat{A}(\zeta, \delta/4, n : \text{EX3})$;
for each call of EX3 by $\hat{A}$, **do**
        call EX until an example (x, y) is found such
        that $h_1(x) \neq h_2(x)$; give (x, y) to $\hat{A}$;
end
return the concept h_4 given by
$$h_4(x) = \begin{cases} h_1(x) \text{ if } h_1(x) = h_2(x) \\ h_3(x) \text{ otherwise} \end{cases};$$

end

Notice that algorithm $\hat{A}$ simulates the sources EX2 and EX3 and that these simulations need not terminate. We will probabilistically account for this difficulty later on.

The proof of correctness for $\hat{A}$ runs by induction on the height of the recursion. (Consider the computational tree created by the recursion in $\hat{A}$. The height of a call of $\hat{A}$ is the height of the computational tree rooted at $\hat{A}$.)

Inductive hypothesis::   If g is the concept returned by $\hat{A}$, with probability at least $(1 - \delta)$, $P(f \Delta g) \leq \varepsilon$.

Basis: The height of the recursion is zero. That is, $\varepsilon \geq \varepsilon_0$, and $\hat{A}$ calls A. Surely, the hypothesis holds.

Induction: Assume that the hypothesis holds for calls of $\hat{A}$ to a certain height i and prove true for height $i + 1$.

Consider a call of $\hat{A}$ at height $i + 1$. There are two possible termination points for $\hat{A}$, one in which it returns h_1 and the other in which it returns the composite h_4.

Suppose that $\hat{A}$ returns h_1. To do so, $\hat{A}$ makes $\dfrac{16}{\varepsilon^2 \delta}$ calls of EX and checks whether h_1 agrees with a fraction of at least $(1 - \varepsilon/2)$ of the examples obtained. In essence, $\hat{A}$ estimates $P(f = h_1)$. Using Chebyshev's inequality, we can show that this estimate will be to a precision of $\varepsilon/2$, with probability at least $(1 - \delta/4)$. Given that the estimate is to a precision of $\varepsilon/2$, if it is at least $(1 - \varepsilon/2)$, then the actual value of $P(f = h_1)$ must be at least $(1 - \varepsilon)$. Thus, if $\hat{A}$ outputs h_1, then with probability at least $(1 - \delta/4)$, $P(f \neq h_1) \leq \varepsilon$.

Suppose that $\hat{A}$ returns the composite concept h_4. By the definition of h_4, $h_4(x) \neq f(x)$ if either of the following hold:

(a) $h_1(x) = h_2(x) \neq f(x)$.

(b) $h_1(x) \neq h_2(x)$ and $h_3(x) \neq f(x)$.

Thus, we can write,

$$
\begin{aligned}
P(f \Delta h_4) &= P(f \neq h_4) \\
&= P(h_1 = h_2 \neq f) + P\left[(h_1 = h_2) \cap (h_3 \neq f)\right].
\end{aligned}
\tag{8.1}
$$

Notation: In the interest of brevity, we use arithmetic expressions to denote sets. For instance, $h_1 = h_2 \neq f$ is shorthand for the set $\{x \mid h_1(x) = h_2(x) \neq f(x)\}$.

We assume that $\hat{A}$ halts, in that its simulations of the sources EX2 and EX3 terminate successfully. Later, we will account for this probabilistically.

Now, h_1 is obtained by running $\hat{A}(\zeta, \delta/4, n : \text{EX})$. We assume that $\hat{A}(\zeta, \delta/4, n : \text{EX})$ succeeds in constructing h_1 within ζ of f. Later, we invoke the inductive hypothesis to account for this probabilistically. Hence, we have

$$
P(f \Delta h_1) = P(f \neq h_1) \leq \zeta.
\tag{8.2}
$$

Similarly, h_2 is obtained from $\hat{A}(\zeta, \delta/4, n : \text{EX2})$, where EX2 chooses examples according to the distribution P_2 given by

$$P_2(x) = \begin{cases} P\dfrac{(x)}{2P(f=h_1)} & \text{if } f(x) = h_1(x) \\ P\dfrac{(x)}{2P(f \neq h_1)} & \text{otherwise} \end{cases}. \tag{8.3}$$

Again we assume that $\hat{A}(\zeta, \delta/4, n : EX2)$ succeeds in constructing h_2 within ζ of f. Later, we invoke the inductive hypothesis to account for this probabilistically. Hence, we have

$$P_2(f \Delta h_2) = P_2(h_2 \neq f) \leq \zeta. \tag{8.4}$$

Finally, h_3 is obtained by running $\hat{A}(\zeta, \delta/4, n : EX3)$, where EX3 draws examples according to the distribution P_3 given by

$$P_3(x) = \begin{cases} P\dfrac{(x)}{P(h_1 \neq h_2)} & \text{if } h_1(x) \neq h_2(x) \\ 0 \text{ otherwise} \end{cases}. \tag{8.5}$$

Yet again, we assume that $\hat{A}(\zeta, \delta/4, n : EX2)$ succeeds in constructing h_3 within ζ of f. Later, we invoke the inductive hypothesis to account for this probabilistically. Hence, we have

$$P_3(h_3 \Delta f) = P_3(h_3 \neq f) \leq \zeta.$$

Using (8.5) in the above, we get

$$P\left[(h_1 \neq h_2) \bigcap (h_3 \neq f)\right] = P_3(h_3 \neq f)P(h_1 \neq h_2)$$
$$\leq \zeta P(h_1 \neq h_2).$$

Substituting the above in (8.1), we get

$$P(f \Delta h_4) \leq P(h_1 = h_2 \neq f) + \zeta P(h_1 \neq h_2). \tag{8.6}$$

Now,

$$P(h_1 \neq h_2) = 1 - P(h_1 = h_2 \neq f) - P(h_1 = h_2 = f).$$

Substituting in (8.6), we get

$$P(f \Delta h_4) \leq (1 - \zeta)P(h_1 = h_2 \neq f)$$
$$+ \zeta\left[1 - P(h_1 = h_2 = f)\right]. \tag{8.7}$$

We now estimate $P(h_1 = h_2 = f)$ in the above. Clearly,

$$P_2(h_1 = f = h_2) = P_2(h_1 = f) - P_2(h_1 = f \neq h_2).$$

From (8.3), $P_2(h_1 = f) = 1/2$. Let $\gamma = P_2(h_1 = f \neq h_2)$. Therefore, we can write

$$P_2(h_1 = f = h_2) = 1/2 - \gamma.$$

Using (8.3) in the above, we get

$$P(h_1 = f = h_2) = (1/2 - \gamma)2P(f = h_1).$$

Substituting (8.2) in the above, we get

$$P(h_1 = f = h_2) \geq (1/2 - \gamma)2(1 - \zeta). \qquad (8.8)$$

Next, we estimate $P(h_1 = h_2 \neq f)$ in (8.7). Clearly,

$$P_2(h_2 \neq f) = P_2(h_1 \neq f \neq h_2) + P_2(h_1 = f \neq h_2).$$

Substituting (8.4) in the above and rearranging, we get

$$P_2(h_1 \neq f \neq h_2) \leq \zeta - \gamma.$$

Noting that the sets $h_1 \neq f \neq h_2$ and $h_1 = h_2 \neq f$ are identical, and using (8.3) in the above, we have

$$P(h_1 = h_2 \neq f) \leq (\zeta - \gamma)2P(f \neq h_1).$$

Substituting (8.2) in the above, we get

$$P(h_1 = h_2 \neq f) \leq (\zeta - \gamma)2\zeta. \qquad (8.9)$$

Substituting (8.8) and (8.9) in (8.7), we have

$$P(f \Delta h_4) \leq (1 - \zeta)(\zeta - \gamma)2\zeta + \zeta \left[1 - (1/2 - \gamma)2(1 - \zeta)\right]$$
$$= 3\zeta^2 - 2\zeta^3.$$

Let $q(\zeta)$ be the polynomial $3\zeta^2 - 2\zeta^3$. $\hat{A}$ picks $\zeta = q^{-1}(\varepsilon)$. Substituting this choice in the above, we have

$$P(f \Delta h_4) \leq \varepsilon. \qquad (8.10)$$

Note that in order for the recursion in $\hat{A}$ to terminate, $\varepsilon_0 > \zeta > \varepsilon$ should be satisfied. Verify that $q^{-1}(\varepsilon) > \varepsilon$ only in the range $0 < \varepsilon < 1/2$. Furthermore, if $0 < \varepsilon < 1/2$, $\zeta = q^{-1}(\varepsilon) < 1/2$ as well. It follows that ε_0 must be less than $1/2$ as required in the statement of the claim.

Inequality (8.10) is predicated on the assumption that each of the following conditions holds:

(a) $P(f \neq h_1) \leq \zeta$.

(b) $\hat{A}$ halts in its simulation of EX2.

(c) $P(f \neq h_2) \leq \zeta$.

(d) $\hat{A}$ halts in its simulation of EX3.

(e) $P(f \neq h_3) \leq \zeta$.

We now account for these conditions probabilistically.

Condition (a): $\hat{A}(\zeta, \delta/4, n : EX)$ is at height i and, hence, by the inductive hypothesis, with probability at least $(1 - \delta/4)$, $P(f \neq h_1) \leq \zeta$. That is, (a) holds with probability at least $\left[1 - \dfrac{1}{4}\delta \right]$.

Condition (b): $\hat{A}$ makes $\dfrac{16}{\varepsilon^2 \delta}$ calls of EX to estimate $P(f = h_1)$. If the estimate is at least $(1 - \varepsilon/2)$, then $\hat{A}$ halts and returns h_1; otherwise, $\hat{A}$ goes on to simulate EX2. As we noted earlier, Chebyshev's inequality implies that with probability at least $(1 - \delta/4)$, the estimate will be to a precision of $\varepsilon/2$. Thus, the probability that $\hat{A}$ simulates EX2 when $P(f \neq h_1) = 0$ is at most $\delta/4$. Note that $\hat{A}$ will halt in its simulation of EX2 as long as $P(f \neq h_1) > 0$. Hence, the probability that $\hat{A}$ will halt in the "tails" branch of its simulation of EX2 is at least $(1 - \delta/4)$. As for the "heads" branch, assume that (a) holds and, hence, $P(f \neq h_1) \leq \zeta$. Since $\zeta < 1/2$, $P(f = h_1) \geq 1 - \zeta > 0$, and $\hat{A}$ will halt in the "heads" branch of its simulation of EX2.

Combining our observations above, the probability that (a) and (b) hold simultaneously is at least $\left[1 - \dfrac{1}{2}\delta \right]$.

Condition (c): Assume that (b) holds and $\hat{A}(\zeta, \delta/4, n : EX2)$ runs to completion. Since $\hat{A}(\zeta, \delta/4, n : EX2)$ is at height i, by the inductive hypothesis, with probability at least $(1 - \delta/4)$, $P(f \neq h_2) \leq \zeta$.

Combining our observations above, the probability that (a), (b), and (c) all hold simultaneously is at least $\left[1 - \dfrac{3}{4}\delta \right]$.

Condition (d): To show that $\hat{A}$ halts in its simulation of EX2, it suffices to show that $P(h_1 \neq h_2) > 0$. Now,

$$P_2(h_1 \neq h_2) \geq P_2(h_2 = f \neq h_1).$$

$$\geq P_2(f \neq h_1) - P_2(f \neq h_2). \tag{8.11}$$

By (8.3), $P_2(f \neq h_1) = 1/2$. Assuming that (c) holds, $P_2(f \neq h_2) \leq \zeta$. Hence, we can write

$P_2(h_2 = f \neq h_1) \geq 1/2 - \zeta.$

Using (8.3) in the above, we have

$P(h_2 = f \neq h_1) \geq (1/2 - \zeta)2P(f \neq h_1).$

Substituting in (8.11), we have

$P_2(h_2 \neq h_1) \geq (1/2 - \zeta)2P(f \neq h_1).$

Since we have already accounted for the probability of the correctness of the Chebyshev estimate of condition (b), here we can assume it to be correct. Thus, we have that $\hat{A}$ will run EX2 only when

$P(f \neq h_1) \geq \varepsilon/2.$

Hence,

$P(h_1 \neq h_2) \geq (1/2 - \zeta)2(\varepsilon/2).$

Since $\zeta < 1/2$ and $\varepsilon > 0$,

$P(h_1 \neq h_2) > 0.$

It follows that $\hat{A}$ will halt in its simulation of EX3 and that (d) holds.

Combining our observations above, the probability that (a), (b), (c), and (d) all hold simultaneously is at least $\left[1 - \dfrac{3}{4}\delta\right]$.

Condition (e): Assume that (d) holds and, hence, $\hat{A}(\zeta, \delta/4, n : \text{EX2})$ runs to completion. Since $\hat{A}(\zeta, \delta/4, n : \text{EX3})$ is at height i, by the inductive hypothesis, with probability at least $(1 - \delta/4)$, $P(f \neq h_3) \leq \zeta$.

Combining our observations above, the probability that (a), (b), (c), (d), and (e) all hold simultaneously is at least $(1 - \delta)$.

We now have the following. (1) If $\hat{A}$ returns h_1, then with probability at least $(1 - \delta/4)$, $P(f \Delta h_1) \leq \varepsilon$. (2) If $\hat{A}$ returns h_4, then with probability at least $(1 - \delta)$, $P(f \Delta h_4) \leq \varepsilon$.

Hence, with probability at least $(1 - \delta)$, the concept g returned by $\hat{A}$ is such that $P(f \Delta g) \leq \varepsilon$.

This completes the proof of the claim.

□

We leave it to the reader as an exercise to show that the time and sample complexities of A and $\hat{A}$ are related by small polynomials in the various parameters. See Exercises 8.6 and 8.7.

An interesting point regarding Claim 8.3: Suppose that the claim held for $\varepsilon_0 \geq 1/2$, rather than $\varepsilon_0 > 1/2$. Then A could simply return a random set, i.e., a concept constructed by tossing a coin to decide whether a given instance is a member. $\hat{A}$ would then be able to boost this concept to arbitrary precision. Such boosting sounds improbable and is the subject of Exercise 8.8.

8.6 Summary

We extended the paradigm of PAC learning, releasing the restriction that the concept output by the learning algorithm belong to the target class. In particular, we introduced the notion of learning a target class in terms of a hypothesis class. We found that this extended model of learning does not enlarge the family of classes that can be handled by algorithms of polynomial-sample complexity. However, it does enlarge the family of classes that are tractably learnable with respect to time complexity. We then examined the notion of statistical prediction and argued that it was equivalent to learning the target class in terms of an arbitrary hypothesis class. Formally, we defined prediction to be learning the target class in terms of the Turing machines. Analogously, we defined polynomial-time prediction to be polynomial-time learning of the target class in terms of the polynomial-time bounded Turing machines. Under this definition, we saw that deterministic finite automata, the linear-threshold networks, and the Boolean formulae are not polynomial-time predictable unless the Rivest-Shamir-Adleman cryptographic assumptions break down. Since polynomial-time prediction is a limiting case of learning in terms of a polynomial-time computable representation, it followed that the above classes are not efficiently learnable in terms of any polynomial-time computable representation. Finally, we examined the problem of confidence and precision boosting of learning and prediction algorithms. Surprisingly enough, such boosting is possible. We established a confidence boosting result that could be used for learning algorithms (and, consequently, prediction algorithms) since it preserved the hypothesis class of the learning algorithm. Our precision boosting results preserved the hypothesis class only for prediction algorithms, and, therefore, can be used only for them.

Additional readings on the topics of this chapter are suggested in the Bibliographic Notes.

8.7 Exercises

8.1.   A Boolean threshold function is defined as follows. Consider n variables $a_1, a_2, \ldots, a_n$. Let S be a subset of these variables and let $k \in \mathbf{N}$. As usual, a string $x \in \Sigma^n$ is to be viewed as an assignment to the variables. The Boolean threshold function f, corresponding to S and k, takes on the value 1 on x if x sets at least k of the variables in S to 1; else, $f(x) = 0$. Notice that f is the indicator function of a set. We call the class of all such sets the class F of Boolean threshold sets. Also, the binary encodings of the (S, k) pairs form a representation R_F for F.

Akin to Corollary 3.1, it can be shown that if $NP \neq RP$, the class F is not polynomial-time learnable in R_F. Let G be the class of all half-spaces defined on N^n, for all $n \in N$. On G, place the representation R_G consisting of the binary encodings of the coefficients of the planes defining the half-spaces in G. Show that with respect to R_F, F is polynomial-time learnable in R_G.

8.2.   State and prove a weak converse to Theorem 8.5. That is, give the analog of Theorem 3.4 on the necessity of an Occam fitting when the target class and the hypothesis class are distinct.

8.3.   Show that $R_{T(p(n))}$ is strongly closed under exception.

8.4.   Show that with respect to the representation of the nondeterministic finite automata (NFA), the regular sets are not polynomial-time predictable, i.e., the NFA are not polynomial-time predictable.

8.5.   Consider the following alternative to the algorithm of Claim 8.3 for precision boosting.

> **Prediction Algorithm $\hat{A}$**
> **input:** ε, δ, n;
> **example source:** EX;
> **begin**
>   run $A(\varepsilon_0, \delta_1, n : \text{EX})$ k times to construct
> k hypothesis $h_1, h_2, \ldots, h_k$;
>   output h_*, where $h_*(x)$ is the
>   majority vote of $h_1, h_2, \ldots, h_k$;
> **end**

Are there good values of δ_1 and k (as functions of the inputs) that will make this an efficient alternative?

8.6.   Algorithm $\hat{A}$ of Claim 8.3 needs a fair coin. Show that the fair coin can be eliminated by using the random source of examples to simulate coin tosses. In light of this result, revisit Exercise 3.8.

8.7.   Show that the expected run time of $\hat{A}$ in Claim 8.3 is polynomial in the time complexity of A and other parameters. To do so, estimate the expected time taken by $\hat{A}$ to simulate EX2 and EX3. Using the methods of Claim 8.2 or by other means, modify $\hat{A}$ so that it halts deterministically rather than probabilistically.

8.8.   In Claim 8.3, suppose that A identifies its output in a representation R that is computable in time $p(n)$. Estimate the time required to test for membership in the concepts identified by $\hat{A}$.

Notice that Claim 8.2 does not require $\varepsilon_0 < 1/2$, while Claim 8.3 does. Can this restriction on Claim 8.3 be removed? If not, how close can ε_0 be to 1/2?

8.9.   Estimate the sample complexity of algorithm $\hat{A}$ of Claim 8.3. Estimate the space complexity of $\hat{A}$ as well. You should find that the sample complexity varies as $1/\varepsilon$ but that the space complexity varies as $\log(1/\varepsilon)$. The significance of these estimates is that prediction needs very little scratch space compared to the size of the examples seen, implying that what is learned can be stored in compressed form.

8.10.   Prove or disprove the following (the converse of Theorem 8.6):

Let F be a class of concepts with a representation R_F. With respect to R_F, let F be polynomial-time predictable. Then, there exists class G with polynomial-time computable representation R_G such that (a) F is polynomial-time learnable in terms of R_G; and (b) G is polynomial-time learnable in R_G.

Notice that Example 8.1 and Exercise 8.1 do not violate this converse.

8.11.   Show that the results of Claim 8.1 and 8.3 (or 8.2) can be combined to simultaneously boost the confidence and the precision of a prediction algorithm.

8.8 Bibliographic Notes

The paradigm of prediction was introduced by Haussler, Littlestone, and Warmuth (1988). Example 8.1 is from Pitt and Valiant (1988). Theorems 8.1 and 8.2 are adapted from Haussler, Littlestone, and Warmuth (1988). The same paper deals with the prediction of concept classes defined on uncountable domains and gives an interesting algorithm for prediction by constructing certain graphs. Theorems 8.3 through 8.6 are "folk" theorems in that they were widely known if not published. Theorem 8.7 is adapted from Board and Pitt (1990). Theorem 8.8 is from Kearns and Valiant (1989). Its proof requires the results of Pitt and Warmuth (1988), (1990), who develop the notion of prediction-preserving reducibility and, based on this, construct a complexity hierarchy. For a general discussion on Turing machines and their binary encodings, see Hopcroft and Ullman (1979). For a discussion on trapdoor functions, see Yao (1982) and Rivest (1990). For a discussion on the Rivest-Shamir-Adleman public-key cryptosystem, see Rivest, Shamir, and Adleman (1978) and Rivest (1990). Claim 8.1 is another "folk" theorem. Claim 8.2 is from Kearns (1988), while Claim 8.3 is from Schapire (1990). An alternate proof of Claim 8.3 involving an iterative algorithm (rather than a recursive one) may be found in Freund (1990). Exercise 8.1 is from Pitt and Warmuth (1990). Exercises 8.2 and 8.3 are from Board and Pitt (1990). Exercise 8.4 is from Kearns (1988). Exercises 8.6 and 8.7 are from Schapire (1990). Exercise 8.10 is an open problem at this time, although a relevant result appears in Blum and Singh (1990).

9

Conclusion

In this chapter we view the results of the previous chapters from a broader perspective, examine their limitations, and survey some recent research directions. We also briefly touch upon the relationship between the results presented in this book and the AI literature.

9.1 The Paradigm

In Chapter 1 we noted that the paradigm of identification in the limit was resistant to the imposition of complexity measures of practical significance. The PAC learning paradigm overcame this resistance by measuring the success of the learning algorithm probabilistically. This achievement in itself is insufficient justification for the elaborate study of a paradigm. Indeed, in Chapter 1 we claimed that the PAC learning paradigm lent itself to analysis, while being a reasonable model of the natural learning process. The results presented in the book certainly bear testimony that the model lends itself to analysis. What justification do we have for the latter claim?

Suppose that there exist theories in physics that explain certain natural phenomena, each theory holding within some range of conditions. A theoretical physicist who proposes a new and unified theory of the phenomena, will have to test his theory against experimental data, as well as against the existing theories in their range of validity. If the new theory violates some of the existing theories, then it is likely to be suspect. On the other hand, if the new theory agrees with the existing theories, it is given added credibility. The same criteria hold for us. If the PAC model of learning meshes well with existing theories, then it is lent added credibility.

One example of such a mesh is that we were able to derive the principle of Occam's Razor within the PAC model. Recall the principle of Occam's Razor of Section 3.3: "The simplest explanation of the observed phenomena is most likely to be a correct one." Suppose that we were to apply this principle to learning algorithms. We would construct an algorithm that would output the shortest hypothesis consistent with the examples seen. In Chapter 3, we showed that such an application of Occam's Razor is mathematically valid in that the learning algorithm constructed above would indeed generalize well from the examples. Actually, we went a little further to obtain an asymptotic form of Occam's Razor. Specifically, we showed that it is sufficient for the learning algorithm to pick a hypothesis that is asymptotically shorter than the examples, rather than pick the *simplest* hypothesis. In this sense we can reformulate the principle of Occam's Razor: "Picking asymptotically simpler explanations of the observed phenomena is likely to produce a good hypothesis."

Occam's Razor is based on philosophical observations and has been a useful rule of thumb for centuries since its formulation. That we were able to formally derive this rule points to our paradigm being a well-founded model of the natural learning process.

Another factor in support of the PAC paradigm is its robustness. It is reasonable and traditional to consider a scientific theory to be well founded if small changes in the parameters of the theory do not lead to wildly different predictions resulting from theory. We observed two situations wherein our paradigm exhibits robustness in the face of changes.

Firstly, we observed that the results of the model are not strongly dependent on the length parameter n in the following sense. In Chapter 2, we saw that eliminating the length parameter n as input to the learning algorithm more or less left the results of that chapter invariant. Specifically, the family of concept classes that are polynomial-sample learnable does not depend on whether n is provided as input to the learning algorithm. The same invariance carried over to the time complexity results of Chapter 3. That is, the family of concept classes/representations that are polynomial-time learnable does not depend on whether n is provided as input to the learning algorithm.

Secondly, we saw that the results of the model are not strongly dependent on the confidence parameter δ or the error parameter ε. Specifically, in Chapter 8 we showed that if we had a learning algorithm that worked only for some fixed value of δ, it would be possible to construct a learning algorithm that works for arbitrarily small values of δ. We also showed that if we had a prediction algorithm that worked only for some fixed value of $\varepsilon < 1/2$, it would be possible to boost the precision of the algorithm to arbitrarily small values of ε. Furthermore, if the algorithm enjoyed the property of one-sided error, the boosting could be done while preserving this property. In essence, the PAC paradigm requires a learning algorithm to succeed for all values of the error and confidence parameters. While this requirement appears rather stringent, it is sufficiently natural that its elimination does not alter the class of concept learning problems that we would consider computationally feasible.

The foregoing stands evidence to the robustness of the PAC learning paradigm, providing support to its being a good model of the natural learning process. But our evidence is based primarily on theoretical aesthetics. As with the theoretical physicist and the new theory, we must also validate the PAC paradigm by testing it against experimental data on various fronts. On one front, we need successful practical applications based on the results obtained within the paradigm. The results of Li (1990) on algorithms for the inference of DNA sequences is a step in this direction. On a second front, we need to relate the paradigm to experimental observations made within the realm of the behavioral sciences. If the model survives these stipulations, it will likely evolve into a good and robust model of the natural learning process, enjoying a range of support from various quarters.

9.2 Recent and Future Directions

Despite the success of the basic PAC model as evidenced by the results presented in this book, many interesting learning problems are intractable within its bounds. For instance, the rather fundamental problem of learning the deterministic finite automata is intractable within the basic PAC model, as shown in the hardness results of Chapters 6 and 8. However, the augmented framework of Chapter 6 involving membership queries permitted an algorithm for this problem. This augmented framework has been the subject of recent research, with several interesting results reported in the literature. Angluin (1988) presents a comprehensive and general discussion of PAC learning with queries. Raghavan and Schach (1990) show that switch configurations are polynomial-time learnable with membership queries, while Angluin, Frazier, and Pitt (1990) obtain a similar result for conjunctions of Horn clauses. Maass and Turan (1990) offer a general lower bound on the sample complexity of PAC learning with membership queries.

A shortcoming of the basic PAC paradigm is that it does not explicitly address the issue of *on-line* learning, i.e., the PAC learning algorithm learns in "batch mode." First, the algorithm enters the training phase in which it sees examples, and then it outputs a hypothesis to be used in the performance phase. In the on-line situation, the learning algorithm would continuously process examples and improve its hypothesis. Littlestone (1988) proposes a model for examining the behavior of on-line learning algorithms, with the attendant complexity measure of mistake-bounds. Within the model, the learning algorithm receives from the domain of interest a stream of unlabeled instances presented in arbitrary order. At each instance, the learning algorithm predicts the value of the target concept and the algorithm is told whether its prediction is correct. The maximum number of times the algorithm makes an incorrect prediction, the maximum being taken over all concepts in the target class and all presentation orders of the instances, is the *mistake-bound* of the algorithm. It is desirable that an algorithm have a small mistake-bound and run in time polynomial in the various parameters at each instance of the input stream. Littlestone exhibits algorithms that are efficient in the above sense for various concept classes that he calls linearly separable. For instance, the class of concepts representable by a single layered linear-threshold network is a linearly separable class. Littlestone's algorithms are particularly parsimonious when the number of inputs to the network are large compared to those that are actually relevant to the output of the network. Using a technique of Angluin (1988) (see the generate and test algorithm of Exercise 2.10), Littlestone shows that an on-line learning algorithm can be converted into a PAC learning algorithm. Indeed, this is a simple transformation and preserves the polynomial time complexity of the on-line algorithm. However, the converse is not so straightforward. Ignoring efficiency considerations, a PAC learning algorithm can be converted into an on-line learning algorithm. But the transformation will not preserve the polynomial time complexity of the learning algorithm. In fact, Blum (1990) shows that assuming the existence of the trapdoor functions proposed by Goldreich, Goldwasser, and Micali (1986), there exists a class of concepts that is efficiently PAC learnable, but not efficiently learnable in the on-line model.

Another restriction of the basic PAC model is that the prior information of the learning algorithm is evidenced only in the definition of the target class. In practice, the prior information may take on other forms. For instance, the probability distribution over the domain of interest may be restricted to be of a particular form, say the normal or the uniform distribution. In this case, the full generality of the PAC model is unduly restrictive of the target classes that are efficiently learnable. To overcome this restriction, it is desirable to parametrize the PAC model over the class of probability distributions to be faced by the learning algorithm. Benedek and Itai (1988) identify necessary and sufficient conditions for the uniform learnability of classes of concepts (the analog of Theorem 4.4) when the class of distributions consists of a single distribution. Natarajan (1989a) obtains similar results for the uniform learnability of classes of concepts over general classes of probability distributions, as well as for classes of functions over a single probability distribution. Haussler (1989) presents results that generalize both of the above. Li and Vitanyi (1989) study learnability over the class of "simple" distributions, where a simple distribution is one that is dominated by a recursively enumerable distribution. They show that there exists a universal distribution P_u such that learnability over P_u implies learnability over all simple distributions.

An important practical consideration that is ignored in the basic PAC model is that of noise in the source of examples. Amongst others, Quinlan (1986) and Schlimmer and Granger (1986) present some heuristic studies of learning in the presence of noise. This noise can take on various forms and is usually modeled in three categories in the theoretical studies reported in the literature. First, we have *classification* noise: Let β be a real in the range $[0, 1)$. If EXAMPLE returns (x, y), with probability at most β, an adversary makes an arbitrary choice for the label y of the example. Second, we have *attribute* noise: If EXAMPLE returns (x, y), an adversary is permitted to randomly flip the bits of the string x, but not the label y. Specifically, with probability at most β, the adversary sets the ith bit of x to be 0 or 1 by tossing a fair coin. Third, we have *malicious* noise: At each call of EXAMPLE, with probability at most β, an adversary is permitted to replace the example returned by EXAMPLE with an arbitrary example of his choice. Angluin and Laird (1988) explore PAC learning in the presence of classification noise. They show that in general, constructing the concept in the hypothesis class that best fits the examples seen is sufficient when $\beta < 1/2$. However, a naive search for this best-fit hypothesis is computationally intractable. Using an alternative technique, they extract a noise-tolerant learning algorithm for the k-CNF concepts. Kearns and Li (1988) examine learning in the presence of malicious errors and present an upper bound on the amount of malicious noise that can be tolerated. Shackelford and Volper (1988) present an algorithm for learning k-DNF in the presence of attribute noise. Sloan (1988) attempts to unify the models of noise and shows some upper bounds on the amount of noise that can be tolerated. In all, the topic of PAC learning in the presence of noise calls for much additional research. For instance, it would be interesting to see which of the classes of concepts known to be efficiently learnable or predictable in the basic PAC model remain so in the presence of a reasonable amount of noise.

9.3 An AI Perspective

The results presented in this book are largely theoretical in direction. The experimentalist within the artificial intelligence school is bound to wonder where these results fit in his or her scheme of things. In a sense, it is too early to give a substantial answer to this question. In fact, one of the purposes of this book is to make the theoretical results accessible to a wider audience, so that this question will find a natural answer. Yet, we will attempt to say a few words on this issue.

In the AI literature, learning algorithms and problems are broadly classified under two categories, *inductive learning* and *explanation-based learning*. See Michalski, Mitchell, and Carbonell (1986), Shavlik and Diettrich (1990). In inductive learning, the learning algorithm has a *bias* and is required to construct a good approximation to a target concept from examples. The bias of the algorithm refers to its preference to output some hypotheses over others. In our terminology, the bias is the prior information. Thus, inductive learning corresponds directly to the concept learning problem within the PAC learning paradigm. Specifically, the prior information of the PAC learning algorithm constitutes its bias and determines the target class of the learning problem. The algorithm is given random examples and is required to construct an approximation to the target concept. While most of this book concerns concept learning in the PAC setting, inductive concept learning represents but a small fraction of the learning problems that arise in the practical situation.

Explanation-based learning (EBL) is of a slightly different flavor. In this paradigm, the learning algorithm is given a complete description of what is to be learned, say a concept or a function. (This description is called the "domain theory" in the literature.) But the description is not in a form that permits efficient evaluation. The learning algorithm is to transform the given description into an efficient form, using the examples that are provided to it. Hence, in EBL, learning serves to reduce the computational complexity of a task and is primarily a reorganization of existing information. EBL also models such learning problems as learning to solve games and puzzles. Take Rubik's cube, for instance. When we buy a cube for the first time, we get complete instructions on its solution. Specifically, we know that:

(a) The object of the puzzle is to place the cube in the configuration in which the colors on each face of the cube match.

(b) The cube can be twisted and turned to achieve new configurations, but is not to be taken apart and reassembled during the course of solving a particular instance of the puzzle.

This information is sufficient for us to solve any instance of the puzzle simply by employing an exhaustive trial-and-error strategy of all possible solution paths. However, such a strategy takes too long. As we experiment with the cube, we study solutions to sample instances of the puzzle. Based on these solutions, we construct rules that constitute a heuristic algorithm for efficiently solving the puzzle. Thus, the role of the examples here is to reorganize the information we have on the cube in order to reduce the computational complexity of our solution procedure.

With some modifications, the PAC criteria can be applied to the EBL paradigm as well, as is done in Natarajan and Tadepalli (1988), Natarajan (1989c), and Cohen (1989). These papers study the EBL problem in an abstract setting. The first paper considers the case in which the learning algorithm is provided with solutions to randomly chosen instances. The second paper considers the case in which the learning algorithm is provided with "exercises"—randomly and benevolently chosen instances without solutions. However, these papers do not offer a full analysis of the EBL paradigm, leaving considerable room for exploration.

In all, the results obtained so far within the PAC model and its variants have but dented the body of learning problems that are interesting in the practical situation. Perhaps this dent will grow with time.

Notation

A:	learning algorithm.
B:	evaluation algorithm for a representation.
$\mathbf{B}$:	class of all Borel sets on $\mathbf{R}^k$.
C:	closure algorithm for a representation under exceptions.
$\mathbf{D}_{VC}$:	Vapnik-Chervonenkis dimension.
$\mathbf{D}_G$:	generalized dimension.
$\mathbf{D}$:	asymptotic dimension.
I_S:	indicator function of set S.
e:	base of the natural logarithm.
f, g, h:	concept or function.
$f^{[n]}$:	projection of concept f on $\Sigma^{[n]}$.
$f^{[n_1][n_2]}$:	projection of function f on $\Sigma^{[n_1]} \times \Sigma^{[n_2]}$.
F, G, H:	class of concepts or functions.
$\mathfrak{F}$:	final states of an automaton.
l:	length of a name in a representation.
$l_{min}(f, R)$:	shortest name for f in representation R.
$\ln$:	natural logarithm.
$\log$:	logarithm in base 2.
M:	finite automaton.
$\mathbf{N}$:	the natural numbers.
n:	length parameter.
NP:	the complexity class NP.
$O()$:	order of magnitude; see Section 2.3.

P:	the complexity class P.
Pr $\{E\}$:	probability of event E.
Pr $\{A/B\}$:	conditional probability of A given B.
P:	probability distribution.
P^m:	$m$fold product distribution of P.
$P(q)$:	the expectation of random variable q, taken with respect to P.
$P_{(m)}(q)$:	mean value of q on m random observations chosen according to P.
$P(S)$:	for set S, $P(S) = P(I_S)$, which is the weight of P on S.
Q:	fitting for a representation.
$\mathbb{Q}$:	set of states of an automaton.
r:	name for a concept in a representation.
R:	representation for a class of concepts or functions.
R:	the set of real numbers.
RP:	the complexity class RP.
s:	sample complexity of learning algorithm; number of states in a DFA.
S:	set, or its indicator function.
$\lvert S \rvert$:	cardinality of set S.
S^m:	$m$fold cartesian product of S.
2^S:	power set of S.
t:	time complexity of a learning algorithm.
$\lvert x \rvert$:	length of string x.
x^m:	sequence of m items.
$[x^m]$:	set of elements occurring in the sequence x^m.
ε:	error parameter.
δ:	confidence parameter.
Δ:	symmetric difference operator, $f\Delta g = \{x \mid f(x) \neq g(x)\}$.
$\varnothing$:	null set.
λ:	null string.

π:	permutation.
τ:	transition function of an automaton.
σ:	sequence of examples.
Σ:	the binary alphabet.
Σ^*:	set of all strings of finite length on Σ.
Σ^n:	set of all strings of length n on Σ.
$\Sigma^{[n]}$:	set of all strings of length at most n on Σ.
$\theta(E)$:	truth value of predicate E.
$\Omega()$:	order of magnitude; see Section 2.3.

Bibliography

Abe, N., and Warmuth, M. (1990). On the computational complexity of approximating distributions by probabilistic automata, in *Proceedings of the 3rd Annual Workshop on Computational Learning Theory*, pp. 52–66.

Adleman, L. M., and Huang, M-D. A. (1987). Recognizing primes in polynomial time, in *Proceedings of the 19th ACM Symposium on Theory of Computing*, pp. 462–469.

Angluin, D. (1982). A note on the number of queries needed to verify regular languages, *Information and Control*, Vol. 51, No. 1, pp. 76–87.

Angluin, D. (1986a). Types of queries for concept learning, Tech. Rep. YALEU/DCS/TR-479, Dept. of Computer Science, Yale University, New Haven, CT.

Angluin, D. (1986b). Learning regular sets from queries and counterexamples, Tech. Rep. YALEU/DCS/TR-464, Dept. of Computer Science, Yale University, New Haven, CT.

Angluin, D. (1987). Learning *k*-bounded context-free grammars. Tech. Rep. YALEU/DCS/RR-557, Dept. of Computer Science, Yale University, New Haven, CT.

Angluin, D. (1988). Queries and concept learning, *Machine Learning*, Vol. 2, No. 4, pp. 319–342.

Angluin, D. (1989). Negative results for equivalence queries, *Machine Learning*, Vol. 5, No. 2, pp. 121–150.

Angluin, D., and Laird, P. (1988). Learning from noisy examples, *Machine Learning*, Vol. 2, No. 4, pp. 343–370.

Angluin, D., and Smith, C. H. (1983). Inductive inference: Theory and methods, *Computing Surveys*, 15, pp. 237–269.

Angluin, D., Frazier, M., and Pitt, L. (1990). Learning conjunctions of Horn clauses, in *Proceedings of the 31st IEEE Symposium on Foundations of Computer Science*, pp. 186–192.

Angluin, D., Hellerstein, L., and Karpinski, M. (1989). Learning read-once formulas with queries, Tech. Rep. UCB/CSD 89/528, Computer Science Division,

University of California, Berkeley. Full version to appear in *Journal of the ACM*.

Assouad, P. (1983). *Densite et Dimension*, Annales Institute Fourier Grenoble, 33 (3), pp. 233-282.

Baum, E., and Haussler, D. (1989). What size net gives valid generalization? *Advances in Neural Information Processing Systems*, D. Touretsky, Ed., Morgan Kaufmann, San Mateo, CA, pp. 81-90.

Ben-David, S., Benedek, G. M., and Mansour Y. (1989). A parametrization scheme for classifying models of learnability, in *Proceedings of the 2nd Annual Workshop on Computational Learning Theory*, pp. 285-303.

Benedek, G., and Itai, A. (1988). Learnability by fixed distributions, in *Proceedings of the 2nd Annual Workshop on Computational Learning Theory*, pp. 80-90.

Berman, P., and Roos, R., (1987). Learning one-counter languages in polynomial time, in *Proceedings of the 28th IEEE Symposium on Foundations of Computer Science*, pp. 61-67.

Blum, A. (1990). Separating distribution-free and mistake-bounded learning models over the Boolean domain, in *Proceedings of the 31st IEEE Symposium on Foundations of Computer Science*, pp. 211-218.

Blum, A., and Rivest, R. (1988). Training a 3-node neural network is *NP*-complete, in *Proceedings of the 1988 Annual Workshop on Computational Learning Theory*, pp. 9-18.

Blum, A., and Singh, M. (1990). Learning functions of k-terms, in *Proceedings of the 2nd Annual Workshop on Computational Learning Theory*, pp. 144-153.

Blumer, A., Ehrenfeucht, A., Haussler, D., and Warmuth, M. (1987). Occam's razor, *Information Processing Letters*, Vol. 24, No. 6, pp. 377-380.

Blumer, A., Ehrenfeucht, A., Haussler, D., and Warmuth, M. (1990). Learnability and the Vapnik-Chervonenkis dimension, *Journal of the ACM*, Vol. 36, No. 4, pp. 929-965.

Board, R., and Pitt, L. (1990). On the necessity of Occam algorithms, in *Proceedings of the 22nd ACM Symposium on Theory of Computing*, pp. 54-63.

Brownlee, K. A. (1960). *Statistical Theory and Methodology in Science and Engineering*, John Wiley and Sons, New York.

Cohen, W. W. (1989). Solution path caching mechanisms which provably improve performance. Tech. Rep. DCS-TR-254, Dept. of Computer Science, Rutgers University, New Brunswick, NJ.

Daley, R., and Smith, C. H. (1986). On the complexity of inductive inference, *Information and Control*, Vol. 69, No. 1, pp. 12–40.

Ehrenfeucht, A., and Haussler, D. (1988). Learning decision trees from random examples, in *Proceedings of the 1988 Workshop on Computational Learning Theory*, pp. 182–194.

Ehrenfeucht, A., Haussler, D., Kearns, M., and Valiant, L. G. (1989). A general lower bound on the number of examples needed for learning, *Information and Computation*, Vol. 82, No. 3, pp. 247–261.

Feller, W. (1957). *An Introduction to Probability Theory and Its Applications*, John Wiley and Sons, New York.

Freund, Y. (1990). Boosting a weak learning algorithm by majority, in *Proceedings of the 3rd Annual Workshop on Computational Learning Theory*, pp. 202–216.

Gao, Q., and Li, M. (1989). The minimum description length principle and its application to online learning of handprinted characters, in *Proceedings of the 11th International Joint Conference on Artificial Intelligence*, pp. 843–848.

Garey, M. R., and Johnson, D. S. (1979). *Computers and Intractability*, W. H. Freeman and Company, New York.

Gill, J. (1977). Computational complexity of probabilistic Turing machines, *SIAM Journal on Computing*, Vol. 6, No. 4, pp. 675–695.

Gold, E. M. (1967). Language identification in the limit, *Information and Control*, Vol. 10, pp. 447–474.

Gold, E. M. (1972). System identification via state characterization, *Automatica*, Vol. 8, pp. 621–636.

Gold, E. M. (1978). Complexity of automaton identification from given data, *Information and Control*, Vol. 37, No. 3, pp. 302–320.

Goldreich, O., Goldwasser, S. and Micali, S., (1986). How to construct random functions, *Journal of the ACM*, Vol. 33, No. 4, pp. 792–807.

Golub, G. H., and Van Loan, C. F. (1983). *Matrix Computations*, Johns Hopkins Press, Baltimore, MD.

Haussler, D. (1989). Generalizing the PAC model for neural nets and other learning applications. Tech. Rep. UCSC-CRL-89-30, Dept. of Computer Science, University of California, Santa Cruz, CA. Also, in *Proceedings of the 30th IEEE Symposium on Foundations of Computer Science*, pp. 40–45.

Haussler, D., and Long, P. (1990). A generalization of Sauer's lemma, Tech. Rep. UCSC-CRL-90-15, Dept. of Computer Science, University of California, Santa Cruz, CA.

Haussler, D., Kearns, M., Littlestone, N., and Warmuth, M. (1988). Equivalence of models for polynomial learnability, in *Proceedings of the 1988 Workshop on Computational Learning Theory*, pp. 42–55. Full version to appear in *Information and Computation*.

Haussler, D., Littlestone, N., and Warmuth, M. (1988). Predicting 0,1 functions on randomly drawn points, in *Proceedings of the 29th IEEE Symposium on Foundations of Computer Science*, pp. 100–109.

Hawking, S. (1986). *A Brief History of Time*, Bantam Books, New York.

Hong, J. W. (1988). On connectionist models, unpublished manuscript.

Hopcroft, J. E., and Ullman, J. D. (1979). *Introduction to Automata Theory, Languages and Computation*, Addison-Wesley, Reading, MA.

Ishizaka, H. (1990). Polynomial time learnability of simple deterministic languages, *Machine Learning*, Vol. 5, No. 2, pp. 151–164.

Johnson, D. (1990). A catalog of complexity classes, in van Leeuwen, J., ed., *Handbook of Theoretical Computer Science*, Vol. A, MIT Press, Cambridge, MA.

Judd, J. S. (1987). Learning in networks is hard, in *Proceedings of the 1st IEEE International Conference on Neural Networks*, San Diego, CA, pp. II_685–II_692.

Judd, J. S. (1990). *Neural Network Design and the Complexity of Learning*, MIT Press, Cambridge, MA.

Kearns, M. (1988). Thoughts on hypothesis boosting, unpublished manuscript.

Kearns, M., and Li, M. (1988). Learning in the presence of malicious errors, in *Proceedings of the 20th ACM Symposium on Theory of Computing*, pp. 267–279.

Kearns, M., and Schapire, R. E. (1990). Efficient distribution-free learning of probabilistic concepts, in *Proceedings of the 31st IEEE Symposium on Foundations of Computer Science*, pp. 382–391.

Kearns, M., and Valiant, L. G. (1989). Cryptographic limitations on learning Boolean formulae and finite automata, in *Proceedings of the 21st ACM Symposium on Theory of Computing*, pp. 433–444.

Kearns, M., Li, M., Pitt, L., and Valiant, L. G. (1987a). Recent results on Boolean concept learning, in *Proceedings of the 4th International Conference on Machine Learning*, pp. 337–352.

Kearns, M., Li, M., Pitt, L., and Valiant, L. G. (1987b). On the learnability of Boolean formulae, in *Proceedings of the 19th ACM Symposium on Theory of Computing*, pp. 285–295.

Li, M. (1990). Towards a DNA sequencing theory, in *Proceedings of the 31st IEEE Symposium on Foundations of Computer Science*, pp. 125–133.

Li, M., and Vitanyi, P. M. B. (1989). A theory of learning simple concepts under simple distributions, in *Proceedings of the 30th IEEE Symposium on Foundations of Computer Science*, pp. 34–39.

Lin, J-H, and Vitter, J. S. (1989). Complexity issues in learning by neural nets, in *Proceedings of the 2nd Workshop on Computational Learning Theory*, pp. 118–133.

Linial, N., Mansour, Y., and Rivest, R. L. (1988). Results on learnability and the Vapnik-Chervonenkis dimension, in *Proceedings of the 1988 Workshop on Computational Learning Theory*, pp. 56–68.

Littlestone, N. (1988). Learning quickly when irrelevant attributes abound: A new linear threshold algorithm, *Machine Learning*, Vol. 2, No. 4, pp. 285–318.

Long, P., and Warmuth, M. (1990). Composite geometric concepts and polynomial predictability, in *Proceedings of the 3rd Annual Workshop on Computational Learning Theory*, pp. 273–287.

Maass, W., and Turan, G. (1990). On the complexity of learning from counter examples and membership queries, in *Proceedings of the 31st IEEE Symposium on Foundations of Computer Science*, pp. 203–210.

Michalski, R., Mitchell, T., and Carbonell, J. (1986). *Machine Learning: An Artificial Intelligence Approach*, Morgan Kaufmann, San Mateo, CA.

Minsky, M., and Papert, S. (1969). *Perceptrons*, MIT Press, Cambridge, MA.

Natarajan, B. K. (1989a). Probably approximate learning over classes of distributions, to appear in SIAM Journal on Computing.

Natarajan, B. K. (1989b). On learning sets and functions, *Machine Learning*, Vol. 4, No. 1, pp. 67–97.

Natarajan, B. K. (1989c). On learning from exercises, in *Proceedings of the 2nd Workshop on Computational Learning Theory*, pp. 72–81.

Natarajan, B. K. (1989d). Some results on learning, Tech. Rep. CMU-RI-TR-89-6, The Robotics Institute, Carnegie Mellon University, Pittsburgh, PA 15213.

Natarajan, B. K. (1991). Probably approximate learning of sets and functions, to appear in *SIAM Journal on Computing*.

Natarajan, B. K., and Tadepalli, P. (1988). Two new frameworks for learning, in *Proceedings of the Fifth International Symposium on Machine Learning*, pp. 402–415.

Nilsson, N. (1990). *The Mathematical Foundations of Learning Machines*, Morgan Kaufmann, San Mateo, CA.

Osherson, D. N., Stob, M., and Weinstein, S. (1986). *Systems That Learn*, MIT Press, Cambridge, MA.

Parzen, E. (1960). *Modern Probability Theory and its Applications*, John Wiley and Sons, New York.

Pearl, J. (1988). *Probabilistic Reasoning in Intelligent Systems*, Morgan Kaufmann, San Mateo, CA.

Pitt, L. (1989). Inductive inference, DFA's and computational complexity, Tech. Rep., UIUCDCS-R-89-1530, University of Illinois, Urbana, IL.

Pitt, L., and Valiant, L. G. (1988). Computational limitations on learning from examples, *Journal of the ACM*, Vol. 35, No. 4, pp. 965-984.

Pitt, L., and Warmuth, M. (1988). Reductions among prediction problems: On the difficulty of predicting automata, in *Proceedings of the 3rd Conference on Structure in Complexity Theory*, pp. 60-69.

Pitt, L., and Warmuth, M. (1989). The minimum consistent DFA problem cannot be identified within any polynomial, in *Proceedings of the 21st ACM Symposium on Theory of Computing*, pp. 421-432.

Pitt, L., and Warmuth, M. (1990). Prediction preserving reducibility, *Journal of Computer and System Sciences*, Vol. 41, No. 3, pp. 430-467.

Pollard, D. (1986). *Convergence of Stochastic Processes*, Springer-Verlag, New York.

Preparata, F. P., and Shamos, M. I. (1985). *Computational Geometry: An Introduction*, Springer-Verlag, New York.

Quinlan, J. R. (1986). The effect of noise on concept learning, in Michalski, R., Mitchell, T., and Carbonell, J., eds., *Machine Learning: An Artificial Intelligence Approach*, Morgan Kaufmann, San Mateo, CA.

Quinlan, J. R., and Rivest, R. L. (1989). Inferring decision trees using the minimum length description principle, *Information and Computation*, Vol. 80, No. 3, pp. 227-248.

Raghavan, P. (1988). Learning in threshold networks, in *Proceedings of the 1988 Workshop on Computational Learning Theory*, pp. 19-27.

Raghavan, V., and Schach, S. R. (1990). Learning switch configurations, in *Proceedings of the 3rd Workshop on Computational Learning Theory*, pp. 38-51.

Rissanen, J. (1978). Modeling by shortest data description. *Automatica*, Vol. 14, pp. 465-471.

Rissanen, J. (1986). Stochastic complexity and modeling. *Annals of Statistics*, Vol. 14, No. 3, pp. 1080–1100.

Rivest, R. (1987). Learning decision lists, *Machine Learning*, Vol. 2, No. 3, pp. 229–246.

Rivest, R. (1990). Cryptography, in van Leeuwen, J., ed., *Handbook of Theoretical Computer Science*, Vol. A, MIT Press, Cambridge, MA.

Rivest, R., and Schapire, R. E. (1987). Diversity-based inference of finite automata, in *Proceedings of the 28th IEEE Symposium on Foundations of Computer Science*, pp. 78–87.

Rivest, R., Shamir, A., and Adleman, L. (1978). A method for obtaining digital signatures and public-key cryptosystems, *Communications of the ACM*, Vol. 21, No. 2, pp. 120–126.

Rumelhart, D. E. and McClelland, J. L. (1986). *Parallel Distributed Processing*, MIT Press, Cambridge, MA.

Sakakibara, Y. (1988). Learning context-free grammars from structural data in polynomial time, in *Proceedings of the 1988 Workshop on Computational Learning Theory*, pp. 330–334.

Schapire, R. (1990). The strength of weak learnability, *Machine Learning*, Vol. 5, No. 2, pp. 197–227.

Schlimmer, J. C., and Granger, R. H. (1986). Incremental learning from noisy data, *Machine Learning*, Vol. 1, No. 3, pp. 317–354.

Shackelford, G., and Volper, D. (1988). Learning k-DNF with noise in the attributes, in *Proceedings of the 1988 Workshop on Computational Learning Theory*, pp. 97–103.

Shavlik, J., and Diettrich, T. (1990). *Readings in Machine Learning*, Morgan Kaufmann, San Mateo, CA.

Shvaytser, H. (1990). A necessary condition for learning from positive examples, *Machine Learning*, Vol. 5, No. 1, pp. 101–113.

Sloan, R. (1988). Types of noise in data for concept learning, in *Proceedings of the 1988 Workshop on Computational Learning Theory*, pp. 91–96.

Solovay, R., and Strassen, V. (1977). A fast Monte Carlo test for primality, *SIAM Journal on Computing*, Vol. 6, No. 1, pp. 84–85.

Statman, R. (1987). Private communication.

Tarjan, R. E. (1983). *Data Structures and Network Algorithms*, SIAM Publications, Philadelphia, PA.

Valiant, L. G. (1984). A theory of the learnable, *Communications of the ACM*, Vol. 27, No. 11, pp. 1134–1142.

Vapnik, V. N. (1989). Inductive principles for empirical dependencies, in *Proceedings of the 2nd Workshop on Computational Learning Theory*, pp. 3–24.

Vapnik, V. N., and Chervonenkis, A. Ya. (1971). On the uniform convergence of relative frequencies, *Theory of Probability and its Applications*, Vol. 16, No. 2, pp. 264–280.

Weiss, S. M., and Kulikowski, C. A. (1991). *Computer Systems That Learn*, Morgan Kaufmann, San Mateo, CA.

Yao, A. C. (1982). Theory and application of trap door functions, in *Proceedings of the 23rd IEEE Symposium on Foundations of Computer Science*, pp. 80–91.

Subject Index

A
admissible learning algorithm 26
axis-parallel rectangles 17, 48, 76

B
bias 7
binomial distribution 95
Bilinear Confinement 15
Boolean formula
    binary encoding of 42
    DNF 71
    k-CNF 37, 70
    k-DNF 37
    k-term-DNF 70, 173
    monotone monomial 16
    monomial 36
    threshold function 193
boosting
    confidence 180
    precision 182
Borel sets 94
bounded precision network 144

C
Chebyshev's inequality 58, 76
class
    concept 9
    function 99
    hypothesis 169
    target 9, 169
concept 8
    class of 9
    graph of 22
    learning class of 14
    target 8

confidence parameter 11
consistent concept 22
context-free grammar 146
    sentential forms of 39, 71
convex polygons 95
countable domain 7
cubic polynomial 102

D
DFA 128
DNA 199
data compression 57
decision list 71
dimension
    asymptotic 20, 105
    generalized 104
    Vapnik-Chervonenkis 18
discriminant 39

E
equivalence queries 145
error parameter 11
example 8
EXAMPLE 11
exceptions 59
    closure under 59, 127, 156
expert system 123
explanation-based learning 201

F
finite automata 125
fitting 47, 110
    generalized Occam 174

Occam 51
function
    class 99
    diameter of class of 120
    domain of 99
    graph of 22
    indicator 8
    learning class of 100
    range of 99
    target 99
    total 99

G

generalized dimension 104
generalized shattering 102
generate and test 38, 180
gradient descent 156
graph of function or concept 22

H

half-spaces 86, 165
hyperplanes 164
hypothesis class 169

I

indicator function 8
intervals, finite union of 58

L

learning algorithm 11
learning in terms of 171
learning operator 26
least concept 31
length parameter 11
linear-threshold network 147
linear transformation 115

M

Manhattan curve 69
minimum description length 58
measurability 94
membership queries 130
metric 118

metric dimension 124
minimal fitting 63
minimally consistent 32
minimum DFA 129
mistake bounds 200
monotone monomial 16, 46

N

name of function or concept 42
neural network 148
noise
    attribute 201
    classification 201
    malicious 201

O

observation table 131
    closed 131
    self-consistent 132
Occam's Razor 51
one-sided error 31, 63
    precision boosting 182
on-line learning 199

P

PAC 2
perfect matching 112
permutation function 107, 108, 112
polynomial expansion 111
polynomial-sample learnability 15, 101, 170
polynomial-time
    computable representation 49
    fitting 47
    learnability 45, 110, 171
    prediction 177
prediction 175
    time complexity of 176
    space complexity of 195
prefix-closed 130
prior knowledge 7
probability distribution on the reals 4
projection 20, 100

R

randomized algorithm 67

random polynomial-time fitting 49

real RAM 96

representation
  for class of concepts 42
  for class of functions 109

right invariance 131

Rivest-Shamir-Adleman function 178

Rubik's cube 202

S

sample complexity 14, 75, 101

Set-Splitting 156

shattering 17

shattering lemma 19
  generalized 104

small DFA problem 129

suffix-closed 130

T

target class 9, 169

Three-Unit Training 156

threshold 147

time complexity 45

total function 99

trap door function 178

U

uncountable domain 73, 113

uniform learnability 75, 114

usually polynomial-time learnability 51

V

Vapnik-Chervonenkis dimension 18

well-behaved class 84